In Defense of Politicization of Human Rights

In Defense of Politicization of Human Rights

The UN Special Procedures

ELVIRA DOMÍNGUEZ-REDONDO

OXFORD
UNIVERSITY PRESS

OXFORD
UNIVERSITY PRESS

Oxford University Press is a department of the University of Oxford. It furthers the University's objective of excellence in research, scholarship, and education by publishing worldwide. Oxford is a registered trademark of Oxford University Press in the UK and certain other countries.

Published in the United States of America by Oxford University Press
198 Madison Avenue, New York, NY 10016, United States of America.

CIP data is on file at the Library of Congress
ISBN 978-0-19-751670-6

1 3 5 7 9 8 6 4 2

Printed by Integrated Books International, United States of America

Note to Readers

This publication is designed to provide accurate and authoritative information in regard to the subject matter covered. It is based upon sources believed to be accurate and reliable and is intended to be current as of the time it was written. It is sold with the understanding that the publisher is not engaged in rendering legal, accounting, or other professional services. If legal advice or other expert assistance is required, the services of a competent professional person should be sought. Also, to confirm that the information has not been affected or changed by recent developments, traditional legal research techniques should be used, including checking primary sources where appropriate.

(Based on the Declaration of Principles jointly adopted by a Committee of the American Bar Association and a Committee of Publishers and Associations.)

To Delfín

Contents

Acknowledgments xi
Abbreviations xiii

Introduction: Testing the Impact of Politicization on Human Rights 1

One. Creation, Institutionalization, and Development of Public and Confidential Special Procedures 7
1. Introduction 7
2. The "Human Rights Pillar": Unintended Creation of Special Procedures 9
   A. The "Missing" UN Main Body: From Commission to Council 10
   B. Self-denied Competence for Addressing Human Rights Violations (1947–1967) 14
   C. Setting the Change of Direction: Resolutions 1235 (XLII) and 1503 (XLVIII) 20
3. First Geographic Mandates 22
4. First Thematic Mandates 26
5. Confidential Special Procedures 29
6. Conclusions 32

Two. The Politics of Reforming Special Procedures 35
1. Introduction 35
2. Contesting Special Procedures' Use of International Treaties as Benchmark 37
   A. Legal Basis to Examine Conventional Obligations 39
   B. Application of Treaties in Handling Individual Communications 43
3. Reforming and Rationalizing Special Procedures: A Blessing in Disguise 45
   A. Reforms under the Commission on Human Rights (1974–2006) 47
   B. Human Rights Council (2006–2019) 51
      i. Successive Waves of Reform: Much Ado about Nothing? 52
      ii. The Code of Conduct for Special Procedures 55
      iii. Withdrawing for Reform: United States of America and the Council 64
4. Conclusions 66

Three. Growing Organically: A "System" of Special Procedures 69
1. Introduction: Building a System by Coordinating Mandates 69

2. Political Decisions: Collective Mandates 70
3. Mandate Holders Initiatives 74
A. Joint Activities and Coordination between Mandate Holders 75
B. Attempt to Codify Model Rules for Fact-Finding Mechanisms 79
C. Filling the Gap: Publication and Standardization of Methods of Work 81
4. Collective Initiatives: Annual Meetings and Coordination Committee 87
5. Institutional Coherence: Role of the Office of the High Commissioner for Human Rights 93
6. Conclusions 95

Four. Shuttling between Diplomacy and Expertise in Developing Methods of Work 97
1. Introduction 97
2. The Lights and Shadows of Improvising Methods of Work 98
A. Doing It All: Multidimensional Approach to Mandates 99
B. Autonomy and Fragmentation 101
i. Armed Conflicts and Applicability of International Humanitarian Law 102
ii. Non-state Actors 104
C. Political Influence Determining Disparity in Working Methods 108
i. Country and Thematic Mandates 108
ii. Categories of Human Rights 111
3. Publicity Governing the Activities of Special Procedures 117
A. The Annual Report 118
B. Beyond the Annual Report: The Challenges of Publicity 119
4. Conclusions 122

Five. Implementation of Methods of Work 125
1. Introduction 125
2. Communications 125
A. Pioneering the Intervention of UN Bodies on Behalf of Individual Cases of Violations 126
B. Mainstreaming Communications as Standard Practice of All Special Procedures 128
C. Methods of Work to Handle Communications of Human Rights Violations 131
D. The Lights and Shadows of the Communications System 134
3. Visits 137
4. Codification and Clarification of Human Rights Standards 143
A. Conceptualization of Human Rights Issues through the Delimitation of Competence 145
i. Determining the Scope of Mandates 145

ii. Replicating the Treaty Bodies: General Comments and Deliberations 148
B. Codification of New International Human Rights Instruments 150
C. Handbooks and Guidelines 153
D. Risk of Fragmentation: The Case of "Hate Speech" 154
5. Conclusions 157

Six. Politics of "Independence": Position of Special Procedures within the United Nations 161
1. Introduction 161
2. The Politics of Selecting and Naming Mandate Holders 162
3. Independent from Whom? Mandate Holders' Standing within and outside the United Nations 165
4. The Politics of Funding: Office of the High Commissioner for Human Rights 170
5. Relationship with Other UN Organs: General Assembly and Security Council 173
6. Conclusions 178

Final Remarks 181

Annex 197
Bibliography 199
Index 217

Acknowledgments

I wish to express my gratitude to Inga Winkler for supporting a very enriching personal and professional experience as visiting scholar at the Institute for the Study of Human Rights at Columbia University, where I started writing this book, in April 2018.

Thanks to Kathleen Cavanaugh, Michelle Farrell, Jose Antonio Guevara Bermudez, and Magdalena Sepulveda Carmona for comments on earlier versions of the book. It is a privilege to benefit from the caring environment provided by all my colleagues at Middlesex University. Among them, I would like to name Cathal Doyle, Anthony Cullen, Erica Howard, Lughaidh Kerin, Philip Leach, Susan Pascoe, Giulia Pecorella, and Lijun Zhao, for your disposition to generously support me on every occasion it mattered.

I would also like to thank Merel Alstein, Blake Ratcliff, and Seth Meera for believing in this project and their professional support from its inception. Very special thanks to my family. To Lily, my mother in law, for feeding my body and soul with much more than delicious food when I most needed it. To Basti, my mum, for your love; for opening the doors to a world full of exciting possibilities, despite all the odds. Thanks to Radha and Delfin, for filling my life with your wisdom, music, and laughter. To Joshua, the magic maker.

Abbreviations

ACHR	American Convention on Human Rights
AI	Amnesty International
CHR	Commission on Human Rights
Dec.	Decision
ECHR	European Convention on Human Rights
GA	General Assembly
HRC	Human Rights Council
ICCPR	International Covenant on Civil and Political Rights (ICCPR)
ICERD	International Convention on the Elimination of All Forms of Racial Discrimination
ICESCR	International Covenant on Economic, Social and Cultural Rights
OAS	Organization of American States
OHCHR	Office of the High Commissioner for Human Rights
Res.	Resolution
SC	Security Council
SG	Secretary General
UDHR	Universal Declaration of Human Rights
UN	United Nations
WG	Working Group
WGAD	Working Group on Arbitrary Detention
WGAD	Working Group on Arbitrary Detention
WGEID	Working Group on Enforced and Involuntary Disappearances

Introduction

Testing the Impact of Politicization on Human Rights

> *Over the 18 years that I have been following this commission there have been few occasions on which I have felt encouraged by the session and this year was almost certainly the epitome of procrastination, politicization, even hypocrisy.* (Constance Jones, 31st session of the UN Commission on Human Rights, 1975)[1]

International human rights have been largely understood and articulated as limitations to state sovereignty, leading to the widely shared view that only expert-driven non-politicized work can ultimately hold states accountable for not upholding them. This approach has had significant success but comes up against the boundaries of states' political will and actual influence in implementing human rights. The creation of the Human Rights Council, intensifying states' prominence within the system, especially through the establishment of the Universal Periodic Review, was an advance met with initial resistance by academic and practitioner communities. This book questions the blunt critique of "politicization" as not nuanced enough to understand progress, through the lenses of the Special Procedures of the Human Rights Council. These mechanisms are ideally located in the system to analyze the impact of politicization on the international human rights system. Depending on a political decision to be established and renewed, they are particularly sensitive to political factors. However, they are also held by independent experts. The scope of thematic mandates is universal preventing the application of bias associated with politically driven processes. By their own

[1] As cited by Rachel Brett, "To Be or Not To Be. Report of the 61st session of the UN Commission on Human Rights," Quarker United Nations Office, (Geneva, August 2005): 1, available at: http://olddoc.ishr.ch/hrm/archive/CHR61/Quakers_report.pdf.

In Defense of Politicization of Human Rights. Elvira Domínguez-Redondo, Oxford University Press (2020).
© Oxford University Press. DOI: 10.1093/oso/9780197516706.001.0001

nature they mitigate the political interest that dominate the governments represented in the Human Rights Council, the selectivity of its actions, and the application of (real or perceived) double standards. Nonetheless, their birth, growth, and continuing relevance is directly linked to the politicization that permeates every aspect of their life cycle.

In the last decade, commentators have focused their attention on the flaws of international human rights. This book addresses some among them, starting with an explanation of the conceptual, normative, and institutional challenges that resulted in a United Nations organigram where human rights occupied a diminished status. It culminates with the author's view on structural weakness of the system of Special Procedures. Some reproaches directed at international human rights are overarching and poorly demarcated in terms of institutions, concepts, norms, or the territorial, temporal, personal, or material scope they cover. These criticisms are often based on unchallenged presumptions. Among those, probably the most universally accepted, repeated by scholars, civil society organizations, and any other actor engaging international human rights, including (paradoxically) intergovernmental and governmental bodies, is the presumption that "politicization" is pernicious for human rights. International human rights, understood as legal standards, institutions, or actors are governed by international law, characterized by the central role of the state in creating and implementing norms. In other words, international law's distinctive feature remains its politicization. Confronted with similar scenarios, states will react differently depending on geopolitical considerations, because they have the right to do so. Any analysis of the international human rights agenda within international law parameters will necessarily conclude that it suffers from politicization.

The chapters that follow test the hypothesis that politicization should be unwelcome and somehow mitigated if not eliminated, using the most politicized UN human rights bodies, as a subject of analysis. Trusted to independent experts, the life cycle of Special Procedures of the Human Rights Council are intrinsically linked to the political decisions that result in their precarious legal foundations. In the language of the United Nations, the qualifying "Special" of the mechanisms under review does not refer to out of the ordinary, unusually important, or good but to their temporary nature. States represented in an intergovernmental body can decide what mechanism to create, eliminate, or modify depending on political coordinates. Contrary to conventional wisdom, international politicization of the human rights agenda has fostered positive progress.

In the fifty years of their existence, Special Procedures have grown in number and scope but have merited little attention in academic literature until recently. By September 2019, eighty independent experts were mandate holders of fifty-five Special Procedures. Of those, forty-three are categorized as "thematic mandates," focusing on a range of human rights issues such as arbitrary detention, violence against women, albinism, or water and sanitation.[2] The remaining twelve, known as "geographic mandates," address the situation of human rights in Belarus, Cambodia, Central African Republic, Democratic Peoples' Republic of Korea, Eritrea, Islamic Republic of Iran, Mali, Myanmar, Somalia, Sudan, and the Palestinian Territories. This book constitutes the first comprehensive study of the UN Special Procedures as a system; covering their history, methods of work, institutional status, and relationship with current critiques of the international human rights system, from their creation in 1947 until the forty-first session of the Human Rights Council (July 2019).[3]

It has taken a long time for experts in international human rights to devote the same consideration to the work of Special Procedures as to UN treaty bodies. The negotiated and fragmented creation of Special Procedures hindered their consideration as a category of human rights mechanisms. This determined that, when they attracted scholarly attention, they were mostly tackled selectively, with greater attention on thematic mandates focusing on "traditional" civil and political rights. The allegedly increased politicization of the Commission on Human Rights was a catalyst for its disappearance and the creation of the Human Rights Council in 2006. This development drew considerable attention to Special Procedures, since their future became a central issue in the most radical reform ever sustained by the UN institutional framework in the field of human rights. However, the difficulty of analyzing the work of dozens of mechanisms that continue to operate with a wide margin of autonomy, influenced by the political consensus that results in their creation and the imprint of the individuals taking over the mandates, explains the continuous scarcity of publications covering all Special

[2] The full list can be found on the OHCHR website at: https://www.ohchr.org/EN/HRBodies/SP/Pages/Welcomepage.aspx.

[3] All online addresses cited were valid by January 10, 2020.

Procedures, in comparison with materials focusing on specific aspects of their methods of work or mandates.

The book systematically analyzes the contribution of Special Procedures to the human rights machinery, their ambiguous institutional standing, and the risks associated with their growth in number and importance. Special Procedures remain more exposed to geopolitical factors than other human rights monitoring bodies composed of independent experts. The decisions about the creation of Special Procedures, the renewal of mandates, the selection of individuals to serve in these roles, and the reactions to Special Procedures' findings and conclusions are made by a governmental body. This ensures the political relevance of their activities but increases their vulnerability to governmental pressure. The research supporting the arguments advanced in the chapters that follow demonstrates that politicization is at the root of the most remarkable contribution of Special Procedures, including their development of pioneering methods of monitoring the behavior of states, and the emergence of international standards with states' endorsement.

The human rights cause seems to call for a collective ethical stand by states purporting to promote and protect them. The human rights agenda is a useful lens to analyze the compliance of states with international norms, as well as in studying the strategies deployed by allegedly impartial experts to monitor such compliance using legal standards as a benchmark, because it is apparent that the antagonistic relationship between law and politics is based on assumptions that defy easily observable facts. The changes in the composition of intergovernmental bodies to better reflect geographical representation have been accompanied by alarm bells of their impact on human rights protection. These fears have never materialized. Beyond the damaging impact of politicization, other assumptions are challenged throughout the book, such as the advantages of absolute independence and autonomy of experts monitoring human rights violations or the alleged contrast between positions held by states belonging to the Western and Other States Group and the rest.

Human rights are articulated as "rights" carrying normative force. This signals an expectation that any breach should be associated with an undesirable consequence for the state responsible for the breach, with a right to complain and seek remedies available to the victim. Human rights defenders, scholars, and practitioners are prone to promote the benefits of judicial or quasi-judicial mechanisms for the implementation of human rights. Yet, the intrinsic features of law, with a specialized language that requires the mediation of legal experts imply certain alienation of popular mobilization.[4] The authority of law makes legal norms more resilient to contestation than issues framed as political. The alleged "depoliticization" and professionalization of the human rights movement may result in the exclusion of the people whose welfare it purports to advance.[5]

Many current criticisms of the international human rights agenda have been articulated over decades by commentators from developing countries that have evaluated the international human rights movement from a neocolonialist perspective. These voices have found more recent echo in the work of scholars with powerful platforms. The heightened criticisms of international human rights standards, institutions, philosophical foundations, and stakeholders may constitute a much higher threat to their survival than their politicization. It is imperative to empirically analyze and contest these criticisms before they take further root, particularly since these critiques are based on widespread presumptions of policies and institutions that this book seeks to highlight as ill-founded. The urgency of contesting these criticisms lies in undermining their power to effectively dismantle crucial protection mechanisms without alternative solutions to replace them, potentially leaving vast swathes of humanity beyond the protection of any rights agenda.

[4] Robert Knox, "Against Law-sterity" 6 *Salvage* (November 2018), available at: http://salvage.zone/in-print/against-law-sterity/?fbclid=IwAR17KyPW03hOM_MjJJk4mFwszuZO8_oC-tlSJsSplD_0_6SL9paIQPBMnuM.

[5] Chidi A. Odinkalu, "Why More Africans Don't Use Human Rights Language," 2(1) *Human Rights Dialogue* (2000): 3.

One
Creation, Institutionalization, and Development of Public and Confidential Special Procedures

1. Introduction

The instigation, design, and establishment of Special Procedures are arguably the most potent legacy among many of the activities and achievements of the erstwhile UN Commission on Human Rights. The history of how Special Procedures were first envisaged, considered, mooted, negotiated, and created impacted the evolution of the Commission and the internationalization of human rights. Equally important, for those interested in tracking the development of post–Second World War international relations, the trajectory of these mechanisms provide key insights into both the overall direction and the conduct of politics concerning not only human rights but also development and issues concerned with peace and security at the United Nations. They correspondingly serve as a backdrop to many contemporary global concerns in how they are articulated, defended, and responded to, at and by multilateral organizations.

This chapter outlines the key events leading to the birth of the first public and confidential Special Procedures as a positive outcome of what was a highly politicized process. The first section explains the rationale underpinning the polar change of direction of the Commission on Human Rights, from a position where it initially denied its own competence to address human rights violations, to its decision to create subsidiary fact-finding bodies with exactly such purpose. The shared origin of public Special Procedures and the design of mechanisms for handling complaints addressing human rights violations that can result in the establishment of confidential Special Procedures are scarcely represented in the literature, especially in comparison with the development of other aspects of the mechanisms and the substantive content

In Defense of Politicization of Human Rights. Elvira Domínguez-Redondo, Oxford University Press (2020).
 DOI: 10.1093/oso/9780197516706.001.0001

of human rights. One of the primary reasons for this deficit is that any comprehensive coverage of the origin, characteristics, and current structures of Special Procedures requires that the confidential complaint mechanisms and Special Procedures are addressed simultaneously. In addition, the ad hoc nature of their establishment against political realities of the time led to a nonlinear history that is often difficult to classify.

Special Procedures trace their origin to the first ad hoc monitoring bodies established by the Commission on Human Rights to examine specific human rights violations. At their inception, it is inconceivable that the governments represented in the Commission had any motivation for creating a new category of human rights monitoring bodies. Instead, state members initiating this process were responding to specific situations of human rights violations relying on the competence, agreed by states in 1967 that the Commission should address gross and systematic violations of human rights. In the following years, subsidiary bodies were established to either investigate and report on the situation of human rights in a country or to study a phenomenon of violations of human rights worldwide that were either perceived or presented as being systemic and/or widespread. The autonomy enjoyed by the first mandate holders in deciding their methods of works resulted in significant diversity of methods, and the absence of standardized United Nations rules of procedures for fact-finding missions was an additional factor in the difficulty of studying and presenting these mechanisms. The resolutions creating or renewing such mandates, based on political decisions, were understandably vague leaving plenty of margin for interpretation and the determination of work practices. The activist leanings of mandate holders, the contexts of each procedure, and the relative differences in perspectives of the holders were a further contributing factor for widely differing methodologies adopted.

The absence of an agreed framework coupled with inconsistency in their operations means that any analysis of the historical development of Special Procedures needs to study the creation of each mandate individually. This changed to a certain extent when mandate holders and the Secretariat of the United Nations began to support the activities and coordinate the work leading up to their designation and treatment as a sui generis category within the UN institutional framework.

The following sections will focus on the political coordinates that explain the creation of the Special Procedures as subsidiary bodies of the former Commission on Human Rights. The first section describes the relevant geopolitical coordinates that determined the absence of a specific human rights main organ in the institutional design of the United Nations. It outlines the main features and functioning of the Commission on Human Rights and the Human Rights Council that came to replace it in 2006. This framework propitiated a timid approach to human rights and a self-denial of competence to address human rights violations for over two decades. The decolonization process transformed the international community and the United Nations in particular, as reflected in the composition of the UN bodies, including the Commission on Human Rights. It also effected the obsolescence of the doctrine of non-competence, resulting in the creation of the first Special Procedures focusing on specific territories. The new-found diversity of political views within existing UN organs led to difficulties in gaining clear majorities toward specific action. When it became impossible to obtain a majority of votes within the Commission to scrutinize particular countries for human rights violations, a new approach was developed to investigate specific situations of human rights.

The immediate antecedent to this was the attempt by some states to negotiate the competing interests of other states, motivated by an emerging and increasingly vocal global civil society, that were becoming adept at operating within the UN machinery. That pressure to act in the face of systematic human rights violations led to the establishment of the so-called "Charter-based" bodies, which in turn sowed the seed for a system of public Special Procedures that continues to coexist with a confidential complaint procedure.

2. The "Human Rights Pillar": Unintended Creation of Special Procedures

When the first mechanisms we now call Special Procedures were established, state members of the Commission on Human Rights did not intend to create a new category of human rights bodies. The first Special Procedures were portrayed as "fact-finding" missions by the United Nations[1] and by the scholarship at the time,[2] or as a "1235

[1] *See Further promotion and encouragement of human rights and fundamental freedoms including the question of the programme and methods of work of the Commission*, UN Doc. E/CN.4/1273 (1 December 1977), paras. 38–41.

[2] *See, e.g.*, Robert Miller, "United-Nations Fact-Finding Missions in the Field of Human Rights" *Australian Year Book of International Law* (1970–73): 40; Stephen B. Kaufman, "The necessity for rules of procedure in ad hoc United Nations Investigations" 18 (4) *The American University Law Review* (1969): 739; and Egon Schwelb and Philip Alston, "The Principal Institutions and Other

procedure."[3] It took twenty years for the Commission on Human Rights to broaden its scope of action vis-à-vis human rights violations and a further decade to confirm it had competence to establish monitoring mechanisms to investigate situations of gross violations of human rights. This delay is explained by the general reluctance of the founding states of the United Nations in guaranteeing the same level of relevance to human rights as for other objectives of the Organization despite their prominence in the UN founding documents. A key element to overcome was the provision of Article 2(7), which guaranteed "exclusive state sovereignty" on all matters that fell within "the domestic jurisdiction of States." For a fledgling global body to place restrictions on its members was a challenge, especially in light of the demise of the United Nations' predecessor, the League of Nations.

A. The "Missing" UN Main Body: From Commission to Council

The reluctance to create strong human rights provisions arises despite a clear articulation of the so-called "three pillars" of the United Nations, meant to reflect the main purposes of the Organization as enshrined in the UN Charter. These were identified as: (1) the promotion and protection of human rights; (2) development; and (3) maintenance of international peace and security. It is, however, well known that the exclusive group of states that prepared the founding documents of the United Nations at Dumbarton Oaks were focused on creating a collective security arrangement, with human rights issues, especially when occurring within the domestic jurisdiction of states, ranking extremely low among their priorities.[4] It was the role played by non-governmental organizations from the United States of

Bodies Founded Under the Charter" in Vasak (ed.), *The International Dimensions of Human Rights* (UNESCO, 1982, vol. 1): 232, 294–6.

[3] The terminology "1235 procedure" was used to refer to all mechanisms created by the UN Commission on the basis of the competence contained in Resolution 1235 (XLII) distinguishing between "public general procedures" and "public special procedures"; *see, e.g.*, José Antonio Pastor Ridruejo, "Les procédures publique spéciales de la Commission de Droits de l'Homme des Nations Unies" 228 R.C.A.D.I. 183 (1991): 209; Henry Steiner and Philip Alston, *International Human Rights in Context. Law, Politics, Morals. Text and Materials* (2nd ed. Oxford University Press, 2000): 620–3.

[4] Mary A. Glendon, "The Forgotten Crucible: The Latin American Influence on the Universal Human Rights Idea" 16 *Harvard Human Rights Journal* (2003): 27, 27–8.

America and Latin American countries, that advocated for the adoption of a declaration that would define a catalogue of human rights, that proved decisive in strengthening the provisions of the Charter on human rights during the San Francisco Conference.[5] Despite some reluctance, the preamble and substantive articles (Articles 1.3, 55 c) and 56) of the UN Charter reference human rights, while other articles contain provisions of an institutional nature (Articles 13.1.b), 60, 62.2, and 68) to support their development. The decision to establish two main bodies of the United Nations to address development (the Economic and Social Council) and peace and security (the Security Council) was not replicated for the human rights pillar. Instead, the creation of a UN human rights body was delegated, under Article 68 of the Charter, to the Economic and Social Council (ECOSOC).[6] State founders were equally unprepared to agree on a catalogue of rights,[7] a significant reflection of their disinclination to accept any proposal that had the potential to erode their sovereignty through the establishment of a regime that might have implied conferring the United Nations with powers to intervene in domestic affairs of the member states.[8] The original decision of the Commission of Human Rights not to address and engage with human rights violations, adopted in the early days of the United Nations, has to be understood in this context.

It is perhaps a reflection of the ambitious nature of the UN mandate, instigated and driven by divergent views of states, civil society organizations, and other relevant actors, that a need to reform the Organization has loomed over it since its very inception. This led one author to consider the articulation of a need for reform as one of the "primary products of the UN system."[9] Over the seven decades of its existence there have been several waves of reform that have directly impacted the growth and development of Special Procedures, as will be analyzed in detail in chapter two. Among them, the most dramatic reform culminated with the decision, in 2006, to

5 Ibid.

6 *See* Louis B. Sohn, "The Human Rights Law of the Charter" 12 *Texas International Law Journal* (1977): 129; Eibe H. Riedel and Jan-Michael Arend, "Article 55(c)" in Bruno Simma (ed.), *The Charter of the United Nations: A Commentary* (2nd ed. Oxford University Press, 2002).

7 Paolo Wright-Carozza, "From conquest to constitutions: retrieving a Latin American tradition of the idea of human rights" 25(2) *Human Rights Quarterly* (2003): 281.

8 As reflected in Article 2.7 of the UN Charter: "Nothing contained in the present Charter shall authorize the United Nations to intervene in matters which are essentially within the domestic jurisdiction of any state or shall require the Members to submit such matters to settlement under the present Charter (. . .)."

9 Edward C Luck, *Reforming the United Nations: Lessons from a History in Process* (Academic Council on the United Nations System, 2003): 2.

terminate the Commission on Human Rights altogether, and to replace it with a Human Rights Council.[10] One of the most significant differences between the former Commission and the Council lies in their institutional positioning within the United Nations. Instead of being a subsidiary organ of ECOSOC, the Human Rights Council is a subsidiary organ of the General Assembly. In technical terms this "elevated" human rights issues bringing them closer to the development and peace and security pillars, in having "principal organ" status at the United Nations. However, this "upgraded" position was considered more a reflection of the hope expressed by then Secretary General Kofi Annan, who instigated this reform.[11] It found little political support among states and commentators.[12] Following a complex process of reform[13] the General Assembly confirmed the subsidiary status of the Human Rights Council in 2011, but decided to reconsider the question of whether to maintain such status between 2021 and 2026.[14] The different status conferred to the human rights pillar is reflected in the location of the Human Rights Council and the main headquarters of the Office of the High Commissioner for Human Rights (OHCHR), based in Geneva. A change of status may have involved migrating the Secretariat supporting human rights mechanisms as well as the Human Rights Council to New York where the other main organs of the United Nations have their principal presence. There was some reticence, however, that such a move could involve an "image problem."[15]

The current membership of the Human Rights Council consists of governmental representatives of forty-seven instead of the fifty-three member states represented in the Commission. In order to fulfill the criteria of equitable geographical distribution, the Council was established with reduced representation of Western and Latin American states in favor of a larger

[10] GA Res. 60/251, 15 March 2006.

[11] On the recommendation to establish the Human Rights Council as a main organ of the UN, see *Note transmitting report of the High-Level Panel on Threats, Challenges and Change, entitled "A More Secure Word: Our Shared Responsibility*, UN Doc. A/59/565; *see also In Larger Freedom: towards development, security and human rights for all: Report of the Secretary-General: Addendum: Human Rights Council: Explanatory Note*, UN Doc. A/59/2005/Add.1, 23 May 2005, para. 183.

[12] *See Summary of the open-ended informal consultations held by the Commission on Human Rights pursuant to Economic and Social Council decision 2005/217 prepared by the Chairperson of the 61st session of the Commission*, UN Doc. A/59/847-E/2005/73, 29 July 2005, paras. 12, 27–8, 51, 57, and 63.

[13] On reforms, *see* chapter two.

[14] GA Res. 65/281, *Review of the Human Rights Council*, 17 June 2011, para. 3.

[15] *See* Universal Rights Group, *Vision 2021—What is the General Assembly's 2021–2026 review, and how might the Human Rights Council usefully contribute* (Universal Rights Group, Jan. 2019): 4.

presence for Asian and African states.[16] The antagonistic attitude of these regional groups towards Special Procedures raised well-founded fears of the impact of the new composition of the Council in relation to the future of these mechanisms.[17] Unlike the Commission, that used to meet once a year, the Council meets at least three times every year for a total period of no less than ten weeks. Other new features of the Council include a reduced ratio of states required to convene special sessions when an emergency arises (one-third instead of a majority), the creation of the *Universal Periodic Review*, and a more sophisticated selection process of state members. Like its predecessor, the Human Rights Council's mandate includes promotional and protective human rights powers. Its meetings are public and any member states, observer states, and non-governmental organizations with consultative status before ECOSOC can participate in the discussions.

In addition to public discussions, the Human Rights Council can approve resolutions and decisions with different purposes, including: (1) making recommendations with regard to the promotion and protection of human rights to state members, the General Assembly, or its subsidiary bodies; (2) determining the provision of advisory services, technical assistance, and capacity-building; and (3) creating subsidiary bodies to assist the Council in performing its tasks. The Human Rights Council inherited the main mechanisms to monitor human rights performance from the Commission, with the confidential complaint procedure and Special Procedures among them. In addition, the Human Rights Council is required to conduct assessments of the situation of human rights in every state of the world under the Universal Periodic Review mechanisms operative since 2008.

[16] Member states of the United Nations are grouped into five unofficial regional groups to consider the purposes of GA Res. 1991 (XVIII) of 17 December 1963, 33/138 of 19 December 1978, and 2847 (XXVI) 20 December 1971. For an updated list, *see* United Nations Handbook 2019–2020 (New Zealand: Ministry of Foreign Affairs and Trade, 2019): 15–7. *See also* Sam Daws, "The Origin and Development of UN Electoral Groups" in Ramesh Thakur (ed.), *What Is Equitable Geographic Representation in the Twenty-first Century?* (UN University, 1999): 11–29. On the proposals tabled by these regional groups, *see* chapter two. The Asian Group changed its name to Group of Asia and the Pacific Small Island Developing States (Asian Pacific Group, APG) in 2011.

[17] *See* Marc Bossuyt, *International Human Rights Protection. Balanced, Critical, Realistic* (Intersentia, 2016): 60, 198–9; *see also* Veronique Joosten, *The UN Human Rights Council at work: From high hopes back to reality* (United Nations Association Flanders Belgium, 2006): 10.

B. Self-denied Competence for Addressing Human Rights Violations (1947–1967)

The idea that human beings deserve special legal protection lies at the foundation of the modern conception of the system of promotion and protection of human rights at the domestic, regional, and universal levels. It is therefore unsurprising that the creation of human rights mechanisms was accompanied by demands for the widening of their jurisdiction to the subjects it is meant to serve: the individual rights-bearers, whose inherent dignity and worth the system has promised to uphold. This seemingly simple task was in fact complicated due to the manner in which international law itself evolved: as primarily existing to regulate the activities between states, with individuals within the state considered as falling within their exclusive jurisdiction. Any "international" activities that expressed concern or proposed solutions for these subjects would necessarily have to penetrate the layer of state sovereignty, a key facet of statehood, and one guarded jealously, largely reinforced with the experience of colonization that was still alive at the time of the creation of the United Nations. The accepted subject-hood of individuals, and more importantly a legitimacy toward concern for their rights, involved a complex trajectory that has been discussed elsewhere. Suffice to say that despite its lofty expression as an ideal, it took a long time for the United Nations to open its apparatus to individuals.

On February 16, 1946, the ECOSOC created the UN Commission on Human Rights complying with the mandate contained in Article 68 of the UN Charter.[18] Originally composed of nine members, the Commission was established with the main task of submitting:

> proposals, recommendations and reports to the Council regarding: a) an international bill of rights; b) international declarations or conventions on civil liberties, the status of women, freedom of information and similar matters; c) the protection of minorities; d) the prevention of discrimination on grounds of race, sex, language or religion.[19]

This mandate was extended to "any other matter concerning human rights" in June 1946.[20] The membership of the body was enlarged to eighteen members,

[18] ECOSOC Resolution 5(1) of 16 February, UN Doc. E/RES/5(I)-E/27 (22 February 1946): Section A. *See also* UN Doc. E/20 of 15 February 1946.

[19] Ibid.

[20] ECOSOC Resolution 9(II) 21 June 1946, UN Docs. E/56 and Rev.1 and E/84 (June 1946).

a number that grew over the years to ensure an equitable geographical representation. When the Commission was replaced by a Human Rights Council in 2006, it had grown to consist of fifty-three states members.[21]

During its second session in 1947, the ECOSOC created the Sub-Commission for the Prevention of Discrimination and the Protection of Minorities, renamed the Sub-Commission on the Promotion and Protection of Human Rights in 1999 to better reflect the scope of its work.[22] This body of experts significantly influenced the creation and practice of Special Procedures.[23] Often perceived as the rebel daughter of the Commission, it was replaced in 2016 by an Advisory Committee consisting of eighteen experts with the mandate of functioning as a think tank for the Council.[24] This meant, in practice, a curtailment of the Sub-Commission mandate that was accepted as a lesser evil than any allowance toward the implementation of other proposals seeking to significantly undermine the competences and independence of Special Procedures. This development also signals the fragility of expert bodies daring to overstep the confines of their mandates. The political majority required to create and renew Special Procedures has nonetheless proven to be effective in protecting them from a similar fate.

In 1947, ECOSOC endorsed the view of the Commission of Human Rights by which it declared that it had "no power to take any action in regard to any complaints concerning human rights."[25] This was perceived as a regression in comparison to the minority petitions system established by the League of

[21] The Commission's membership became twenty-two in 1961 (ECOSOC Res. 845 (XVII) 3 August 1961); increasing to thirty-two in 1966 (ECOSOC Res. 1147 (XLI) 4 August 1966), forty-three in 1979 (ECOSOC Res. 1979/36, 10 May 1979); and fifty-three in 1992 (ECOSOC Res. 1990/48, 25 May 1992).

[22] The Sub-Commission was established in 1974 (*see Report of the First Session of the Commission on Human Rights' Commission on Human Rights: Report to the Economic and Social Council on the 1st session of the Commission held at Lake Success, New York, from 27 January to 10 February 1947*, UN Doc. E/259, paras. 18–20). Composed by twelve expert members, it was expanded to fourteen in 1959 (ECOSOC Res. 728E (XXVIII) 30 July 1959), eighteen in 1966 (ECOSOC Res. 1074G (XXXIX) 28 July 1965), and twenty-six in 1969 (ECOSOC Res. 1334 (XLIV) 31 May 1968). It was renamed Sub-Commission for the Promotion and Protection of Human Rights in 1999 (ECOSOC Res. 1999/256 of 27 July 1999).

[23] On its mandate and influence in the creation and evolution of Special Procedures, *see* Asbjørn Eide, "The Sub-Commission on Prevention on the Elimination of Racial Discrimination," in Alston (ed.), *The United Nations and Human Rights. A Critical Appraisal* (Clarendon Press, 1992): 211.

[24] HRC. Res. 5/1 *Institution Building of the United Nations Human Rights Council*, 18 June 2007, paras. 65–84.

[25] UN Doc. E/259 (Supp.) (n. 22): para. 22, and ECOSOC Res. 75 (V) of 5 August 1947 in *Resolutions adopted by the Economic and Social Council during its 5th session from 19 July to 16 August 1947*, UN Doc. E/573 (2 September 1947).

Nations[26] as it denied a right of petition to individuals deriving directly from the UN Charter.[27] ECOSOC was also effectively contradicting itself: it was only a year earlier that it had expressed the view that the Commission's role was to:

> assist the appropriate organs of the United Nations in the task defined for the General Assembly and the Economic and Social Council in Articles 13, 55, and 62 of the Charter, and that it might aid the Security Council in the task entrusted to it by Article 39 of the Charter, by *pointing to cases where violation of human rights may constitute a threat to the peace*.[28]

Several initiatives to overturn this self-denial stance, led by the Sub-Commission on the Prevention of Discrimination and Protection of Minorities,[29] the Sub-Commission on the Freedom of Information and the Press,[30] and the Secretariat,[31] proved unsuccessful in shifting this position at the time.

Within the United Nations, the only individual complaint procedure in force established under the authority of the UN Charter (Article 87) was operated by the Trusteeship System,[32] the successor to the mandate system under the League of Nations.[33] From 1961, the so-called Committee of the

[26] Maxime Tardu, "Human Rights Complaint Procedures of the United Nations: Assessment and Prospects" in Jürgen Jekewitz et al. (eds.), *Des Menschen Recht zwischen Freiheit und Verantwortung. Festchrift für Josef Partsh zum 75. Geburstag* (Duncker & Humblot, 1989): 287, 287–8.

[27] H. Lauterpacht, *International Law and Human Rights* (Praeger, 1950): 177–88. *See also* J.W. Bruegel, "The Right to Petition an International Authority" 2 *International and Comparative Law Quarterly* (1953): 542.

[28] *See Report of the Commission on Human Rights to the 2nd session of the Economic and Social Council*, UN Doc. E/38 (17 May 1946): 228, and E/38/Rev.1 (21 May 1946): 408 [emphasis added]. *See also* Nabiel J. Fareed, *The United Nations Commission on Human Rights and its work for human rights and fundamental freedoms* (Diss. Washington State University, 1979): 82–3.

[29] *Report of the 2nd session of the Sub-Commission on the Prevention of Discrimination and the Protection of Minorities, Lake Success, N.Y., 13 June to 27 June 1949*, UN Doc. E/CN.4/351-E/CN.4/SUB.2/78 (29 June 1949), paras. 26–30, *esp.* para. 29. *See also Report of the 3rd session of the Sub-Commission on the Prevention of Discrimination and the Protection of Minorities, Lake Success, N.Y, 9 to 27 January 1950*, UN Doc. E/CN.4/359-E/CN.4/SUB.2/119 (30 January 1950), paras. 17–21 and draft resolution VI.

[30] *See Report of the 3rd session of the Sub-Commission on Freedom of Information and of the Press to the Economic and Social Council*, UN Doc. E/1369–E/CN.4/SUB.1/98/REV.1 (24 June 1949), paras. 22–8.

[31] *Report of the Secretary General on the present situation with regard to communications concerning human rights*, UN Doc. E/CN.4/165 (2 May 1949), *esp.* para. 13. *See also* Schwelb and Alston (1982) (n. 2): 271–2.

[32] *See* A.J.R. Groom, "The Trusteeship Council: A Successful Demise" in Paul Taylor and A.J.R. Groom, *The United Nations at the Millennium. The Principal Organs* (Continuum, 2000): 142.

[33] For historic precedents of the right to petition internationally prior and during the League of Nations period, *see* Donald P. Parson, "The Individual Right of Petition: A Study of Methods Used by

24 (Decolonization Committee) monitored the situation of human rights in non-self-governing territories using individuals as sources of information. The Special Committee on Apartheid, established in 1962 by the General Assembly, also dealt with petitions.[34] However the individuals benefiting from access to these international mechanisms were very limited.[35]

While ECOSOC Resolution 75 (V) declared a lack of competence in dealing with allegations of human rights violations, it also sought to establish a symbolic procedure to process the thousands of communications transmitted by individuals concerning alleged violations of human rights that had begun to arrive at the Secretariat since the creation of the United Nations. The scattered data available fails to provide an insight of the number of communications received by the Secretariat. For instance, the Commission on Human Rights reported that over 25,000 communications were referred to it between April 3, 1951, and May 7, 1952, compared to 2,118 communications received during the period May 7, 1952, to March 7, 1953.[36] Following several amendments, a procedure to handle communications was established by ECOSOC Resolution 728F (XXVIII) of July 30, 1959.[37] Defined by John Humphrey, then Director of the United Nations Division on Human Rights,

International Organizations to Utilize the Individual as a Source of Information on the Violations of Human Rights" 13 *Wayne Law Review* (1966–7): 678, 678–88.

[34] *See* GA Res. 1761 (XVII), "The policies of *apartheid* of the Government of the Republic of South Africa" (6 November 1962), operative para. 5,

[35] *See* John Carey, "The United Nations' Double Standards on Human Rights Complaints" 60 *American Journal of International Law* (1996): 792; *see also* Nigel Rodley, "Monitoring Human Rights by the U.N. System and Nongovernmental Organizations" in Kommers and Loescher (eds.), *Human Rights and American Foreign Policy* (University of Notre Damme Press, 1979): 157, 161–2.

[36] *See Commission on Human Rights Report of the Ninth Session, 7 April–30 May 1953*, UN Doc. E/2447-E/CN.4/689 (6 June 1953), para. 293.

[37] *See Resolutions: Economic and Social Council Official Records, 28th Session, 30 June–31 July 1959*, UN Doc. E/3290 (1959) p. 19. The Resolution consolidates in one document minor amendments introduced to ECOSOC Res. 75 (V) (n. 25). The amendments can be found in ECOSOC Res. 116 A (VI) 1 March 1948, *Resolutions adopted by the Economic and Social Council during its 6th Session from 2 February to 11 March 1948*, UN Doc. E/777 (12 March 1948); ECOSOC Res. 192 A(VIII) 9 February 1949, *Resolutions: Official Records of the 8th Session of the Economic and Social Council, 7 February–18 March 1949*, UN Doc. E/1310 (15 March 1949); and 454 (XIV) 28 July 1952 *Resolutions: Official Records of the Economic and Social Council 14th Session, 20 May–1 August 1952*, UN Doc. E/2332 (31 December 1952). *See also* proposals to modify the procedure contained in *Report of the* Ad Hoc *Committee on Communications: Commission on Human Rights, 2nd Session*, UN Doc. E/CN.4/64-E/600, supp. 6 (1947) (14 December 1947): 7 and 8; *Report of the Session of the Sub-Commission on the Prevention of Discrimination and the Protection of Minorities, Lake Success, N.Y. 13 June to 27 June 1949*, UN Doc. E/CN.4/351-E/CN.4/SUB.2/78 and Corr. 1 and 2 (29 June 1949), paras. 26–32; *Report of the 3rd Session of the Sub-Commission on the Prevention of Discrimination and the Protection of Minorities, Lake Success, N.Y., 9 to 27 January 1959*, UN Doc. E/CN.4/358-E/CN.4/SUB.2/119 (30 January 1950), paras. 17–21; and *Communications: Memorandum by the Secretary General*, UN Doc. E/CN.4/361 (14 March 1950).

as "the most elaborate wastepaper basket ever intended,"[38] the Secretariat compiled a public list of communications dealing with human rights "principles" and a confidential summary of communications concerning human rights violations.[39] States concerned received a copy of the human rights communications and were provided with the opportunity to reply. The authors of human rights communications were informed that their communication was to be handled in accordance with this procedure, with a reminder that the Commission had no power to take any action regarding any complaint concerning human rights.[40] At the end of each session, the Commission took note of the receipt of the compiled lists of communications and restated its position as being one where no action was possible, until 1959, when this formality was finally dropped.[41]

This way of circulating communications became the basis of the confidential "1503 procedure," pertaining to the number of the 1970 ECOSOC Resolution 1503 (XLVIII) creating it.[42] The 1503 procedure, explained later, was reformed amid the wider reforms undertaken in 2000[43] and, following the creation of the Human Rights Council, was replaced by the current "complaint procedure."[44]

[38] John P. Humphrey, *Human Rights and the United Nations: A Great Adventure* (Transnational Publishers, Inc. 1984): 28.

[39] *See* UN Doc. E/259 (Supp.) (n. 22), paras. 21 and 23; and ECOSOC Res. 75 (V) (n. 25). *See also Report of the Sub-Committee on the Handling of Communications: Commission on Human Rights*, UN Doc. E/CN.4/14/Rev. 1 (5 February 1947); and *Report of the Sub-Committee on the Handling of Communications: Commission on Human Rights*, UN Doc. E/CN.4/14/Rev. 2 (6 February 1947), paras. 2 and 5.

[40] *See* ECOSOC Res. 728 F(XXVIII) of 30 July 1959, which consolidates minor amendments to ECOSOC Res. 75 (V) (n. 25) introduced by: ECOSOC Res. 116 A (VI) 1 March 1948, UN Doc. E/777 (n. 37); 112 A (VI) [on these amendments see also suggestions by the Committee ad hoc on Communications in UN Doc. E/CN.4/64-E/600, supp. 6 (14 December 1947) 7–8; and suggestions of the Sub-Commission concerning its own role in the study of communications in UN Doc. E/CN.4/351 (n. 29); E/CN.4/358 (n. 37); and E/CN.4/361 (n. 37)]; 192 A (VIII) 9 February 1949, UN Doc. E/1310 (n. 37). *See also Report of the 3rd Session of the Commission on Human Rights, Lake Success, N.Y., 24 May to 18 June 1948*, UN Doc. E/800 (28 June 1948); 275 B (X) 17 February 1950, *Resolutions: Economic and Social Council Official Records, 5h year, 10th session, 7 February–6 March 1959*, UN Doc. E/1661 (18 April 1950); and *Report of the 5th Session of the Commission on Human Rights to the Economic and Social Council, Lake Success, N.Y., 9 May–20 June 1949*, UN Doc. E/1371(SUPP)-E/CN.4/350 (23 June1949), pp. 12 and 13. In addition, ECOSOC Res. 728 F(XXVIII) ends the distinction between state members of the Commission and non-state members regarding the receipt of a copy of the communications [formerly established by paragraph e) of Res. 75 (V) (n. 25) and 454 (XIV) of 28 July 1952].

[41] ECOSOC Res. 15 (XV) of 8 April 1959. *See also Methods Used by the United Nations in the Field of Human Rights*, UN Doc. A/CONF.32/6 (1967).

[42] ECOSOC Res. 1503 (XLVIII) of 27 May 1970.

[43] ECOSOC Res. 2000/3 (16 June 2000), *Procedure for dealing with communications concerning human rights*.

[44] *See* HRC Res. 5/1 (n. 24).

Geopolitical factors were decisive in making the non-competence stance of the Commission unsustainable. Key among these was the decolonization process, which dramatically changed the composition of the United Nations. Between 1945 and 1960, forty-five countries and 800 million persons (a quarter of the inhabitants of the planet) achieved independence from colonial rule.[45] By 1967, 57 percent of the 127 UN member states were relatively new Asian and African states.[46] The new "Third World" majority at the United Nations supported the creation of human rights monitoring mechanisms. The contribution of newly independent states to the change of direction of the United Nations toward human rights is often downplayed or explained as motivated by the risk of marginalization as second-rate countries with consequent reduction of foreign aid.[47] Whatever the motivations driving their political agendas, Asian and African states have always been key actors in shaping human rights mechanisms. This reality is obscured by relatively simplistic North versus South discourses on human rights that appear to rely on imbedded assumptions that are rarely supported by evidence.

Between 1960 and 1963, the General Assembly created a Special Committee to monitor the implementation of the *Declaration of Independence to Colonial Countries and Peoples*[48] with competence to carry out its task by employment of all available means.[49] It commissioned the second-ever UN fact-finding mission concerning the observance of human rights[50] to investigate allegations of human rights violations of the Buddhist community in

[45] R. Aracil, J. Oliver, and Antoni Segura, *El mundo actual. De la Segunda Guerra Mundial a nuestros días* (2nd ed. Universitat de Barcelona, 1998): 123; M.J. Peterson, "General Assembly" in Weiss and Daws (eds.), *The Oxford Handbook on the United Nations* (Oxford University Press, 2007): 97, 106–9; and Sally Morphet, "States Groups at the United Nations and Growth of Member States at the United Nations" in Paul Taylor and A.J.R Groom (eds.), *The United Nations at the Millennium. The Principal Organs* (Continuum, 2000): 224, table 8.1.

[46] On the impact of the new UN memberships on the composition of the Commission on Human Rights, *see* Fareed (1979) (n. 28): 71–6.

[47] Tardu (1989) (n. 26): 288–9; *See also* S. Chesterman, T.M. Franck, and D.M. Malone, *Law and Practice of the United Nations* (Oxford University Press, 2008): 457–8.

[48] *Declaration on the Granting of Independence to Colonial Countries and Peoples*, GA Res. 1514 (XV) 14 September 1960.

[49] *The Situation with Regard to the Implementation of the Declaration on Granting of Independence to Colonial Countries and Peoples*, General Assembly Resolution 1654 (XVI) 27 November 1961, para. 5.

[50] The first one was established by ECOSOC Res. 350 (XII) 17 March 1951, to investigate the question of forced labor as a means of political coercion or punishment for holding or expressing political views. Its final report can be found in *Report of the* Ad Hoc *Committee on Forced Labour*, UN Doc. E/2431 (1953), paras. 7–547. A comprehensive study of other fact-finding bodies created by the United Nations between 1945 and 1964 can be found in the *Report of the Secretary General on methods of fact-finding*, UN Doc. A/5694 (1 May 1964).

South Vietnam;[51] additionally, it designated a Special Committee on the apartheid policies of the government of South Africa.[52] The first "treaty bodies" make their appearance during these years too, with the adoption of the two Covenants on Civil and Political Rights and Economic and Social Rights (1966), as well as the Convention on the Elimination of All Forms of Racial Discrimination (1965). The Commission's self-denied competence to deal with human rights violations was at odds with other UN bodies, particularly taking into account its role as the main UN human rights institution.

C. Setting the Change of Direction: Resolutions 1235 (XLII) and 1503 (XLVIII)

The unanimous condemnation of apartheid should be considered the decisive instigator of the creation of a fact-finding mission, which set the basis for the first "Special Procedure." The Chairman of the General Assembly's *Special Committee on the Policies of Apartheid of the Government of South Africa* called upon the Commission on Human Rights, on February 3, 1947, to carry out an international investigation of charges of torture and ill-treatment of South African prisoners and other persons in police custody.[53] This request required the Commission to claim competence for such action, overturning its twenty-year denial of such powers.

In March 1967, the Commission appointed an Ad Hoc Working Group of Experts on the situation of human rights in southern Africa[54] and a Special Rapporteur on the politics of apartheid.[55] The Commission also sought authorization from its parent body, ECOSOC, to deal with other situations of human rights violations in the future.[56] The authorization became effective

[51] *See Report of the United Nations Fact-Finding Mission to South Viet-Nam*, UN Doc. A/5630 (7 December 1963). For the precedents of this Mission, *see* Kaufman (1969) (n. 2): 752–5.

[52] UNGA Res. 1761 (XVII) (6 November 1962). *See* Theo van Boven, "Chartering New Grounds in Human Rights" in Coomans et al. (eds.), *Human Rights from Exclusion to Inclusion; Principles and Practice. An Anthology from the Work of Theo van Boven* (Kluwer Law International, 2000): 3; and R.B. Ballinger, "UN Action on Human Rights in South Africa" in Evan Luard (ed.), *The International Protection of Human Rights* (Thames and Hudson, 1967): 248, *esp.* 257–66.

[53] *See* Miller (1970–3) (n. 2): 43.

[54] CHR Res. 2 (XXIII) 6 March 1967.

[55] CHR Res. 7(XXIII) 16 March 1967.

[56] *See* CHR Res. 8 (XXIII) and 9 (XXIII) (both 16 March 1967). *See also* ECOSOC Res. 1102 (XL) 4 March 1966 and 1164 (XLI) 5 August 1966; and GA Res. 2144 (XXI) 26 October 1966, determining the change of direction of the Commission. Former proposals can be found in reports of the Commission on Human Rights on its annual sessions of 1962 (UN Doc. E/3616/Rev.1-E/CN.4/832/Rev.1); 1963 (UN Doc. E/3743-E/CN.4/857); 1964 (UN Doc. E/3873-E/CN.4/874), and 1966 (UN Doc. E/4184-E/CN.4/916).

that same year with the adoption of ECOSOC Resolution 1235 (XLII). The text of Resolution 1235 (XLII) restricted the sources of information available to the Commission to those contained in the communications listed by the Secretary General pursuant to ECOSOC Resolution 728 F (XXVIII) of July 30, 1959. However, a particular reading of the 1235 resolution in conjunction with others approved by the Commission on Human Rights, the General Assembly, and ECOSOC, as well as the public nature of the annual sessions of the Commission on Human Rights, privileged an interpretation according to which the Commission—and the former Sub-Commission for the Promotion and Protection of Minorities—were authorized to use all sources of information to investigate situations of human rights violations. This interpretation was contested and the object of several legal analyses within the United Nations, but this reading of the Resolution 1235 (XLII) prevailed and was decisive in terms of the birth of two different procedures, one public and one confidential, to deal with allegations of human rights violations: the so-called "1235" and "1503" procedures.[57]

The confidential information included in the list prepared according to Resolution 728 F (XXVIII) was processed within the framework of the so-called 1503 procedure. At the time, the rules contained in Resolution 1503 were understood as creating "the first procedure within the framework of the United Nations under which private individuals and non-governments [could] raise complaints about violations of human rights within a State and [had] those complaints investigated and reported upon by an impartial international body."[58] All the other sources of information became the object of public scrutiny, either in the context of the public annual sessions of the Commission on Human Rights or under what would become known as the system of Special Procedures.[59]

Resolution 1503 (LXVIII) was meant to spell out the details of the procedure mandated in the 1235 resolution, not to create two different mechanisms. The possibility of both treatments was a positive step derived from the interpretation referred to earlier. However, early accounts of the

[57] *See* Bertrand G. Ramcharan, *The concept and present status of the international protection of human rights. Forty Years after the Declaration* (Martinus Nijhoff Publishers, 1989): 65–70. *See also* Theo van Boven, "The United Nations Commission on Human Rights and violations of human rights and fundamental freedoms" 18 *Netherlands International Law Review* (1968): 374, 380–2.

[58] Antonio Cassese, "The Admissibility of Communications to the United Nations on Human Rights Violations" 5 *Human Rights Journal* (1972): 375.

[59] A detailed account of the circumstances leading to this result can be found in Elvira Domínguez-Redondo, "La Comisión de Derechos Humanos a Debate: El Procedimiento 1503," 2 *Revista Iberoamericana de Derechos Humanos* (2006): 34.

approval of Resolutions 1235 (XLII) and 1503 (XLVIII) reflect an understanding that communications could only be dealt with under the confidentiality of the 1503 procedure. In the words of Howard Tolley:

> The unintended result was the creation of two procedures for considering violations—one public, under Resolution 1235, *without benefit of the communication*—and a separate, confidential procedure for reviewing communications.[60]

The scope of the 1503 procedure was universal in terms of countries and rights covered by it. Admissibility criteria to submit a complaint were framed by the then Sub-Commission for the Prevention of Discrimination and the Protection of Minorities in its Resolution 1 (XXIV) in 1971.

After its first substantial reform in 2000, the 1503 procedure was renamed as a "complaint procedure" in 2007,[61] while retaining its original objective: to reveal a consistent pattern of gross and reliably attested violations of human rights. Thus, while the mechanism is largely nourished by individual complaints, it does not seek to redress individual cases but rather to address patterns of violations, in cooperation with the state concerned, with the confidentiality of the procedure meant to facilitate such cooperation. Within that context, individuals submitting complaints act as witnesses and sources of information, rather than victims or/and parties of a process. A possible outcome of this procedure is the creation of new Special Procedures, as explained below.[62]

3. First Geographic Mandates

In March 1969, the Commission established its second "fact-finding" mission, this time to investigate human rights allegations concerning Israel's

[60] Howard Tolley, "The Concealed Crack in the Citadel: The United Nations Commission on Human Rights' Response to Confidential Communications" 6 *Human Rights Quarterly* (1984): 420, 429 [emphasis added]. The divergent position of states on this issue is summarized in UN Doc. E/CN.4/1273/Add.1-5 (n. 1). *See also* Theresa Gonzáles, "The Political Sources of Procedural Debates in the United Nations: Structural Impediments to Implementation of Human Rights" 13 *New York University Journal of International Law* (1981): 427; and Sidney Liskowsky, "Coping with the Question of the violation of human rights and fundamental freedoms" VIII(4) *Human Rights Journal* (1975): 883.

[61] ECOSOC Res. 2000/3 (n. 43) and HRC Res. 5/1 (n. 24).

[62] *See* section 5.

violation of the 1949 Geneva Convention relative to the Protection of Civilian Persons in Time of War, in the territories occupied in the aftermath of the 1968 "Six-Day War."[63] This mechanism was created as a result of the difficulties faced in nominating members of the General Assembly Committee to Investigate Israel Practices Affecting the Human Rights of the Palestinian People and Other Arabs of the Occupied Territories.[64] Once the Committee became operative, the Commission's Working Group on the same topic ended its mandate. While many name this body as the "second" Special Procedure created by the Commission, its existence was limited to provisionally replacing a mandate taken over from the General Assembly.[65]

It was not until 1975 that the Commission addressed another country's human rights situation, despite attempts made by the former Sub-Commission on Prevention of Discrimination and Protection of Minorities to promote the investigation of other territories in 1968.[66] Both the investigation on the policy of apartheid and the occupied Arab territories had been the object of worldwide condemnation, actions by the General Assembly and the Security Council.[67] It was thus relatively easy to justify them as not pertaining to the domestic affairs of a state by their own nature and therefore not in open conflict with Article 2.7 of the UN Charter.[68] This explains the

63 CHR Res. 6(XXV) 4 March 1969.

64 GA Res. 2443(XXIII) 19 December 1968. *See* Kurt Herndl, "Recent Developments concerning United Nations fact-finding in the field of human rights" in Nowak, Sterurer, and Tretter (eds.), *Progress in the Spirit of Human Rights. Festchrift für Felix Ermacora* (Engel, 1988): 1, 11; *see also* Nigel Rodley, "The United Nations and Human Rights in the Middle East" 38(2) *Social Research* (1971): 217, 238–9.

65 *See, e.g.*, Miko Lempinen, *Challenges Facing the System of Special Procedures of the United Nations Commission on Human Rights* (Åbo Academi University, 2001): 139–44; Ingrid Nifosi, *The UN Special Procedures in the Field of Human Rights* (Intersentia, 2005): 15; Marc Limon and Hilary Power, *History of the United Nations Special Procedures Mechanism* (Universal Rights Group, 2014): 6.

66 The Sub-Commission's tabled proposals for investigations on Greece and Haiti, were not welcome by the Commission. *See Report of the Sub-Commission on Prevention of Discrimination and Protection of Minorities to the Commission on Human Rights, Geneva, 25 September–12 October 1967*, UN Doc. E/CN.4/947-E/CN.4/Sub.2/286, 32–41 (4 December 1967), in particular Res. 3(XX) 6 October 1967. On discussions concerning the powers of the Sub-Commission to recommend actions, *see Report of the 21st Session of the Sub-Commission on Prevention of Discrimination and Protection of Minorities to the Commission on Human Rights, Geneva, 7–25 October 1968*, UN Doc. E/CN.4/976-E/CN.4/Sub.2/294-E/4475 (18 November 1968): 58–79; *see also* Peter Haver, "The United Nations Sub-Commission on Prevention of Discrimination and Protection of Minorities" 21 *Columbia Journal of Transnational Law* (1982): 103; Tom J. Farer, "The UN and Human Rights: More than a Whimper, Less than a Roar" in Roberts and Kingsbury (eds.), *United Nations, Divided World. The UN's roles in international relations* (Clarendon Press, 1988): 95, 127–31; Maxime E. Tardu, "Procedures of the United Nations Organization: Procedures of General Scope" in *Human rights: the international petition system* Vol. I, Part I, Section IA (Oceana Publications, 1979): 28.

67 *See, e.g.*, SC Res. 134 (1960) 1 April 1960 and 181 (1963) 7 August 1963.

68 *See e.g.*, Felix Ermacora, "Human Rights and Domestic Jurisdiction (article 2 paragraph 7 of the Charter)" 124 RCADI (1968): 375, 406–23; Ballinger (1967) (n. 52): 248, *esp.* 257–66; Rodley (1971) (n. 64); Antônio Cançado Trindade, "Co-existence and co-ordination of mechanisms of

lack of resistance enjoyed by the Commission when it decided the mandates on southern Africa. It is also reflected, in sharp contrast with the highly controversial discussions that have followed the birth and life of every other geographic mandate since, the almost unanimous political support enjoyed by the Commission in relation to decisions addressing this territory, including the designation of a separate point in its agenda or the two-year extension of its mandate in 1969.[69]

The Commission's decision to create a Working Group on the situation of human rights in Chile in 1975 signaled a radical change of direction.[70] The events instigating its creation were influenced by international outcry and were in parallel to other interventions by the United Nations and regional bodies. Yet unlike the two previous situations, they could not be ascribed to a question of racist policy or decolonization, as those used as the title of Resolution 1235(XLII).[71] The situation of human rights violations under scrutiny was clearly one traditionally considered within the domestic affairs of a state. The creation of the Working Group resulted in strong contestation by states of the legitimacy of actions decided by the Commission, and it represents the first example of the political confrontations accompanying the creation of a country-specific mandate to date and the calls for their removal from the system.[72]

Even among governments supporting the creation of the Working Group on Chile, there was an attempt to present the situation as unique and to highlight that it could not be "used as a precedent for future United Nations

international protection of human rights (at global and regional levels)" 202 RCADI (1987) 35–42. A survey of the UN actions regarding apartheid can be found in the *Report of the Special Rapporteur Study of Apartheid and Racial Discrimination in Southern Africa*, UN Doc. E/CN.4/949/Add.3, chap. V (1967).

[69] With the exception the South African government, which opposed UN actions based on Article 2.7 of the UN Charter. *See* Ballinger (1967) (n. 52): 251–71. Early debates concerning the competence of the Commission on Human Rights to establish the Group can be found at *Commission on Human Rights: Report of the 23rd session, 20 February–23 March 1967*, UN Doc. E/4322(SUPP)-E/CN.4/940 (1 January 1967), paras. 220–35.

[70] CHR Res. 8(XXI) (27 February 1975); *see also* Sub-Commission Res. 8(XXVII) (21 August 1974) and UNGA Res. 3219 (XXIX) (6 November 1974).

[71] Question of the violation of human rights and fundamental freedoms, including policies of racial discrimination and segregation and of apartheid, in all countries, with particular reference to colonial and other dependent countries and territories.

[72] On the debate generated over the Chilean mandate, *see* Gonzáles (1981) (n. 60). On subsequent attempts to remove country-specific mandates, *see* Elvira Domínguez-Redondo, "UN Public Special Procedures under Damocles' Sword—Two Particular Innovations: Mechanisms for the Appointment of Mandate-holders and the Adoption of a Code of Conduct for Special Procedures Mandate-holders of the Human Rights Council" (2008) 29 HRLJ 32, 35–6.

activities in the field of human rights,"[73] although other states supported the idea that the Chilean experience could be extended to other similar situations across the globe.[74]

In any case, the mandate on Chile opened the door to other geographic mandates, and, in the following years, geographic procedures rapidly extended the scope of their actions around the world. The Commission entrusted mandates to the Secretary General on the situation of human rights in Cyprus (1975),[75] Kampuchea (1978),[76] and Nicaragua (1979).[77] In 1979, it also decided for the first time to use the possibility of public scrutiny—and the appointment of a Special Rapporteur—to study the situation of a country that was being investigated at the time under the confidential 1503 procedure (Equatorial Guinea).[78] In 1978, the General Assembly provided the final endorsement needed, settling the Commission's competence to create geographic mandates. After acknowledging and welcoming the work carried out by the Ad Hoc Working Group on the Situation of Human Rights in Chile, it called upon the Commission to use it as basis for its future actions when dealing with consistent patterns of gross violations of human rights.[79]

The endorsement of the General Assembly confirmed the merits of the Special Procedures as a tool to guide future actions of the Commission at a crucial time. The adoption of Resolution 1235 (XLII) was facilitated by the absence of any other body able to deal with human rights violations within the United Nations. The approval of Resolution 1503 (XLVIII) had already prompted some governments to argue that every situation and communication on human rights violations should follow the confidential route

[73] Statement by the Representative of Yugoslavia, *Summary Record of the 70th Meeting: 3rd Committee, held on Thursday, 7 December 1978, General Assembly*, UN Doc. A/C.3/33/SR.70 (8 March 1979), para. 47.

[74] *See*, for instance, the statements by the Representatives of the United States of America, Canada and Austria, *Summary Record of the 70th Meeting: 3rd Committee, held on Thursday, 7 December 1978, General Assembly*, UN Doc. A/C.3/33/SR.70 (8 March 1979), paras. 6, 14, and 32; *see also* statement by the Representative of Australia, *Summary Record of the 69th Meeting: 3rd Committee, held on Wednesday, 6 December 1978, General Assembly, 33rd Session*, UN Doc. A/C.3/33/SR.69 (12 December 1978), para. 79.

[75] CHR Res. 4 (XXXI) 13 February 1975.

[76] CHR Res. 9 (XXXIV) 8 March 1978.

[77] CHR Res. 14(XXXV) 13 March 1979.

[78] ECOSOC Res. 1979/35, 10 May 1979. A summary of actions addressing the situation in the country can be found in the first report of the Special Rapporteur (Study of the Human Rights Situation in Equatorial Guinea-by Professor Fernando Volio Jimenez, Special Rapporteur, appointed in accordance with Resolution 15 (XXXV) of the Commission on Human Rights, UN Doc. E/CN.4/1371 (12 February 1980), paras. 5–23. *See also* section II.D.

[79] UNGA Res. 33/176 (10 December 1978).

established in 1970.[80] After all, such states argued that Resolution 1235 (XLII) only provided competence, not a procedure to deal with human rights violations—and as seen earlier, the letter of the text seemed to restrict sources to those contained in Resolution 728F(XXVIII).[81] The creation of public mandates on southern Africa and support for this action prevented the proposals to prosper. However, it was the decision to create the Chilean mandate that ended the discussion on whether two routes of dealing with human rights violations—one public and one confidential—had been created. By 1978, several human rights treaties had entered into force—significantly the two Covenants on Civil and Political Rights and Economic, Social and Cultural Rights—which raised again the question of the necessity of retaining the mechanisms established by the Commission.[82] However, by the time this debate was ignited, Special Procedures were consolidated enough to prevent their removal.

4. First Thematic Mandates

The Commission's expansion of members in 1980[83] reinforced membership from the "Non-Aligned" group of countries, which, contrary to some pessimistic prognosis, facilitated the proliferation of geographic mandates and contributed to the creation of the first thematic Special Procedures.[84] In a

[80] Nigel Rodley, "Towards a more effective and integrated system of human rights protection by the United Nations," UN Doc. A/CONF.157/PC/60/Add.6 (1 April 1993), para. 14.

[81] Theo van Boven, "United Nations and Human Rights. A Critical Appraisal" in Antonio Cassese (ed.), *UN Law/Fundamental Rights. Two topics in International Law* (Sijthoff Noordhoff, 1979): 119, 121–4; and Tolley (1984) (n. 60): 425–9.

[82] Although these discussions were generally on the 1503 procedure and attempts to eliminate or reform it. *See* UN Commission on Human Rights Res. 16(XXIV) of 7 March 1976 and resulting report by the Secretary General *Analysis of existing United Nations procedures for dealing with communications concerning violations of Human Rights*, UN Doc. E/CN.4/1317 (8 February1978). *See also* Theo van Boven, "Creative and Dynamic Strategies for Using United Nations Institutions and Procedures: The Frank Newman Files" in Coomans et al. (2000) (n. 52): 89, 90–5.

[83] See n. 21.

[84] On the pessimist forecast environment of the 1980's session of the Commission, resulting from the extension of members, the invasion of Afghanistan and the Andrei Sakharov case, *see* International Commission of Jurist: "UN Commission on Human Rights (Commentaries, 36th session)" 24 *International Commission of Jurists/Review* (1980): 29–36; Howard Tolley, "'Decision-Making' at the United Nations Commission on Human Rights, 1979–1982" 5(1) *Human Rights Quarterly* (1983): 25–57. On the non-aligned group positions within the United Nations, *see* Sally Morphet, "States Groups at the United Nations and Growth of Member States at the United Nations" in Paul Taylor and A.J.R Groom (eds.), *The United Nations at the Millennium. The Principal Organs* (Continuum, 2000): 224, 237–43.

remarkable development, oral interventions of non-governmental organizations during the Commission's sessions referred to any country, whether or not their study was included in the agenda, simplifying the creation of new geographic procedures.[85] Special Procedures rapidly became the main focus of the Commission's agenda with their reports discussed under a growing number of points, consolidating their position in the Organization.

The expansion of territories coming under the scrutiny of the Commission also fueled tensions in what was a particularly dark period of the United Nations' history. Between 1979 and the mid-80s, the United Nations witnessed an intensification of the Cold War confrontation, a proliferation of new categories of armed conflicts to which it was unable to respond due to the use of Security Council vetoes by the United States and its Allies or the Soviet Union, accusations of application of "double standards," along with allegations of espionage within the Secretariat (exacerbated by the departure of the Director of the Human Rights Division, Theo van Boven),[86] a general disagreement on the role of the United Nations when dealing with human rights, and the claim of involvement in war crimes of a former UN Secretary General, Kurt Waldheim.[87] The translation of these conflicts to the Commission's negotiations resulted in a historic milestone for the evolution of Special Procedures: the creation of thematic mandates.

The situation leading to the creation of the first thematic procedure is well documented, arising in the context of disappearances in Argentina. Under pressure from well-organized civil society organizations, the Commission

[85] The circulation of written statements was restricted by the rules contained in ECOSOC Res. 1919 (XLVIII) of 5 May 1975, although they have not been respected in practice. *See* Maya Prasad, "The Role of Non-Governmental Organizations in the New United Nations Procedures for Human Rights Complaints" 5(1) *Denver Journal of International Law and Policy* (1975): 441–62. Several opinions on the topic were issued by the UN Office of Legal Affairs: *Circulation of Written Statements: Opinion Dated 28 April, 1977 from the Office of Legal Affairs to the Under-Secretary for Political and General Assembly Affairs; Principles for the Issuance and Circulation of Written Statements by NGOs: Legal Analysis Dated May, 1977; Oral Statements in the Commission on Human Rights: Legal Analysis (1978); Written Statements by Non-Governmental Organizations: Legal Analysis Dated 22 February, 1984*, reproduced in Bertrand G. Ramcharan (ed.), *The principle of legality in International Human Rights Institutions. Selected Legal Opinions* (Martinus Nijhoff Publishers, 1997): 349–55. *See also* Rodley (1993) (n. 80): paras. 30–1.

[86] The reports surrounding this event are worth reading for those who are interested in the dark side of the Secretariat and its not so independent role, *see* Eric G. Berman, *Bringing a new life to UN human operations* (United Nations Associations of the United States of America, 1998): 12; Ian Guest, *Behind the Disappearances. Argentina's Dirty war against human rights and the United Nations* (University of Pennsylvania Press, 1990): 80; Evan Luard, *The United Nations. How It Works and What It Does.* (2nd ed. Macmillan, 1994): 118 and 119; Tolley, *The U.N. Commission on Human Rights* (Westview Press, 1987): 32.

[87] Adam Roberts and Benedict Kingsbury, "The UN's roles in a divided world," in Roberts and Kingsbury (1988) (n. 66): 1, *esp.* 11–4.

was compelled to react. The Director of the Human Rights Division, Theo van Boven, actively supported campaigns led by the International Commission of Jurists and Amnesty International. Several international organizations had adopted measures on the topic, including UNESCO, the Organization of American States, the 1980 Conference on Women's Rights, and the sixth UN Congress of the United Nations for the prevention of crime and treatment of offenders.[88] The General Assembly, ECOSOC, and the Sub-Commission all called upon the Commission to address the issue.[89] However, the accusations of selectivity in the choice of countries and the diplomatic maneuvers of the Argentinian government, then under scrutiny by means of the confidential 1503 procedure, were impossible to overcome in order to reach the necessary votes to create a public geographic mandate.[90] A different strategy was then followed, and the proposals for a Special Procedure on Argentina were replaced by proposals for the creation of a Working Group to study the phenomenon of disappearances taking place anywhere in the world. The government targeted was notorious, and the draft resolution circulated to establish the working group was known as the "Argentinian Resolution."[91] Still, the lack of reference within the text of the resolution to Argentina, allowed the adoption of Resolution 20 (XXXVI) of February 29, 1980, by which the Commission decided to appoint, for a year, a Working Group to examine questions relevant to enforced or involuntary disappearances of persons. A few months later, the Sub-Commission dared to submit a proposal for a specific mechanism, similar to habeas corpus to deal with particularly urgent cases of disappearances.[92] The proposal was not approved but inspired future work of the Working Group on Enforced Disappearances.

Following this example, many other Special Procedures with thematic mandates were created. Most are still in force, although some have changed

[88] *See, e.g.*, David Kramer and David Weissdbrodt, "The 1980 U.N. Commission on Human Rights and the Disappeared" 3 *Human Rights Quarterly* (1981): 18; Hurst Hannum, "Human Rights and the United Nations: Progress at the 1980 U.N. Sub-Commission on Prevention of Discrimination and Protection of Minorities" 3 *Human Rights Quarterly* (1981): 1.

[89] *See* ECOSOC Res. 1979/38 of 10 May 1979; GA Res. 33/173 of 20 December 1978; Sub-Commission Res. 5 (XXXII)B 5 September 1979 (*Report of the Sub-Commission on Prevention of Discrimination and Protection of Minorities on its 32nd Session, Geneva, 20 August–7 September 1979*, UN Doc. E/CN.4/1350-E/CN.4/Sub.2/435, 3 October 1979).

[90] *See* Guest (1990) (n. 86). *See also* Patrick J. Flood, *The Effectiveness of UN Human Rights Institutions* (Praeger Publishers, 1998): 50–61.

[91] Nigel S. Rodley, "The Evolution of the United Nations Charter-based Machinery of the Protection of Human Rights" 1 *European Human Rights Law Review* (1997): 4, 6.

[92] "Question of the human rights of persons subjected to any form of detention or imprisonment; Subcommission Res. 18 (XXXIII) (11 September 1980), UN Doc. E/CN.4/-E/CN.4/Sub.2/459 (1980): 75.

denomination or composition over the years. The short existence of the Special Rapporteur on human rights and mass exoduses, created in 1981 for a year and not renewed, is an exception among thematic Special Procedures that have otherwise survived indefinitely once established.[93]

5. Confidential Special Procedures

Similar to "Public Special Procedures," "Confidential Special Procedures" are held by independent experts to monitor the situation of a state and report to the Human Rights Council under the confidentiality of the complaint procedure.[94] The Commission on Human Rights created several such confidential Special Procedures before this competence was expressly acknowledged by ECOSOC[95] and, subsequently, by the Human Rights Council.[96] For instance, a confidential Special Procedure was created in 2004 to address the situation of human rights in Uzbekistan.[97] In 2005, the Commission extended the mandate of the independent expert (Michèle Picard), and, after considering her report,[98] the newly created Human Rights Council[99] decided to discontinue the consideration of the human rights situation in Uzbekistan in 2007.[100] In 1999, the Commission terminated similar confidential Special Procedures on Chad, Armenia, and Azerbaijan.[101] Douré M'Bam Diarra (1996) and Emma Aouij (1996–7) were appointed independent experts on the situation of human rights in Chad.[102] The mandate was terminated

[93] CHR Res. 29(XXXVII) (31 March 1981). The first and only report of the Special Rapporteur can be found in "Study on Human Rights and Massive Exoduses-Sadruddini Aga Khan, Special Rapporteur," UN Doc. E/CN.4/1503 (31 December 1982).

[94] HRC Res. 5/1 (n. 24), para. 109 c.

[95] ECOSOC Res. 2000/3 (n. 43), para. 1. *See also* CHR Dec 2000/109 (26 April 2000).

[96] HRC Res. 5/1 (n. 24), para. 109 c.

[97] *See Report of the Secretary General on the situation of human rights in Uzbekistan*, UN Doc. A/61/526 (18 October 2006), para. 31.

[98] The independent expert's report was examined by the Human Rights Council in September 2006. The Report on the situation of human rights in Uzbekistan (restricted) was circulated as UN Doc. E/CN.4/2006/WG.16/R.3 (5 January 2006), *see United Nations Document Index* (Vol. 9 No. 3, October–December 2006) Part 2, UN Doc. ST/LIB/SER.N/34 (Part 2) (United Nations, 2008) 1300.

[99] The mandate was extended by the HRC Dec 1/102 (30 June 2006), Annex, in the context of the transfer of responsibilities and mandates from the Commission to the Council.

[100] "Report to the General Assembly on the 4th Session of the Human Rights Council," UN Doc. A/HRC/4/123 (12 June 2007), paras. 119–21.

[101] "Commission on Human Rights Report on the Fifty-Fifth Session," UN Doc. E/1999/23-E/CN.4/1999/167 (1999), paras. 246–8.

[102] *See* "Commission on Human Rights Report on the 52nd Session, (18 March–26 April 1996)," UN Doc. E/1996/23(SUPP)-E/CN.4/1996/177 (1996) 286–7: CHR Dec. 1996/101 (19 March 1996); "Commission on Human Rights Report on the Fifty-Fourth Session (16 March–24 April 1998)," UN Doc. E/1998/23-E/CN.4/1998/177 (1998), paras. 419 and 282–3: CHR Dec. 1998/101 (17 March

in favor of providing advisory services and technical cooperation to the country.[103] Hugh Templeton was appointed independent expert on the situation of human rights in Armenia and Azerbaijan in 1996,[104] but his mandate was short-lived since the Commission decided, the same year, to discontinue consideration of these territories under the 1503 procedure.[105] Confidential Special Procedures have also existed, in the past, concerning the situation of human rights in Uganda (1978–81)[106] and Haiti (1981–7).[107] On several occasions, the Commission requested the Secretary General to designate the expert or to exert his good offices with the government concerned.[108]

The confidentiality of the complaint procedure has made it difficult to know whether an independent expert has been appointed to examine a territory. The official information available is restricted to public statements made by the Chair of the Human Rights Council regarding the territories examined under this mechanism,[109] compiled and published by the OHCHR.[110]

1998); *see also* Carlos Villán Durán, *Curso de Derecho Internacional de Los Derechos Humanos* (Trotta, 2002): 638.

103 CHR Dec. 1999/102 (22 April 1999).

104 CHR Dec. 1996/101 (n. 102).

105 UN Doc. E/1996/23(SUPP)-E/CN.4/1996/177 (n. 102) 365, para. 382; *see also* Villán Durán (2002) (n. 102) 638.

106 This was the first confidential Special Procedure established by the Commission, *see* Report of the Secretary-General on the Effective functioning of the various mechanisms established for the supervision, investigation and monitoring of the implementation of the treaty obligations entered into by states in regard to human rights and of the existing international standards in this regard, UN Doc. E/CN.4/1994/42 (14 February 1994), para. 73 and fn. 4. On the unsuccessful attempts to make this situation public, *see* Tardu (1989) (n. 26): 574–5; Gonzáles (1981) (n. 60): 457–8; and R.B. Lillich and Hurst Hannum, *International Human Rights. Problems of Law, Policy and Practice* (3rd ed. Aspen Pub, 1995): 16–32.

107 *See* CHR Res. 1987/13 (2 March 1987), preliminary para. 1, referring to the confidential report of the Special Representative of the Commission, UN Doc. E/CN.4/1987/R.2 (1987); on different experts designated for this territory, *see* America Watch Staff: Reverting to Despotism: Human Rights in Haiti (Human Rights Watch, 1990), 137, 140, and 141.

108 Until 1997, the Secretary General would have facilitated direct contact with governments, acting under the 1503 procedure, with Armenia and Azerbaijan (1995); Chad (1994–5 and 1997); Equatorial Guinea (1977–8); Ethiopia (1979–80); Haiti (1981–3 and 1986); Myanmar (1990–1); Paraguay (1978–90); Somalia (1992); Sudan (1992); Uruguay (1979–84); and Zaire (1992), *see* M. Francisca Ize-Charrin, "1503: A serious Procedure" in Gudmundur, et al. (eds.), *International Human Rights Monitoring Mechanisms: Essays in Honour of Jakob Th. Möller* (Martinus Nijhoff Publishers, 2001): 293, 304 (fn. 7).

109 The result of a confidential agreement, this practice commenced in 1978 and by 1984, the list expanded to countries no longer examined by the Commission. This practice was later codified by Resolution 2000/3 (n. 43) and HRC Res. 5/1 (n. 24). *See* Nigel Rodley (1997) (n. 91); Christian Tomuschat, "Human Rights in a World-Wide Framework. Some Current Issues" in *Zeitschrift für Ausländisches Öffentliches Recht Und Völkerrecht. Begründet von Viktor Bruns* (Kohlhammer, 1985): 547, 579–80; and Peter Kooijmans, "Introduction to the International Systems of Protection of Human Rights," *Recueil des Cours, Strasbourg Institut International des Droits d l'Homme* (1986): 6, 17.

110 *See* "List of situations referred to the Human Rights Council under the Complaint Procedure since 2006" OHCHR at: http://www.ohchr.org/Documents/HRBodies/ComplaintProcedure/Situat

To the author's knowledge, the Human Rights Council has not established any new confidential Special Procedure since its creation in 2006.

In some instances, the decision to discontinue reviewing the situation of the state concerned under the confidential procedure in favor of taking up public consideration of the matter has resulted in the creation of new geographic public Special Procedures. Equatorial Guinea (1979) was the first country subjected to this treatment due to its lack of cooperation with the Commission.[111] An emblematic example of the relationship between the 1503 (now complaint) procedure and Special Procedures is represented by the manner in which the Commission tackled the situation of human rights in Haiti. Following the creation of a confidential Special Procedure to examine Haiti in 1986, the report submitted by the appointed Special Representative was later made public in 1987 by the same resolution deciding the creation of a public Special Procedure.[112] Other public Special Procedures, preceded by an examination of the country under the confidential 1503 procedure, include: Afghanistan, Liberia, Myanmar, Rwanda, Chile, Democratic Republic of Congo (Zaire), El Salvador, Guatemala, Iran, Somalia, Sudan, and Uzbekistan.[113] In the lifetime of the Human Rights Council, Eritrea has also become a country examined under a public Special Procedure as an outcome of the complaint procedure.[114] Despite numerous voices demanding its elimination,[115] it has endured for half a century, revealing states' support

ionsConsideredUnderComplaintProcedures.pdf. However, the confidentiality does not cover civil society organizations and other sources of information. Therefore unofficial—scattered and not always verifiable—information is available elsewhere, *see* Felix Ermacora, "Procedure to deal with human rights violations. A hopeful start in the United Nations?" 7 *Human Rights Journal* (1974): 670, 684; Tolley (1984) (n. 60) 442, 446, 448, and 454; Rodley (1979) (n. 35): 169–70. Pauline Egret, "Outcomes of the 1503 and 1235 procedures" in Meghna Abraham, *A New Chapter of Human Rights* (International Service for Human Rights and Friedrich Elbert Stifung, 2006), Annex 5.1, available at: http://oldDocishr.ch/handbook/Annexes/CommProcs/1503outcms.pdf.

[111] Confidential CHR Decision of 8 March 1979 and CDH Res. 1979/35 (10 March 1979). A summary of the confidential discussions leading to these decisions is available in the Report of the Special Rapporteur on the situation of human rights in Guinea, UN Doc. E/CN.4/1371 (n. 78), paras. 5–23.

[112] CHR Res. 1987/13 (n. 107), paras. 1 and 11. *See also Report on Haiti by the Expert, Mr. Philippe Texier, prepared in conformity with Commission on Human Rights resolution 1988/51*, UN Doc. E/CN.4/1989/40 (6 February 1989), paras. 1–14; and *Situation of Human Rights in Haiti: Note by the Secretary General*, UN Doc. A/49/513 (14 October 1994), paras. 1–15.

[113] Egret (2006) (n. 110) and Tardu (1989) (n. 26): 311.

[114] *See* HRC Res. 20/20 (6 July 2012) and HRC Res. 21/1 (26 September 2012). *See also* summaries available on the OHCHR website (n. 110).

[115] *See, e.g.*, International Commission of Jurist, "UN Commission on Human Rights" 24 *International Commission of Jurists. The Review* (1980): 29, 34–5; Philip Alston, "Individual Complaints: Historical Perspectives and the International Covenant on Economic, Social and Cultural Rights" in S. Pritchard (ed.), *Indigenous Peoples, the United Nations and Human Rights* (Zed Books Ltd., The Federation Press, 1998): 81, 81–3; Eric Lane, "Mass Killing by Governments: Lawful in the World Legal Order?" 12 *New York University Journal of International Law & Politics*

for its confidential nature and the belief that states may be in a better position to present their viewpoint without being exposed to public pressure while remaining under the threat of a public investigation if they do not cooperate with the procedure.[116]

6. Conclusions

The status conferred to human rights within the United Nations has determined the development of Special Procedures. The diminished importance of human rights compared to the development and security agenda facilitated the self-denied competence to discuss human rights violations based on Article 2(7) of the UN Charter. Other decisions that might have looked less relevant at the time, such as locating the meetings of the Commission on Human Rights and the Secretariat supporting human rights mechanism in Geneva, rather than New York, contributed to detaching the human rights mechanisms from the main organs of the Organization.

The decision to overturn the self-imposed non-competence doctrine of the Commission was intrinsically linked to emerging global political consensus on the need to address specific human rights violations that were already under the radar of the Security Council and the General Assembly, gradually eroding arguments based on the principle of non-intervention in the domestic affairs of states. This consensus led to the creation of ad hoc mechanisms that needed a decision (ECOSOC Resolution 1235) that conferred the eventual competence of the Commission on Human Rights to deal with human rights violations. The Commission's change of direction in 1967 was not, however, accompanied by the adoption of general rules for the establishment of similar mechanisms in the future nor the approval of rules to guide their operationalization. The Commission took a further three years to articulate a procedure, enshrined in ECOSOC Resolution 1503 (XLVIII).

(1979): 239, 268–73; Manfred Nowak, "Proposals for Improving the UN Human Rights Programme" 11 *Netherlands Quarterly of Human Rights* (1993): 153, 156.

[116] Stefan Oeter, "Inspection in international law. Monitoring compliance and the problem of implementation in international law" XXVIII *New York Journal of International Law* (1997): 129, 135. *See also* David Weissbrodt, "Protecting the Right to Life: International Measures against Arbitrary or Summary Killings by Governments" in Bertrand Ramcharan (ed.), *The Right to Life in International Law* (Martinus Nijhoff, 1985): 297, 303; and Eibe Riedel, "Commission on Human Rights" in Wolfrum and Philipp, *United Nations: Law, Policies and Practice* (vol.1, Martinus Nijhoff, 1995): 116, 124.

As many advocated at the time, the procedure laid out in Resolution 1503 constituted the agreed confidential mechanism to deal with all communications related to human rights violations. However, the simple majority rule governing the adoption of decisions by the Commission on Human Rights defied this logic.

When enough states endorsed the creation of a different monitoring mechanism focusing on specific countries with the proviso of reporting their findings publicly, they were created. Thus random political decisions resulted in the establishment of two differentiated means of dealing with human rights violations: one confidential, following the rules of the Resolution 1503 (XLVIII); and one public, which could culminate with the creation of a monitoring body, a Public Special Procedure for which no general rules existed or were established at the time. The term "Special" was used to denote its temporary/ad hoc, nature. Resolution 1503 was also interpreted as allowing the establishment of Special Confidential Procedures that could become public.

The impossibility of garnering enough votes to address the situation of human rights in specific countries acted as the eventual detonator for the establishment of the first of the thematic procedures. When human rights treaty monitoring bodies entered the scene, some states sought to remove the Special Procedures, resuscitating arguments based on Article 2.7 of the Charter and viewing these as superfluous. They were unsuccessful, however, and since then, the only obstacle standing in way of the creation of a new Special Procedure is the absence of enough votes in the Human Rights Council. It is thus unsurprising that several attempts to rationalize the number of Special Procedures have failed.[117] The successive enlargement of the composition of the former Commission and current composition of the Human Rights Council, with greater representation of Asian and African states, has facilitated the growth of thematic mandates, particularly those focused on economic, social, and cultural rights, collective rights, and solidarity rights.[118] Countries belonging to the African and Asian Group, among others, have been staunch defenders of removing country mandates and have put forward this view repeatedly during the many processes of reform that have focused on Special Procedures. Their initiatives have been partially successful. The percentage of country mandates compared to thematic

[117] See chapter three.
[118] On the pernicious consequences of the categorization of rights, *see* chapter four on methods of work.

mandates has declined since 1997. However, it appears unlikely that country mandates will disappear as long as states continue to table resolutions for that purpose, while remaining effective in gathering sufficient support from other members of the Human Rights Council. This modus operandi, as it is often highlighted, cannot guarantee that the seriousness of a human rights violation will be the main indicator leading to the creation of a Special Procedure nor that similar situations of violations will be addressed in the same manner. Nonetheless, there is robust evidence to demonstrate that the former Commission and current Council's decisions target particularly serious situations of human rights violations. While some may escape scrutiny, the situations under consideration are not solely politically motivated but are based on reported and verified facts.[119] Therefore, not every situation of human rights violations that deserves international scrutiny is under the radar of the Human Rights Council, but all those that are warrant it.

[119] For a large statistical analysis comprising all actions adopted by the Commission on Human Rights, targeting specific countries between 1979 and 2001, *see* James H. Lebovic and Erik Voeten, "The politics of shame: The condemnation of country human rights practices in the UNHCR" 50(4) *International Studies Quarterly* (2006): 54; replicating the study for the period 2001–2005, *see* David P. Forsythe and Baekkwan Park, "The Changing of the Guard: From the UN Human Rights Commission to the Council" 29(1) *Human Rights Law Journal* (2008): 3.

Two

The Politics of Reforming Special Procedures

1. Introduction

Having focused on the birth and formation of UN Special Procedures, highlighting facets that have shaped these over the decades, this chapter focuses on their impact and why and how these have contributed to a steady call for reform. The chapter reveals how some of the features characterizing the monitoring activities currently carried out by mandate holders of Special Procedures have attracted vehement critique by some states, leading to successive waves to reform them. Advanced at times by governments willing to weaken their competence and influence, the received wisdom would suggest that these attempts have served to restrict their competence. Yet as will be demonstrated, the reforms have rarely had a negative impact on the implementation of mandates themselves. Conversely, they have strengthened the legal basis for some of their methods of work, such as the treatment of individual communications. Some of the reforms have also contributed to much needed codification and standardization of working methods, creating greater coherence, and, as a consequence, greater global engagement.

Until mandate holders of Special Procedures started convening annual meetings in 1993, twenty-six years after their creation, no forum existed for coordinating activities. Mandate holders adopted and implemented autonomous decisions on the scope of their own mandates, resulting in a myriad of practices that were neither explicitly within their competence nor expressly prohibited. Following well-established practice, if their parent body (the Commission on Human Rights first, the Human Rights Council since 2006) did not object, their actions were deemed valid according to the general principles of law governing the validity of acts of subsidiary bodies of an international organization.[1] A good illustration of this is how, early in the

[1] On this principle, *see* n. 128

In Defense of Politicization of Human Rights. Elvira Domínguez-Redondo, Oxford University Press (2020).
 DOI: 10.1093/oso/9780197516706.001.0001

history of Special Procedures, mandate holders started intervening on behalf of individuals without relying on any specific competence, initially guided by humanitarian concerns, but progressing over time toward determining possible violations of international law by the concerned states. This situation was facilitated by the vagueness of the mandates themselves, created by political decisions, and the consequent absence of standard rules applicable to fact-finding missions or other UN bodies performing monitoring tasks.

The working methods developed by Special Procedures have often subverted the traditional requirement of state consent to monitoring their compliance with international law standards. Paradoxically, the regular attempts by some states to limit the independence and freedom of Special Procedures has resulted in unintended positive outcomes, including a clarification of their scope of competence and the establishment of a stronger legal basis to exercise their most exceptional powers. These powers include undertaking assessments, based on international law, into the existence of violations of human rights in specific contexts, without having to obtain governmental consent or complying with traditional admissibility requirements that would normally pertain to individual petitioners' access to international bodies, most notably the exhaustion of domestic remedies and the existence of a specific binding treaty-based obligation upon a given state to protect a specific right.

The first part of this chapter analyzes the changes made to the working methods of mandate holders that were prompted by direct criticisms of states toward some practices implemented by specific mandate holders of Special Procedures. The second section addresses the nature of the overarching reforms that sought to affect the methods of work of Special Procedures, in particular, the introduction of a Code of Conduct that mandate holders managed to oppose effectively until it was approved in 2007.[2] Other changes introduced through different reforms, such as the procedure by which mandate holders are appointed or their institutional position within the United Nations are addressed in chapter six.

As articulated chapter One, states seeking to highlight the prevalence of systemic or thematic human rights violations often engage in political negotiations with the aim of creating or renovating Special Procedures. While these negotiations often create or reify the existence of a specific mandate, the bid to gain consensus in the Human Rights Council (and its predecessor

[2] HRC Res. 5/2 of 18 June 2007.

the Commission) means that the language used to justify the action is often vague. This has left mandate holders with a degree of freedom to develop their own working methods while sharpening the contours of the mandate itself. Before the standardization of practices, mandate holders often developed improvised methods of work that attracted criticisms based on the source of their competence or their approaches to the mandate. At times, this resulted in successful contestation and modification of well-established practices that may have appeared or were intended to debilitate their position. The following section elaborates on how some of these changes have acted to reinforce, in practice, the legitimacy of working methods of Special Procedures.

2. Contesting Special Procedures' Use of International Treaties as Benchmark

Despite the outspoken support of the United States of America in opposing proposals to narrow or weaken its mandate,[3] China and Cuba[4] as well as the American Association of Jurists[5] contested the quasi-jurisdictional approach adopted by the Working Group on Arbitrary Detention to its mandate. In the treatment of alleged cases of arbitrary detentions, the Working Group adopted an adversarial process with a ninety-day deadline for governments to reply to requests for information, before formulating conclusions, called "decisions," on whether a deprivation of liberty was arbitrary in cases alleging arbitrary detention.[6] The criticism to such an adversarial approach gathered enough support within the Commission on Human Rights, to result in the imposition of a change in the terminology among other measures aimed at loosening the Working Groups' quasi-jurisdictional approach to its mandate.[7] Since 1997, the Working Group issues "views" rather than "decisions"

[3] *See Summary Record of the 29th meeting, held at the Palais des Nations, Geneva, on Thursday, 27 March 1997: Commission on Human Rights, 53rd Session*, E/CN.4/1997/SR.29, para. 32.

[4] Carlos Villán-Durán, *Curso de derecho internacional de los derechos humanos* [International Human Rights Law Course] (Trotta: Madrid, 2002): 806, *esp.* fn.116.

[5] *See Written statement submitted by the American* Association *of Jurists, a non-governmental organization in consultative status (category II)*, UN Doc. E/N.4/1994/NGO/18 (1994).

[6] The Working Group published its methods of work in its first report, including the "Principles applicable in the consideration of cases submitted to the Working Group" and a "Model questionnaire to be completed by persons alleging arbitrary arrest or detention," UN Doc. E/CN.4/1992/40 (1992).

[7] *See* Jeroen Gutter, *Thematic Procedures of the United Commission on Human Rights and International Law: In Search of a Sense of Community* (Intersentia, 2006): 204–8.

in order to emphasize the non-binding nature of its opinions. Clarifications have also been made that governments "are not legally compelled to respond to its communications or recommendations."[8] While this decision would seem to undermine the authority of the Working Groups' evaluations, it can in fact be interpreted as allowing the submission of communications handled by Special Procedures to other international monitoring bodies with treaty-based adjudicatory powers.[9] This rationale was explained by the Chairman of the Working Group in 1997:

> the Working Group recognized that the use of the word "decision" to describe its assessment of the communications submitted to it might give the impression that it was calling into question the force of *res judicata*: for that reason he believed that it would be advisable to replace it with a word such as view, opinion, recommendation or observation.[10]

Since then it has become a permissive customary rule, well established in international law, that states and intergovernmental institutions can discuss and monitor compliance by states with human rights standards, without the express consent of the state concerned. This prerogative has subsequently been widely used by the political bodies of the United Nations because states have accepted "a *droit de regard* in human rights matters in a series of institutions and mechanisms by which compliance of States with international standards is monitored irrespective of whether the target states have acceded to a particular human rights treaty."[11] From the content of General Assembly and Economic and Social Council resolutions establishing Special Procedures, among other measures, and on the basis of consistent practice by the Commission on Human Rights, its own competence to examine questions of human rights violations and to create subsidiary bodies with

[8] Resolution of the Commission on Human Rights 1997/50, 15 April 1997, para. 7. During the same session, Cuba and other countries successfully amended the mandate of the Working Group to distinguish between detention and imprisonment, *see* Michael J. Dennis, "The Fifty-second Session of the UN Commission on Human Rights" 91(1) *American Journal of International Law* (1997): 167–77: 172.

[9] UN Doc. E/N.4/1994/NGO/18 (n. 5), para. 15.

[10] *Summary Record of the 25th meeting, held at the Palais des Nations, Geneva, on Wednesday, 26 March 1997: Commission on Human Rights, 53rd session*, UN Doc. E/CN.4/1997/SR.25, para. 20.

[11] Bruno Simma, "Human Rights" in Christian Tomuschat (ed.), *The United Nations at Age Fifty. A legal perspective* (Kluwer Law International, 1995): 263, 264. *See also* Bruno Simma and Philip Alston, "The Sources of Human Rights Law: Custom, Jus Cogens, General Principles" 12 *The Australian Yearbook of International Law* (1992): 82.

such purpose, became uncontested by the late 1970s.[12] The resolution of the UN General Assembly establishing the Human Rights Council was approved by the vast majority of states worldwide,[13] and expressly confirms this power, by sustaining that "the Council should address situations of violations of human rights, including gross and systematic violations, and make recommendations thereon."[14] In addition, the Council has been endowed with the mandate to undertake a universal periodic review under which the fulfillment by every state of its human rights obligations and commitments is reviewed.[15]

It took longer for states and scholars to agree on whether the erstwhile Commission had competence to intervene on behalf of individuals, following actions with this purpose adopted first by the Commission, but soon delegated to Special Procedures.[16] The activities of the Special Procedures as fact-finding bodies and their assessment of human rights violations based on customary law standards had become well accepted by the mid-1980s. However, two further issues have been settled indirectly through the introduction of measures that may have sought to restrict and damage Special Procedures. The first controversial issue relates to the competence of mandate holders of Special Procedures to evaluate the compliance of states with international law standards on the basis of treaties to which they are not a party. The second pertains to states that have challenged the competence of Special Procedures in handling individual communications. As will be discussed in more detail in chapter four, the distinctions introduced in the content of mandates for Special Procedures dealing with economic, social, and cultural rights and collective rights, meant inter alia, that mandate holders refrained from dealing with individual communications. The structure of the Office of the High Commissioner further supported that approach.

A. Legal Basis to Examine Conventional Obligations

By October 2019, there were nine international human rights treaties establishing a committee of experts to monitor the implementation of their

[12] Egon Schwelb and Philip Alston, "The Principal Institutions and Other Bodies Founded Under the Charter" in Karel Vasak (ed.), *The International Dimensions of Human Rights* (UNESCO, 1982, vol. 1): 232, 275.

[13] Only the United States of America, Israel, Palau, and the Marshall Islands voted against its adoption while Iran, Venezuela, and Belarus abstained.

[14] GA Res. 60/251, 15 March 2006, para. 3.

[15] Ibid., para. 5(e).

[16] *See* Schwelb and Alston (n. 12): 276; *see also* chapter five.

provisions by state parties to them. These are usually referred to as "core international human rights instruments" and include the Covenant on Economic, Social and Cultural Rights,[17] the Covenant on Civil and Political Rights,[18] the International Convention on the Elimination of All Forms of Racial Discrimination,[19] the Convention on the Elimination of All Forms of Discrimination against Women,[20] the Convention against Torture and Other Cruel, Inhuman or Degrading Treatment or Punishment,[21] the Convention on the Rights of the Child,[22] the International Convention on the Protection of the Rights of All Migrant Workers and Members of Their Families,[23] the Convention on the Rights of Persons with Disabilities,[24] and the International Convention for the Protection of All Persons against Enforced Disappearances.[25]

All the committees have competence to report on the state parties' fulfillment of their obligations under those treaties. Additionally, they have competence to deal with complaints from individuals claiming to be victims of violation of human rights if the state parties have provided specific consent to confer this power to them following the procedure set out by the relevant treaty or protocol.[26] This reflects a principle of international law by which the consent to be bound by a treaty is different from the consent needed to endow an international organ with power to monitor compliance.[27] Relying on such principle, Jean Charpentier harshly criticized activities of the Commission on Human Rights for lacking competence to create monitoring mechanisms without the consent of states.[28] Paraphrasing the words of René Cassin in

[17] Adopted on 16 December 1966, entry into force 3 January 1976.

[18] Adopted on 16 December 1966, entry into force 23 March 1976.

[19] Adopted on 21 December 1965, entry into force 4 January 1969.

[20] Adopted on 18 December 1979, entry into force 3 September 1981. Its Optional Protocol conferring the incumbent Committee with competence to address individual complaints was adopted on 10 December 1999 (entered into force 22 December 2000).

[21] Adopted on 10 December 1984, entry into force 16 June 1987. Its Optional Protocol was adopted on 18 December 2002 (entry into force 22 June 2006) establishing a system of preventive visits.

[22] Adopted on 20 November 1989, entry into force 2 September 1990. Two additional Protocols to this Convention were adopted on May 25, 2000, on the rights on the sale of children, child prostitution, and child pornography; and on the involvement of children in armed conflict. Both Protocols entered into force in 2002. A third protocol, allowing individual communications, was adopted in 2014 but is not yet in force.

[23] Adopted on 18 December 1990, entry into force 1 July 2003.

[24] Adopted on 13 December 2006, entry into force 12 May 2008.

[25] Adopted on 20 December 2006, entry into force 23 December 2010.

[26] The Committee of the Rights of the Child will only be able to address individual complaints when the third protocol to the Convention on the Rights of the Child enters into force.

[27] Charpentier, Jean, "Contrôle par les Organisations Internationales de l'exécution des obligations des Etats" 182 (IV) *Recueil de Cours* (1983): 147, 165–87, *esp.* 176.

[28] Ibid. 180.

1951, imposing the obligation to report to an intergovernmental body about obligations deriving from a treaty for state parties to that treaty violates the principles of equality and state reciprocity. States that are not party to the treaty become potential or actual controllers of a set of regulations to which they may not be bound themselves.[29] The closeness of the final vote approving Resolution 1503 (LXVIII) with twelve states voting in favor, twelve against, and three abstentions, illustrates the strong opposition to a procedure that was perceived by many as violating Article 2(7) of the UN Charter in 1970. These states considered that "it imposed upon states procedures to which they had not given their consent in treaty form" constituting therefore "an illegal substitution for the procedure set forth in the Optional Protocol to the UN Covenant on Civil and Political Rights."[30]

The same interpretation had underpinned the commentaries of different scholars questioning the competence of the Working Group on Chile to evaluate the situation of human rights in this territory by referring to the Covenant on Civil and Political Rights (which had entered into force in 1976). Felix Ermacora argued that ratification of the Covenant implied that states:

> have submitted to a *lex specialis* and so may not be subjected to another procedure which might seek for political motives to override the specific convention obligations. Under general international law Chile may be entitled to refuse any commitment under a resolution of a political organ of the UN, if it has undertaken obligations under the Covenant.[31]

Jean-Bernard Marie raised concerns over the Working Group's competence to interpret Article 4 of the International Covenant on Civil and Political Rights unduly replacing the Human Rights Committee.[32] The Chilean government used this argument to challenge the competence of the Working Group vis-à-vis the application of the Covenant, stating that:

[29] René Cassin, "La déclaration universelle et la mise en œuvre des droits de l'homme" 79(II) *Recueil des Cours* (1951): 237–367, at 353 and 354.

[30] Maxime E. Tardu, "Procedures of the United Nations Organization: Procedures of General Scope" in *Human rights: the international petition system* Vol. I, Part I, Section IA (Oceana Publications, 1979): 30.

[31] Felix Ermacora, "UN and human rights in Chile" 1(2) *The Human Rights Review* (1976): 145, 155.

[32] Jean-Marie Bernard, "La situation des droits de l'homme au Chili: enquête de la Commission des droits de l'homme des Nations Unies" 22 *Annuaire Français de Droit International* (1976): 305–35, at 332.

> Chile recognized and respected that Covenant but could not accept that bodies extraneous to it should claim to exercise powers which it did not vest in them. (. . .) His Government would, however, provide information regarding human rights, in accordance with its obligations, to the proper and authorized bodies.[33]

Over a decade later, Rüdiger Wolfrum questioned the competence of the General Assembly or the Economic and Social Council to interpret or develop treaty rights, a power vested in specific committees.[34]

Governmental and non-governmental voices counterargued this interpretation.[35] In addition to the Working Group on Arbitrary Detentions, during the first half of the 1990s, he mandate holders of Special Procedures on arbitrary detention, summary executions, torture, violence against women, independence of lawyers, and judges had expressly asserted the applicability of international instruments to states, independently of their condition as parties of the relevant treaties. However, it remained controversial, and mandate holders of Special Procedures that used treaties as benchmark of compliance were frequently under attack until the question was settled in 1996.[36] Since then, and in direct relationship with pressure led by Cuba, the UN Special Rapporteurs and Working Groups are prevented from referring to treaties as normative bases from which to draw conclusions on human rights violations where the scrutinized state is not a party to the treaties in question.[37] The Working Group on Arbitrary Detention tried to refute arguments challenging its prior practice of relying on different provisions of the Covenant on Civil and Political Rights to evaluate the arbitrariness of a detention whether or not the state concerned was a party, claiming that such provisions had become customary law.[38] However, the Commission on Human Rights endorsed the criticisms, limiting the application of

[33] *Summary record of the 56th meeting: 3rd Committee, held on Thursday, 11 November 1976, New York, General Assembly 31st session*, UN Doc. A/C.3/31/SR.46, para. 31.

[34] Rüdiger Wolfrum, "The Progressive Development of Human Rights: A Critical Appraisal of UN Recent Efforts" in Jürgen Jekewitz, Karl Heinz Klein, Jörg Detlef Kühne, Hans Petersmann, and Rüdiger Wolfrum (eds.), *Des Menschen Recht zwischen Freiheit und Verantwortung. Festschrift für Karl Josef Partsch zum 75. Geburtstag* (Duncker & Humblot, 1989): 67–95, 71.

[35] *See* Marc Bossuyt, "The United Nations and Civil and Political Rights in Chile" 27(2) *International and Comparative Law Quarterly* (1978): 462–71.

[36] *See* Olivier de Frouville, *Les procédures thématiques: une contribution efficace des Nations Unies à la protection des droits de l'homme* (A. Pedone, 1996): 55–6.

[37] On the issues raised by Cuba, *see Report of the Working Group on Arbitrary Detention*, UN Doc. E/CN.4/1993/24 (12 January 1993), paras. 19 and 20.

[38] Report of the Working Group on Arbitrary Detention, UN Doc. E/ CN.4/1993/24 (12 January 1993), deliberation 2.

conventional standards by Special Procedures to state parties of a given treaty,[39] and the Working Group changed its methods of work accordingly.[40] The Code of Conduct of Special Procedures has formally reproduced this rule in its operative Paragraph 6(c) requiring all mandate holders to "[e]valuate all information in the light of internationally recognized human rights standards relevant to their mandate, and of international conventions to which the State concerned is a party."[41] This concession to states that are reticent to accept interferences in their sovereignty has merited criticism as a backward step and a threat for the system of Special Procedures.[42]

In forcing this approach, a set of political decisions have settled the old dispute regarding the distinction between the consent to be bound by a treaty and the consent needed to endow a UN body with competence to monitor state compliance with such treaty. State acceptance of the authority of non-treaty-based organs to review situations pertaining to their conventional human rights obligations has also been reinforced by the creation of the Universal Periodic Review mechanism in 2006, which includes treaties to which states are parties, as one of the criteria under which they are reviewed.[43] The next section explains how Special Procedures have also received competence to deal with individual communications using treaties to which the states are parties as benchmarks, independently of the specific consent required in the case of treaty bodies.

B. Application of Treaties in Handling Individual Communications

The unconditional acceptance by states that Special Procedures can use international human rights treaties when the states are parties implies that they can evaluate individual communications against the same benchmark, even when the state concerned has not consented to the complaints

[39] UN Commission on Human Rights Res. 1996/28, 19 April 1996, para. 5.

[40] Report of the Working Group on Arbitrary Detention, UN Doc. E/ CN.4/1997/4 (17 December 1996), para. 49. The Chairman of the Working Group made its disagreement clear with this position in *Summary Record of the 25th meeting, held at the Palais des Nations, Geneva, on Wednesday, 26 March 1997: Commission on Human Rights, 53rd session*, UN Doc. E/CN.4/1997/SR.25 (n.10), para. 20.

See also Frouville (1996) (n. 36): 55–60.

[41] HRC Res. 5/2 (n. 1).

[42] Frouville (1996) (n. 36): 59.

[43] HRC Res. 5/1 of 18 June 2007, Annex (n. 2), para. A.1.c.

procedure established by the relevant convention. The most salient example is the Working Group on Arbitrary Detentions, which has elaborated on the prohibition of deprivation of liberty in its Deliberation No. 9 (2012).[44] When a state is not a party to the Covenant on Civil and Political Rights, the Working Group assesses the legality of the detention under customary law, relying primarily on the Universal Declaration on Human Rights.[45] For state parties of the Covenant, the Working Group performs this assessment following a procedure that resembles the procedural rules of the Human Rights Committee, whether or not states have ratified the Optional Protocol to the Covenant required for the admissibility of communications by the Human Rights Committee. Since the number of state parties to the Protocol is significantly lower than those parties of the Covenant, the Working Group often constitutes the only avenue to access an international mechanism that will assess the legality of a detention, achieving comparable results to those expected from the maximum instance they could reach within the UN system. This practice was expressly endorsed by states by approving the Code of Conduct, not only for the Working Group on Arbitrary Detention but for the full range of Special Procedures, because it has confirmed both the competence of Special Procedures to handle individual communications (by incorporating admissibility criteria)[46] and to use international conventions when states are a party (without referring to the need of having consented to conventional provisions regarding individual communications).[47] This is a welcome outcome. Special Procedures are the only potential outlet for individual communications regarding a wide range of rights. This is the case for human rights contained in a treaty that states have not ratified—or not accepted the specific competence of a body to address individual communications—or a treaty that does not provide an individual complaints mechanism. Many of the rights covered by Special Procedures are not protected by a specific legal instrument (e.g., indigenous people or extreme poverty). The ability to address individual communications is the direct result of political decisions based on collective consent, rather than the legal requirements associated with conventional mechanisms.

[44] *Report of the Working Group on Arbitrary Detention*, U.N. Doc. No. A/HRC/22/44 (24 December 2012), paras. 37–85.

[45] *See Methods of work of the Working Group on Arbitrary Detention*, UN Doc. A/HRC/36/38 (13 July 2017).

[46] HRC Res. (n. 2), Article 9. *See also* chapter five.

[47] HRC Res. (n. 2), Article 6, c).

3. Reforming and Rationalizing Special Procedures: A Blessing in Disguise

One of the main bones of contention preventing states from reaching a definitive consensus on the text aimed at the creation of a Council was the chasm between states that emphasized the importance of preserving "the" existing system of Special Procedures, against those in favor of "a" system of Special Procedures. The final language adopted in the General Assembly Resolution 60/251 creating the Human Rights Council, refers to "a" system of Special Procedures,[48] validating the view of those who opposed endorsing these mechanisms without modifications.[49] Additionally, the General Assembly called for another review of all Special Procedures. Hence, the creation of a Human Rights Council reopened the question of reforming Special Procedures shortly after the completion of the 2000 "rationalization process."

The dangers of such reform initiatives should not be understated. States seeking to weaken the Special Procedures have been the main instigators of "rationalization" and review processes.[50] For instance, the Asian Group has repeatedly called for the disappearance of the former Item 9 of the Agenda of the Commission, *Question of the violation of human rights and fundamental freedoms anywhere in the world*,[51] and has proposed measures that, had

[48] GA Res. 60/251 (n. 14), operative para. 6.

[49] *Contribution by Cuba-Intersessional Open-Ended Intergovernmental Working Group, on the implementation of operative para. 6 of GA Resolution 60/251 established pursuant Human Rights Council Decision 1/104, 12 December 2006*, section 1.A, at 3 (document available through HRC extranet at: http://www.ohchr.org/EN/HRBodies/HRC/Pages/HRCRegistration.aspx). The Cuban emphasis on the distinction between maintaining "a" system instead of "the" system during discussions is recorded in *Summary Records of the 19th meeting, held at the Palais des Nations, Geneva, on Wednesday, 28 June 2006: Human Rights Council, 1st session, general segment*, UN Doc. A/HRC/1/SR.19 (14 July 2006), para. 24.

[50] Several authors and mandate holders have drawn attention to the attacks suffered by Special Procedures under the disguise of reform over the years. *See* Helena M. Cook, "International Human Rights Mechanisms. The Role of the Special Procedures in the Protection of Human Rights: The Way Forward After Vienna" 50 *International Commission of Jurists. The Review* (1993): 31, 41; Gudmundur Alfredson, "Concluding Remarks: More Law and Less Politics" in Alfredson et al. (eds.), *International Human Rights Monitoring Mechanisms: Essays in Honour of Jakob Th. Möller* (Martinus Nijhoff Publishers, 2001): 913, 918–9. The concern of the experts on the attempts to restrict their activities was raised in the report of the Chairperson of the fourth annual meeting of Special Procedures, UN Doc. E/CN.4/1999/3/Add.2 (5 February 1999), paras. 16–8; *see also* Amnesty International, "2003 UN Commission on Human Rights: A time for deep reflection," AI Doc. IOR 41/025/2002, 1 December 2002.

[51] On the position of the Asian Group, and other countries united under the Like-Minded Group, African Group and members of the Organisation of Islamic Conference to remove country-specific bodies, *see* Elvira Domínguez-Redondo, "Rethinking the Legal Foundations of Control in International Human Rights Law—The Case of Special Procedures" 29(3) *Netherlands Quarterly of Human Rights* (2011): 261–88, 274–5.

they been accepted, would have significantly curtailed the powers of Special Procedures.[52] The mutable set of states assembled under the "Like-Minded Group"[53] have coordinated their actions seeking to significantly undermine the competences and independence of Special Procedures.[54]

Even with the best intentions, subjecting the same procedures to regular reform undermines their credibility and potential impact. Inevitably, it also influences efficiency; scarce resources are devoted to reform, rather than substantive issues. Still, Special Procedures have been strengthened as a direct consequence of these initiatives. The endless "rationalization" process has involved important reflection on their functions, in a better knowledge and visibility of Special Procedures and in addition to greater transparency and standardization of methods of work. Additionally, the reforms have exposed the views of states in relation to Special Procedures, particularly those with increased representation within the Human Rights Council. The following sections summarize the reform initiatives and their outcomes, highlighting some positive results that are often ignored.

[52] *Position paper of the Asia Group on the report of the Bureau of the 54th session of the Commission on Human Rights submitted pursuant to Commission decision 1998/112 (E/CN.41999/104)*, UN Doc. E/CN.4/1999/WG.19/3 (19 August 1999).

[53] In 2005, Mr. Sha Zukang (representative of China) identified the Like-Minded Group of States as comprising: Algeria, Bangladesh, Belarus, Bhutan, China, Cuba, Egypt, India, Indonesia, Iran, Malaysia, Myanmar, Nepal, Pakistan, the Philippines, Sri Lanka, Sudan, Viet Nam, and Zimbabwe, *Summary record of the 2nd meeting held at the Palais des Nations, Geneva, on Monday, 14 March 2005*, UN Doc. E/CN.4/2005/SR.2 (2005), para. 48. In 1999, another contribution suggested a more restricted list where Bangladesh, Indonesia, the Philippines, and Zimbabwe were not included, *see* UN Doc. E/CN.4/1999/WG.19/2 (18 August 1999). A wider list including twenty-eight countries based on statements made before the Human Rights Council in 2014 can be found in: Marc Limon and Toby Lamarque, *The 2015 Human Rights Council* (URG, 17 November 2014), available at: https://www.universal-rights.org/blog/the-2015-human-rights-council/.

[54] UN Doc. E/CN.4/1999/WG.19/2 (n. 53). For a critique on the position of the Like-Minded Group, *see* Miko Lempinen, *Challenges Facing the System of Special Procedures of the United Nations Commission on Human Rights* (Institute for Human Rights, Abo Akademi University, 2001): 248–84 ; José Antonio Almeida, "Reform of the United Nations Commission on Human Rights: Proposals to Restore the Commission's Credibility, Coherence and Consistency" (International Centre for Human Rights and Democratic Development: March 2004); Philip Alston, "Reconceiving the UN Human Rights Regime: Challenges Confronting the New Human Rights Council" 7(1) *Melbourne Journal of International Law* (2006): 185–224, 204–6; The Asian Indigenous And Tribal Peoples Network (AITPN), *LMG: Killing the Commission on Human Rights softly*, UN Doc. E/CN.4/2005/NGO/8 (5 February 2005); SAHRDC, *Rationalization of the Work of the Commission*, UN Doc. E/CN.4/2003/NGO/161 (8 April 2003); SAHRDC, Like Minded Group—Unlikely protectors of human rights, Human Rights Features, HRF/57/02, 29 May 2002.

A. Reforms under the Commission on Human Rights (1974–2006)

In 1974, the Commission introduced the agenda item "Further Promotion and Encouragement of Human Rights" and since then has approved an annual resolution related to the question of reviewing its working methods and those of its subsidiary organs.[55] In 1989, the first resolution of the Commission addressing Special Procedures as a group included a request to examine the "question of increasing the effectiveness of special rapporteurs and representatives."[56] Other resolutions on the issue followed,[57] but no relevant measure was approved until 1998, when the Commission restructured its agenda and appointed its Bureau to undertake a review of its subsidiary mechanisms.[58] Taking into account the report of the Bureau, submitted in 1999—the so-called "Selebi Report"[59]—the Chair of the fifty-fifth session of the Commission announced, through an oral statement, the decision to create an open-ended "Working Group on Enhancing the Effectiveness of the Mechanisms of the Commission on Human Rights."[60] Some of the recommendations included in the Bureau's report were adopted informally

[55] *See* CHR Res. 10 (XXX) 5 March 1974, UN Doc. E/5464(supp)-E/CN.4/1154; 10 (XXXI) 5 March 1975, UN Doc. E/5635(supp)-E/CN.4/1179; 7(XXXII) 3 March 1976, UN Doc. E/5768(supp)-E/CN.4/1213; 26 (XXXIV) 8 March 1978, UN Doc. E/1978(supp)-E/CN.4/1292; 22 (XXXV) 14 March 1979, UN Doc. E/1979/36(supp)-E/CN.4/1347; 28 (XXVI) 11 March 1980, UN Doc. E/1980/13(supp)-E/CN.4/1408; 23 (XXXVII) 10 March 1981, UN Doc. E/1981/25-E/CN.4/1475; 1982/40 of 11 March 1982, UN Doc. E/1982/12(supp)-E/CN.4/1982/30; 1983/51 of 10 March 1983, UN Doc. E/1983/13(supp)-E/CN.4/1983/60; 1984/59 of 15 March 1984, UN Doc. E/1984/14(supp)-E/CN.4/1984/77. *See also* CHR Decisions 4 (XXXIII) 18 February 1977, UN Doc. E/5927(supp)-E/CN.4/1257; 1985/110 of 14 March 1985, UN Doc. E/1985/22(supp)-E/CN.4/1985/66; 1986/107 of 13 March 1986, UN Doc. E/1986/22(supp)-E/CN.4/1986/65; and 1987/108 of 11 March 1987, UN Doc. E/1987/22(supp)-E/CN.4/1987/60. On the attempts to reform the Commission during the 1980s, *see* Howard Tolley, *The UN Commission on Human Rights* (Westview Press, 1987): 154–62.

[56] CHR Res. 1989/48 of 7 March 1989, UN Doc. E/1989/20(supp)-E/CN.4/1989/86, with the title *Special rapporteurs and representatives and other mechanisms established by the Commission on Human Rights.*

[57] CHR Res. 1991/22 of 5 March 1991, UN Doc. E/1991/22(supp)-E/CN.4/1991/91; 1992/39 of 28 February 1992 and 1992/83 of 6 March 1992, UN Doc. E/1992/22(supp)-E/CN.4/1992/84; 1993/58 & 59 of 9 March 1993, UN Doc. E/1993/23(supp)-E/CN.4/1993/122; 1994/97 of 10 March 1994, UN Doc. E/1994/24(supp)-E/CN.4/1994/132; 1995/92 of 8 March 1995 and 1995/93 of 10 March 1995, UN Doc. E/1995/23(supp)-E/CN.4/1995/176; 1996/83 of 24 April 1996, UN Doc. E/1996/23(supp)-E/CN.4/1996/177. *See also* CHR Decision 1997/116 of 15 April, UN Doc. E/1997/23(supp)-E/CN.4/1997/150.

[58] CHR Res. 1998/84 and Decision 1998/112, both of 24 April 1998, UN Doc. E/1998/23(supp)-E/CN.4/1998/177.

[59] *Report of the Bureau of the 54th session of the Commission on Human Rights submitted pursuant to Commission decision 1998/112*, UN Doc. E/CN.4/1999/104 of 3 March 1999.

[60] Statement of the Chairperson, on behalf of the Commission, delivered on 29th April 1999, UN Doc. E/1999/23(supp)-E/CN.4/1999/167, para. 552. *See also* ECOSOC Decision 1999/256 of 27 July 1999.

and with immediate effect in 1999.[61] Especially relevant was the decision, in force since then, to limit to six years any individual's tenure in a given mandate, whether thematic or country-specific.[62] The Commission on Human Rights approved all the recommendations advanced by the Working Group on Enhancing the Effectiveness of the Mechanisms in 2000.[63]

In summary, this reform involved the mild modification of the 1503 procedure and a reduction in the competence of the now defunct Sub-Commission for the Promotion and Protection of Human Rights.[64] The curtailment of the Sub-Commission's mandate was considered a lesser evil than any allowance toward the implementation of other proposals advanced mainly by Asian countries and those grouped under the Liked-Minded Group seeking to diminish the competences and independence of Special Procedures.

In addition to measures advanced by the Chairperson of the fifty-fifth session, the Commission merged the mandates of the Independent Expert on structural adjustment programs and the Special Rapporteur on foreign debt.[65] It also directed mandate holders to allow a "reasonable opportunity" for states to comment on their reports (interpreted as a minimum of six weeks) and to make such comments available.[66] The Working Group also outlined vague guidelines for the standardization of the structure of reports, recommending the adoption of executive summaries facilitating the follow-up of recommendations.[67] Finally, the Commission approved the recommendation by which its Chairperson had to convene a one-day informal meeting with the Third Committee of the General Assembly.[68] The recommendation concerning the publication of the roster of candidates to be considered as mandate holders, on the website of the OHCHR, was endorsed by the Commission, but its implementation was delayed for years.[69]

[61] UN Doc. E/1999/23(supp)-E/CN.4/1999/167 (n. 60) para. 552.

[62] Concerning Recommendation 6 of the Bureau's Report, *see* ibid. In 2000, the Commission endorsed the same limit for mandate holders belonging to working groups (CHR Decision 2000/109 of 26 April 2000). *See also* CHR Decision 2002/114 of 26 April 2002.

[63] CHR Decision 2000/109 (n. 62), endorsed by the ECOSOC Res. 2000/3 of 16 June 2000. For the report of the Working Group, *see Report of the inter-sessional open-ended Working Group on Enhancing the Effectiveness of the Mechanisms of the Commission on Human Rights*, UN Doc. E/CN.4/2000/112 (16 February 2000).

[64] UN Doc. E/CN.4/2000/112 (n. 63), chs. 3 and 4.

[65] The new independent expert mandate was established by CHR Res. 2000/82 of 26 April 2000.

[66] UN Doc. E/CN.4/2000/112 (n. 63), para. 30.

[67] Ibid., para. 32.

[68] Ibid., para. 33.

[69] For this recommendation, Ibid., para. 6. The Asian Group reiterated that recommendation in 2005, *see Initial Discussion Paper on "Enhancing the Effectiveness of the Special Mechanisms of the Commission on Human Rights,"* UN Doc. [ST/]HR/SP/SEM.1/2005/1, Recommendation 6. On the practice developed since, *see* chapter five.

Between 2002 and 2004, the attempt to reform the United Nations on its sixtieth anniversary, launched by former UN Secretary General Kofi Annan, prompted further discussions on reviewing Special Procedures but did not yield specific fruits.[70] It did nonetheless conclude with the Resolution of the Commission on Human Rights 2004/76 of April 21, 2000, identifying challenges faced by Special Procedures and the desirable focus for further reform processes.[71]

Against the backdrop of the discussion that would culminate in the decision to replace the Commission with the Human Rights Council in 2006, the Asian Group revived the question of reviewing the Special Procedures during the last substantial session of the Commission.[72] Despite their antagonistic position toward Special Procedures, the Commission approved the Asian initiative and held a seminar on enhancing and strengthening their effectiveness in October 2005.[73] The seminar was based on a "non-paper"[74] presented by the Asian Group with the support of the Like-Minded Group, advocating for reforms that were perceived as a threat to the future of Special Procedures.[75] The Group recommended strict criteria for the selection of mandate holders that would have, inter alia, made ineligible persons holding a governmental or non-governmental paid position.[76] It also

[70] In his report *Strengthening of the United Nations: An Agenda for Further Change*, UN Doc. A/57/387 (9 September 2002), Action 4, the Secretary General requested the OHCHR to undertake a review of Special Procedures and to report back to him with recommendations on how to enhance their effectiveness. The OHCHR's report can be found in UN Doc. E/CN.4/2004/12/Add.1 (24 February 2004).

[71] However, the resolution was adopted by a recorded vote of 35 against 18 abstentions reflecting the lack of consensus on its content, *see* Marc Limon and Hilary Power, *History of the United Nations Special Procedures Mechanism: Origins, Evolution and Reform* (Universal Rights Group, 2014): 14. A "Compilation of recent documents in relation the enhancement of the working methods of the Commission on Human Rights (1999–2005)" was published by the OHCHR on January 17, 2006, available at: https://www.ohchr.org/Documents/HRBodies/HRCouncil/CompilationDocuments1999-2005.pdf.

[72] The Secretary General's March 2005 report *In Larger Freedom: Development, Security and Human Rights for All*, UN Doc. A/59/2005 (March 2005) proposed the creation of a Human Rights Council in place of the Commission on Human Rights in order to accord human rights a more authoritative position. On the Secretary-General proposals see also references in n. 93.

[73] Decision of the Commission on Human Rights 2005/113, 21 April 2005.

[74] In UN jargon, "non-papers" are written proposals distributed unofficially, without nomenclature. The author of the proposal is identified, and the papers are usually tabled to test if an idea "can fly." Its nonofficial status facilitates its withdrawal if there is no consensus forthcoming. Their distribution is unrestricted, and they are open to public discussion.

[75] UN Doc. *[ST/]*HR/SP/SEM.1/2005/1 (n. 69). As explained above, the Like-Minded Group's Approach to Special Procedures has deserved widespread condemnation.

[76] The Asian Group recommended that "the individuals to be considered for appointment as a mandate-holder should neither be holding a government post nor be a salaried member of an NGO or a member of the Governing Bodies of advocacy groups in the area of the mandate," Asian Group for the 61st session of the Commission on Human Rights *Initial Discussion Paper on "Enhancing the Effectiveness of the Special Mechanisms of the Commission on Human Rights,"* UN

tabled unprecedented limits to the principle of publicity governing the activities of Special Procedures in the context of reaffirming the need of a Code of Conduct to regulate their operations.[77] Canada and New Zealand advocated for the inclusion of a standard feature in media releases highlighting the independence of Special Procedures, a statement that would have suggested mandate holders do not represent the United Nations, a complex matter examined in chapter six.[78]

The Asian proposal introduced a requirement of personal signatures by mandate holders on their letters of allegations addressed to member states (Recommendation 10), a divisive issue that was the object of a resolution in 2003 and became codified practice with the adoption of a Code of Conduct in 2006.[79] The US position paper also favored better standardization of practices and due consideration to states' comments before publicizing outcomes, suggesting a minimum deadline of sixty days to allow a governmental response to mandate holders' standard communications.[80] The Asian Group advocated for introducing the exhaustion of domestic remedies as a criteria of admissibility for communications on human rights violations, which would have rendered "urgent appeals" redundant (Recommendation 9).[81] The African Group went further by suggesting the additional exhaustion of regional remedies.[82] Other recommendations issued by stakeholders participating in the seminar included the Romanian proposal to create a "Special Segment for the Special Procedures," concentrating the examination of their reports in a period of three days, with the aim of mitigating the fragmentation hindering their efficiency and visibility.[83]

Doc. *[ST/]*HR/SP/SEM.1/2005/1, Recommendation 4. On the selection of mandate holders, *see also* Recommendations 1–6.

[77] Recommendation 8 calls for the respect for "confidentiality of information of allegations ensuring that such information should not be sent to media or other organization" as well as for "Guidelines for media interaction such as press releases, press conferences and statements."

[78] *New Zealand and Canadian Input to Discussion on Strengthening and Enhancement of the Special Procedures, 12–14 October 2005*, UN Doc. *[ST/]*HR/SP/SEM.1/2005/9.

[79] The Commission endorsed the Asian view in Decision 2003/113, 25 April 2013 (approved by a narrow majority of 28 votes in favor, 25 against, and 1 abstention). The African Group also supported this proposal, *see Observations of the African Group on the Initial Discussion Paper Entitled "Enhancing the Effectiveness of the Special Mechanisms of the Commission on Human Rights" prepared by the Experts of the Asian Group on Human Rights*, [ST/]HR/SP/SEM.1/2005/7, Recommendation 10.

[80] *Position of the United States of America on the issue of Enhancing and Strengthening the Effectiveness of the Special Procedures of the Commission on Human Rights*, UN Doc. *[ST/]*HR/SP/SEM.1/2005/8.

[81] On "urgent appeals," *see* chapter five.

[82] UN doc., *[ST/]*HR/SP/SEM.1/2005/7 (n. 79) Recommendation 9.

[83] *A Proposal for a Compact Special Segment for the Special Procedures of the Commission on Human Rights*, UN Doc. *[ST/]*HR/SP/SEM.1/2005/3.

Overall, the positions advanced during the 2005 seminar highlighted disagreements among states concerning the best criteria and procedures to select mandate holders, but consensus on the need to address the increase in the number of Special Procedures without clarity on the resources to support them or the fragmentation/duplication originated by this phenomenon.[84] This apparent consensus has been consistently contradicted by governmental actions. While civil society and mandate holders influence the process,[85] the creation of Special Procedures relies exclusively on the will of states and, therefore, curbing their numbers or stopping further growth should have already happened if such consensus was not overridden by interests and agendas favoring the creation of new mechanisms for specific topics.

The different views expressed during the 2005 informal seminar and former discussions on reviewing the mechanisms also revealed a widespread appetite for standardization of working methods and clarity, particularly regarding the handling of letters of allegations as well as the process of verifying their credibility. Within this context, it is puzzling that mandate holders kept fighting the inevitable imposition of a Code of Conduct instead of contributing actively to the elaboration of a set of standards to govern their modus operandi.

B. Human Rights Council (2006–2019)

The quest for reforming the Commission and calls to replace it with another body, including the creation of an International Court for Human Rights, has been a recurrent issue in UN debates tracing back to 1950, but was unsuccessful for decades.[86] The establishment of the Human Rights Council in 2006 was characterized by the overwhelming emphasis on the weaknesses of the Commission on Human Rights without giving adequate credit to its significant achievements. The shameful end of the Commission, with a procedural rather than ceremonial session, is further evidence of the haste to be

[84] The report of the seminar is available in OHCHR, *Enhancing and Strengthening the Effectiveness of the Special Procedures of the Commission on Human Rights*, UN Doc. E/CN.4/2006/116 (12 December 2005).

[85] Jane Connors, "Special Procedures: Independence and Impartiality" in Aoife Nolan, Rosa Freedman, and Thérèse Murphy (eds.), *The United Nations Special Procedures System* (Brill, 2017): 59.

[86] *See* Miko Lempinen, *The United Nations Commission on Human Rights and the Different Treatment of Governments* (Åbo Akademi University Press, 2005): 31–4; *see also* Manfred Nowak, "The Need for a World Court of Human Rights" in Jessica Almqvist and Felipe Gómez Isa (eds.), *The Human Rights Council: Challenges and Opportunities* (FRIDE, 2006): 59–70.

rid of the old body. Only after that final session, nostalgic voices were heard, mainly when it became noticeable that the acclaimed Human Rights Council had little to start with.[87] The lack of clear configuration of the new Council forced the body to dedicate its first year of operations to deciding its agenda, competence, and future of the subsidiary bodies.

Three subjects have occupied the core of the negotiations around the review Special Procedures undertaken by the Human Rights Council. First, the maintenance of geographic procedures in relation with the dispute over selectivity and double standards informing the adoption of country resolutions. Second, the procedure for the appointment of mandate holders. Finally, the adoption of a code of conduct. The vast majority of the members of the African Group, the Asian Group, the Organization of Islamic Cooperation, and the Like-Minded Group have continued to contest the existence of geographic Special Procedures. Ironically, these states are the main advocates of maintaining a separate point in the agenda of the Human Rights Council to address the situation of the Palestinian territories. They also favor the exceptionally undefined deadline for this mandate that was established in 1993 to last "until the end of the Israeli occupation of those territories."[88] This contradictory position has been repeatedly justified by arguing the thematic rather than geographic nature of this Special Procedure, focused on the right to self-determination.[89] Despite protracted contestation, country mandates and country resolutions were retained.

The procedure followed to select mandate holders is explained in chapter six. The following section will therefore focus on the main innovation introduced by the Human Rights Council in relation to Special Procedures: the Code of Conduct.

i. Successive Waves of Reform: Much Ado about Nothing?

Former attempts to reform the Commission or its subsidiary mechanisms were completed with minimal impact on how Special Procedures continued to operate. The creation of a Human Rights Council reinvigorated proposals

[87] Paul Gordon Lauren, "To Preserve and Build on Its Achievements and to Redress Its Shortcomings: The Journey form the Commission on Human Rights to the Human Rights Council" 29 *Human Rights Quarterly* (2007): 307, 309–25; *see also* Amnesty International, "UN Commission on Human Rights ends on a disappointing note. New Council deserves a better start," AI Doc. IOR 41/003/2006, 28 March 2006.

[88] CHR Res. 93/2, 19 February 1993.

[89] *See, e.g.*, Veronique Joosten, *The UN Human Rights Council at work: From high hopes back to reality* (United Nations Association Flanders Belgium, 2006): 23–5.

that succeeded for the first time. Among them, the approval of a Code of Conduct for Special Procedures was perceived as a major setback, first and foremost by the mandate holders.[90] The Western Group drove the reform impetus by trying to address the politicization of an intrinsically political body, an unattainable objective reinforced by Kofi Annan's attempt to overhaul the Organization before the end of his tenure as Secretary General.[91] He aspired to transform the United Nations entirely, predominantly the Security Council and the Secretariat.[92] Annan failed to gain the political support necessary to deal with the most controversial issues and, instead, the salient outcomes of his initiative were reduced to the creation of the Human Rights Council and the Peacebuilding Commission.[93] Hence, the latest failure to renovate the Security Council was disguised by enacting a human rights reform,[94] the usual victim of the "reformitis" syndrome suffered by the UN machinery.[95] Whatever the rationale, states who wished to reduce Special Procedures' scrutiny over their human rights records used this opportunity to advance their "negative reform agenda."[96]

90 Mandate holders have vehemently opposed the approval of a Code of Conduct. *See* Coordination Committee of Special Procedures, *A Note by the Special Procedures' Coordination Committee in Response to Discussions on a Code of Conduct and Annex: Possible Elements of a Code of Conduct* (Geneva, April 13, 2007), available at: http://www2.ohchr.org/english/bodies/chr/special/docs/note_code_of_conduct.pdf.

91 *See* Françoise J. Hampson, "An Overview of the Reform of the Human Rights Machinery" 7(1) *Human Rights Law Review* (2007): 7, 8–10; *see also* Kevin Boyle, "The United Nations Human Rights Council: Origins, Antecedents, and Prospects" in Kevin Boyle (ed.), *New Institutions for Human Rights Protection* (Oxford University Press, 2009): 29.

92 *See* UN Doc. A/59/2005 (n. 72). This report is a response to the proposals contained in the report of the High-Level Panel on Threats, Challenges and Change, *A More Secure World: Our Shared Responsibility*, UN Doc. A/59/565 (December 2004). *See also Investing in the United Nations: For a Stronger Organization Worldwide*, UN Doc. A/60/692 (March 2006), and *Investing in People*, UN Doc. A/61/255 (August 2006). Former proposals from the Secretary General can be found in *Renewing he United Nations: A Programme for Reform*, UN Doc. A/51/950 (1997); and *Strengthening the United Nations: An Agenda for Further Change*, UN Doc. A/57/387 (2002).

93 The UN Peacebuilding Commission was established by a joint resolution of the Security Council and the General Assembly, *see* Res. SC 1645/2005-GA 60/180 of 20 December 2005.

94 Hampson (2007) (n. 90): 7, 9. Marc Bossuyt, *The Human Rights Council: A Doubtful Reform?* (KU Leuven Faculty of Law paper, 2006), at: https://www.law.kuleuven.be/iir/nl/activiteiten/archief/documentatie/OldActivities/HRCBossuyt.pdf.

95 *See* remarks by Marc Bossuyt in *Summary Records of the Fifth Meeting, 28th July 2005*, UN Doc. E/CN.4/Sub.2/2005/SR.5, para. 47. *See also* Edward C. Luck, *Reforming The United Nations: Lessons From A History In Process* (New Haven, Academic Council on the United Nations System, 2003): 2; and Alston (2006) (n. 54): 185.

96 Meghna Abraham, *A New Chapter for Human Rights: A Handbook on Issues of Transition from the Commission on Human Rights to the Human Rights Council* (Friedrich-Ebert-Stiftung and International Service for Human Rights, June 2006): 41; Jeroen Gütter, "Special Procedures and the Human Rights Council: Achievements and Challenges Ahead" 7(1) *Human Rights Law Review* (2007): 93, 104–5.

The support for a Code of Conduct by the African Group, the Organization of Islamic Cooperation, and the Non-Aligned Movement granted enough majority for its approval on June 18, 2007.[97] On the same date, negotiations resulted in the "Institution Building" resolution, a last-minute compromise leaving crucial issues affecting Special Procedures unsettled.[98] Instead, they were deferred until September 2007, when an agreement was reached on some imprecise criteria for nominating candidates.[99] The failure to approve a standardized procedure to review mandates of Special Procedures meant that these appraisals were conducted on a case-by-case basis bringing about the maintenance of all thematic procedures and the termination of the country mandates on Cuba and Belarus.[100]

General Assembly Resolution 60/251—operative paragraphs 1 and 16—called for a full review of the status, work and functioning of the Council within five years, adding uncertainty to the future of the human rights machinery depending on this body. The latest attempt to comprehensively reform Special Procedures resulted in 437 state proposals advocating conflicting views on their independence and accountability (35 percent), state cooperation (17 percent), Secretariat support and management of resources (17 percent), "proliferation" of mandates (7 percent), and implementation and follow-up (5 percent).[101] This process concluded with the adoption of an outcome document on March 25, 2011, which introduced some modifications to the Universal Periodic Review but left Special Procedures "untouched."[102]

The absence of concrete results betrayed the efforts invested in the process by governmental and non-governmental stakeholders and were perceived as another missed opportunity to advance improvements such as the compilation of statistics on cooperation by states with Special Procedures

[97] HRC Res. 5/2 (n. 2). On the political alliance over this issue, *see* Limon and Power (2014) (n. 71): 15.

[98] HRC Res. 5/1 (n. 43).

[99] HRC Decision 6/10, 27 September 2007. On nominations of mandate holders, *see* chapter six.

[100] Meghna Abraham, "Building the New Human Rights Council. Outcome and analysis of the institution-building year" in *Dialogue on Globalization* (Friedrich-Ebert-Stiftung Occasional Papers: August 2007), *esp*. 27–9.

[101] Marc Limon and Ted Piccone, "Human Rights Special Procedures: Determinants of Influence" in *Brookings Institutions & Universal Rights Group Policy Report* (Universal Rights Group, 2014): 10.

[102] Ibid. at 12. For the outcome document, *see Open-ended inter-governmental working group on the review of the work and functioning of the Human Rights Council*, UN Doc. A/HRC/WG.8/2/1 (4 May 2011), adopted by HRC Res. 16/21 of 25 March 2011 and GA Res. 65/281 of 17 June 2011. A summary of the proposals and political alliances can be found in Thomas Colerick, *The Human Rights Council: Is it filling its mission as the world's premier human rights protector?* (Centre for UN Reform, 2 February 2012).

or suggestions for a better oversight and allocation of resources.[103] Instead, the 2011 review served to crystallize opposing governmental positions on Special Procedures.[104] Nonetheless it also represented a small victory because it averted the passing of proposals with the potential to undermine the independence of mandate holders seeking to tighten the Code of Conduct,[105] undertake periodic "rationalization" processes,[106] rewrite the Manual of Operations of Special Procedures,[107] or bar country mandates unless established with the consent of the state concerned.[108]

ii. The Code of Conduct for Special Procedures

The resolution adopting the Code of Conduct was sponsored by the African Group, Colombia, Cuba, and the Islamic Republic of Iran,[109] despite the protracted opposition by mandate holders,[110] civil society organizations, and some states.[111] Chapter five elaborates on the expert status of mandate holders, mainly understood as the need of operating without political interference. The perceived need of a Code of Conduct reflects on the difficulty to find a balance between political decision makers and experts that permeates

103 *See*, for instance, *Contribution of the Special Procedures mandate-holders to the review process* dated October 8, 2010, and available at: http://www2.ohchr.org/english/bodies/chr/special/docs/HRCreview-ContributionSPPP_en.pdf.

104 Limon and Power (2014) (n. 71): 14, and CHR Res. 2004/76, 21 April 2004.

105 *See* proposals for the establishment of a "Legal Committee on Compliance with the Code of Conduct" or similar monitoring mechanism advanced by the Non-Aligned Movement (NAM), the Organization of the Islamic Cooperation (OIC), Bolivia, Cuba, China, Algeria, Iran, Libya, Morocco, and Russian Federation, UN Doc. A/HRC/WG.8/2,1 (Annex IV—Compilation of Proposals), at 55–64: *see also* UN Doc. A/HRC/WG.8/1/CRP.1/Rev.1 (15 November 2010). The text of all proposals submitted can be found on the extranet website of the OHCHR at: https://extranet.ohchr.org/sites/hrc/Pages/default.aspx.

106 The African Group, Algeria, India, Azerbaijan, Sri Lanka, and OIC proposed that the Council should periodically embark on the process of Review, Rationalization and Improvement (RRI) of mandates, *see* UN Docs. A/HRC/WG.8/2,1 and A/HRC/WG.8/1/CRP.1/Rev.1 (n. 105).

107 The representative of Algeria introduced draft resolution A/HRC/2/L.2/Rev.1, sponsored by Algeria (on behalf of the Group of African States), Colombia, and Indonesia. The support of most Asian countries led to HRC Res. 2/1 of 27 November 2006 (approved by 30 votes to 15, with 2 abstentions).

108 African Group, Bangladesh, Democratic People's Republic of Korea, Libya, OIC, and NAM, *see* UN Docs. A/HRC/WG.8/2,1 and A/HRC/WG.8/1/CRP.1/Rev.1 (n. 105).

109 *See* draft resolution in UN Doc. A/ HRC/4/L.6 (21 March 2007), and *Report to the General Assembly on the 4th session of the Human Rights Council*, UN Doc. A/HRC/4/123 (12 June 2007), para. 142.

110 Coordination Committee of Special Procedures (2007) (n. 90); *see also* UN Doc. A/HRC/5/19 (15 June 2007).

111 The minority of states opposing the Code of Conduct were Canada, Czech Republic, Finland, France, Germany, Guatemala, Mexico, Netherlands, Peru, Poland, Republic of Korea, Romania, Switzerland, Ukraine, and United Kingdom; *see* Abraham (2007) (n. 100): 29.

every aspect of international law and international organizations.[112] Experts are never fully trusted, as illustrated by the relationship between governments and international human rights mechanisms. A large number of states are not willing to grant individuals direct access to treaty bodies, despite their decisions not being legally binding. Although ratifications of the core human rights treaties are rising, in all cases, the number of countries that have ratified the optional protocol or treaty article authorizing the appropriate treaty body to review individual complaints is significantly lower. The inter-state complaint mechanisms before treaty bodies remain virtually unused. Conversely, all states of the world have engaged with the Universal Periodic Review, predominantly dominated by governmental interactions. This suggests, in the logic of international law, that states are reluctant to fully rely on expert mechanisms. The need to isolate experts from political influence coexists with mistrust toward expertise and the corollary need of political control. Thus:[113]

> Political decision makers appoint experts, yet experts cannot be trusted to take all perspectives into account and thus need to be subjected to either political scrutiny or a different, higher level of scrutiny by experts.[114]

The stated purpose of the Code of Conduct is to enhance "the effectiveness of the system of special procedures by defining the standards of ethical behaviour and professional conduct that special procedures . . . shall observe whilst discharging their duties" (Article 1). The provisions of the Code complement the General Assembly's Regulations Governing the Status, Basic Rights and Duties of Officials other than Secretariat Officials, and Experts on Mission;[115] the draft manual of Special Procedures must be in consonance with the Code (Article 2). The Code introduces restrictions on their ability to publicize their activities and lays out admissibility criteria for the handling of individual communications and gathering of information. As argued below, these two features have strengthened rather than weakened the standing of Special Procedures. However, the Code of Conduct has also had some

[112] Jan Klabbers, "The virtues of expertise" in Monika Ambrus, Karin Arts, Ellen Hey, and Helena Raulus (eds.), *The Role of "Experts" in International and European Decision-Making Processes* (Cambridge University Press, 2014): 82, 84–5.
[113] Ibid. 82, 84–5.
[114] Ibid. 82, 86.
[115] GA Res. 56/280, 27 March 2002, reprinted in UN Doc. ST/SGB/2002/9 (18 June 2002).

pernicious consequences and, at times, has been used to weaken the work of mandate holders.

a. Publicity Restrictions

The power of the Special Procedures to address human rights violations and effect change is rooted in the publicity given to their work under the stamp of the United Nations.[116] Several of the provisions of the Code of Conduct are specifically aimed at regulating the publicity of their operations with emphasis on avoiding unfettered interaction with mass media. Contrary to other international and regional human rights mechanisms, mandate holders are routinely present in mainstream media, and many Special Rapporteurs have a distinct profile in social media, a feature that originates important tensions with governments and resulted in the first formal invocation of the Internal Advisory Procedure in 2013.[117]

It is worth highlighting that in 2003, Special Procedure mandate holders discussed their relationship with the press and agreed that "no general rules could be established that would dictate them when a press release would be issued."[118] They considered "their ability to establish relations with the press and to use these to further their mandates was an aspect of their independence and their ability to determine their procedures and methods of work,"[119] concluding that they should not be the object of any interference or clearance procedures.[120]

This position is no longer sustainable. Mandate holders must be guided by the principle of discretion in their information-gathering activities (Article 13 of the Code of Conduct) and to "show restraint, moderation and discretion" in the implementation of their mandate (Articles 8 and 12). They must also ensure that the first recipient of their conclusions and recommendations is the concerned government (Article 13). They must take into account "in a comprehensive and timely manner" (Article 6) the information provided by states, which reflects standards expected from a balanced and fair approach to any issue; still, these provisions can be abused. For instance, public

[116] On this principle, *see* chapter four.

[117] Limon and Piccone (2014) (n. 101): 32.

[118] *Report of the tenth meeting of special rapporteurs/representatives, independent experts and chairpersons of working groups of special procedures of the Commission on Human Rights and of the advisory service programme, Geneva 23 to 27 June 2003*, UN Doc. E/CN.4/2004/4, Annex, para. 23.

[119] Ibid., para. 22, 24–7, and 69.

[120] *Report of the eleventh meeting of special rapporteurs/representatives, independent experts and chairpersons of working groups of special procedures of the Commission on Human Rights and of the advisory service programme, Geneva 21 to 25 June 2004*, UN Doc. E/CN.4/2005/5, Annex, para. 27.

announcements of preliminary conclusions following a visit have been considered relevant to protect Special Procedures' independence, limiting potential pressure aimed at changing their views before submitting final reports.

b. Criteria of Admissibility

The attempt to impose a requirement to exhaust domestic remedies through the Code of Conduct, prior to sending communications to Special Procedures referred to earlier, was unsuccessful, as was the proposal requiring the identification of a situation of gross human rights violations for processing urgent appeals.[121] However, the Code of Conduct does introduce criteria of admissibility for allegations of breaches of human rights. Until the approval of the Code of Conduct, those criteria, as well as any other aspect of their methods of work, were decided on a case-by-case basis by mandate holders of Special Procedures.

Regrettably, mandate holders are required to address all communication through diplomatic channels, unless agreed otherwise between a state and the OHCHR (Article 14 of the Code of Conduct). This has had a negative impact on expediting the delivery of urgent appeals compared with the previous practice of transmitting time-sensitive cases directly to the minister of foreign affairs of the state concerned, with a copy forwarded to the relevant Permanent Mission before the United Nations.[122]

Conversely, the Code of Conduct has also introduced positive regulations. Prior to its approval, only the Working Groups on Arbitrary Detention and Enforced Disappearance required some relationship between the author of the communication and the victim coming before them. The Code of Conduct has formalized the need to assess that communications are authored by victims of the human rights violation or by persons or groups "claiming to have direct or reliable knowledge of those violations substantiated by clear information" (Article 9). This is a welcome innovation. The nature, function, and current practice of Special Procedures has changed and increasingly corresponds to a "complaint recourse-mechanism" in addition to their established nature as a "complaint-information procedure."[123] Therefore, the allegations of human rights violations are not only used by

[121] *See* Abraham (2007) (n. 100): 31.

[122] *See* ibid., 31. Coordination Committee of Special Procedures (n. 90); *see also Letter dated 14 June 2007 addressed by the Chairperson of the Coordination Committee of Special Procedures to the President of the Human Rights Council*, UN Doc. A/HRC/5/19 (15 June 2007).

[123] *See* chapter five.

mandate holders to assess the situation of human rights in a specific territory or the causes, prevalence, and remedies of the phenomenon of abuse under their competence worldwide. Many allegations are addressed to identify the existence of individual cases of human rights violations where the victim is considered part of an adversarial procedure. In this scenario, alleged victims should have, at the very least, knowledge that their case is being handled by an international human rights body.

The prior practice, based on an implicit presumption of the "objective interest" of the victim to have her or his case handled by Special Procedures, might have resulted in outcomes manifestly contrary to the principles informing due process and, in particular, the principle of doing no harm.[124] An alleged victim of a human rights violation whose case is handled by a Special Procedure mandate holder was at risk to be subjected to reprisals without even knowing the case was under review by one or several mandates. The risk remains despite this provision, a point elaborated upon in chapter four.

The Code of Conduct (Article 10) allows for continuing the practice of resorting to urgent appeals without the express consent of the victim, striking a better balance between the situation where cases involving loss of life, life-threatening situations, or other imminent or ongoing damage of a grave nature to victims cannot be addressed in a timely manner following the procedure outlined in Article 9.

Some authors have described Special Procedures' mandate holders actions on behalf of individual victims of human rights violations, particularly in relation to the handling of "urgent appeals" as international habeas corpus, underlying the role of these mechanisms to intervene on behalf of individual cases.[125] As explained in chapter five, this competence has rarely been adjudicated to Special Procedures expressly. A significant part of the implementation of working methods by Special Procedures has evolved in practice as fait accompli accompanied, at most, by an emerging opinio juris gradually sanctioning monitoring organs of international organizations to develop their working methods based on their own will in areas arguably outside those originally identified as their zones of competence.[126] Nonetheless, it

[124] This presumption of "objective interest" was advocated by Frouville (1996) (n. 36): 48.

[125] Nigel Rodley, "United Nations Action Procedures against Disappearances, Summary or Arbitrary Executions, and Torture" 8(4) *Human Rights Quarterly* (1986):700–30, at 700; Simma (1995) (n. 11): 273; Tolley (1987) (n. 55): 10.

[126] The hypothesis is advanced by Emmanuele Decaux, "Avant-Propos" in Frouville (1996) (n. 36): 7.

has been difficult to explain the legal foundations supporting the activities developed by Special Procedures without invoking complex legal arguments drawn from the theory of implicit powers, the legal value of "self-executing" resolutions, the prima facie validity of acts of subsidiary organs in international intergovernmental organizations, "ad hoc" consent, or the obligation of states to cooperate for the promotion and protection of human rights.[127]

The formalized approval of admissibility criteria included in the Code of Conduct confirms the competence of all mandate holders to deal with communications, albeit indirectly. Instead of express recognition of the competence of mandate holders to handle, investigate, or reach conclusions over potential human rights violations, this competence is deduced from the setting of admissibility criteria by the Council. The Human Rights Council and its Special Procedures have been endowed with the power to react to human rights violations without the specific consent of the state concerned, not only for the case of situations of human rights violations but also in relation to individual complaints. Resolutions, such as the one establishing the Code of Conduct of the Council and those of the former Commission apply and are valid as long as no superior organ within the organization contradicts them.[128]

From a legal perspective, there is no real difference between the views adopted by the Working Group on Arbitrary Detention or other mandate holders of Special Procedures on the violation of human rights norms and the opinions issued by treaty bodies. None of them are binding, and they share the same underlying purpose: to incite a change of states' attitude based on the "mobilization of shame." The real difference lies in the clear legal foundation of this competence for treaty bodies, which had been largely missing in the case of Special Procedures until the approval of the Code of Conduct.

[127] These grounds are analyzed in some detail in Elvira Domínguez-Redondo, Los procedimientos públicos especiales de la Comisión de Derechos Humanos de Naciones Unidas. Evolución, *Naturaleza y Fundamentación Jurídica [Special Procedures of the Commission on Human Rights: Evolution, Nature and Legal Foundations]* (Universidad Carlos III de Madrid, Madrid, 2003): 720–78 [available in the Library of Universidad Carlos III de Madrid (Spain).

[128] Several opinions of the UN Office of Legal Affairs confirmed this, for instance, *The Extent to which the Commission on Human Rights May Act on Its Own Decisions without Awaiting the Consideration/Approval of its Reports by the Economic and Social Council*, dated 26 June 1978; *Appointment of Special Rapporteurs/Special Representatives*, 10 April 1981, reproduced in Bertrand Ramcharam, *The Principle of Legality in International Human Rights Institutions. Selected Legal Opinions* (Martinus Nijhoff Publishers, 1997): 31, 33–6, 284–5.

c. Ill-intentioned Use of the Code of Conduct

During the drafting negotiations of the Code of Conduct, a significant number of states promoted the idea of creating a body to oversee compliance with the Code. The main mission of this organ would have been to act as a mechanism to discipline Special Rapporteurs who failed to abide by its terms.[129] This initiative was perceived as a threat to the independence of mandate holders due to its potentially intimidating impact that would have facilitated self-censorship as well as the introduction of an adversarial progress.[130] The proposal was unsuccessful, and instead compliance with the Code of Conduct has been left to mandate holders through an "Internal Advisory Procedure to Review Practice and Working Methods," adopted by mandate holders in 2008.[131] It involves a self-regulatory process that allows the "Coordination Committee" to provide good offices in order to settle possible disagreements with states over the compliance of the Code of Conduct.[132]

Since its approval, several states, especially the Russian Federation, have insisted on including reference to the Code of Conduct in resolutions creating or renewing mandates.[133] By July 2019, all resolutions creating or renewing Special Procedures included a reminder of the Code of Conduct in their preamble stressing that the mandate holder shall discharge his or her duties in accordance with its provisions.

It is difficult to measure the impact of the Code of Conduct in facilitating legitimate concerns over mandate holders' behavior. Its implementation remains intrinsically linked to political processes resistant to legal or ethical standards. Many governments have questioned the impartiality and findings of the Special Procedures mandate holders without referring to specific rules of the Code of Conduct. For instance, the 2010 report of the then Special Rapporteur on Torture, Manfred Nowak, was the object of staunch criticisms by Jamaica.[134] When the Working Group on Arbitrary Detention issued

[129] On the proposals advanced by the African Group, the Non-Aligned Movement and the Organisation of the Islamic Conference, *see* Philip Alston, "Hobbling the Monitors: Should U.N. Human Rights Monitors be Accountable?" 52(2) *Harvard International Law Journal* (2011): 561, 566.

[130] Limon and Piccone (2014) (n. 101): 12–3.

[131] *Report on the fifteenth meeting of special rapporteurs/representatives, independent experts and chairpersons of working groups of the special procedures of the Council, held in Geneva from 23 to 27 June 2008*, UN Doc. A/HRC/10/24 (2008), Appendix III.

[132] *See* Najat Maalla M'jid, "The UN Special Procedures System: The Role of the Coordination Committee of Special Procedures" in Nolan, Freedman, and Murphy (n. 85): 131, 136–7; *see also* Alston (2011) (n. 129): 561, 563.

[133] Joosten (2006) (n. 89): 19–21.

[134] Who accused the Rapporteur of making sweeping statements and drawing conclusions not necessarily grounded in evidence, *see Summary record of the 20th meeting of the 3rd Committee of the General Assembly, held on 25th October 2010, 65th session*, A/C.3/65/SR.29 (2010), para. 87.

its controversial view on the Assange Case on December 4, 2015,[135] the British Foreign Secretary responded undermining its authority, describing the Working Group as a group of "lay people not lawyers."[136] Following a visit to the United Kingdom in 2013, the Special Rapporteur on housing, Raquel Rolnik, was portrayed as "a woman from Brazil" by the Chairman of the Conservative Party, who also demanded an investigation by the UN Secretary General claiming the mandate-holder conclusions were influenced by political bias.[137] The British Work and Pensions Secretary also threatened to lodge a "formal complaint" against the Special Rapporteur on Extreme Poverty Philip Alston, over the alleged ill-founded and politically biased conclusions deriving from his visit to the country in 2018.[138] In an unconventional move, during the forty-first session of the Human Rights Council, the United Kingdom relinquished its right to respond orally, simply referring to its written response.[139]

While states do not necessarily rely on the Code of Conduct to criticize Special Procedures, its existence has strengthened governmental arguments with references to a legal/ethical framework. The Special Rapporteur on the situation of human rights and fundamental freedoms of indigenous peoples, Rodolfo Stavenhagen, became the first target when he presented a report on the situation of human rights and indigenous peoples in Asia in 2007.[140] On this occasion, members of the Asian Group alleged the Special Rapporteur had failed to consult with the states concerned before the release of the report breaching Article 6 of the Code.[141] Soon after, states showed

[135] *Opinion No. 54/2015 concerning Julian Assange (Sweden and the United Kingdom of Great Britain and Northern Ireland)*, UN Doc. A/HRC/WGAD/2015.

[136] "Hammond calls U.N. Assange report 'ridiculous,'" *Reuters. World News*, February 5, 2016.

[137] Meabh Ritchie, "Bedroom tax row: Grant Shapps v 'woman from Brazil,'" *Channel4 News*, September 11, 2013, available at: https://www.channel4.com/news/bedroom-tax-un-grant-shapps-brazil-row; *see also* Aoife Nolan and Alice Donald, "Human rights case against welfare reforms keeps growing," *The Conversation*, July 10, 2014, available at: https://theconversation.com/human-rights-case-against-welfare-reforms-keeps-growing-28990.

[138] Robert Booth, "Amber Rudd's to lodge complaint over UN's austerity report," *The Guardian*, May 22, 2019, available at: https://www.theguardian.com/politics/2019/may/22/amber-rudd-to-lodge-complaint-over-un-austerity-report; *see also* Andrew Fagan, "Poverty and Inequality in the UK: Proud to be British?" in *Human Rights Centre Blog* (University of Essex, June 27, 2019), available at: https://hrcessex.wordpress.com/2019/06/27/poverty-inequality-in-the-uk-proud-to-be-british/.

[139] The written response can be found in UN Doc. A/HRC/41/39/Add.3 (2019). For the UK intervention, *see* UN WEB TV Webcast, "Interactive dialogue with Special Rapporteur on extreme poverty and human rights," 14th Meeting, *41st Regular Session Human Rights Council*, 28th June 2019, available at: http://webtv.un.org/meetings-events/security-council/watchbr%20/watch/clustered-id-sr-on-poverty-sr-on-idps-14th-meeting-41st-regular-session-human-rights-council-/6053551884001/?term=&sort=date#player.

[140] UN Doc. A/HRC/6/15/Add. 3 (1 November 2007).

[141] Joosten (2006) (n. 89): 26–7.

their discontent with the Special Rapporteur on extrajudicial, summary, or arbitrary executions by using the Code of Conduct as a channel to reduce the security of tenure enjoyed by mandate holders until then, by forcing a Statement of the President of the Human Rights Council.[142] To date, such statement has not had a practical impact in the renewals of mandates.

In 2009, the same mandate holder was accused of breaching the Code of Conduct for recommending the resignation of the Kenyan Attorney General as a necessary measure to restore trust and combat impunity,[143] leading to the adoption of a Human Rights Council resolution recalling "that it is incumbent on special procedures mandate holders to exercise their functions with full respect for and strict observance of their mandates, as outlined in the relevant Council resolutions providing such mandates, and to comply fully with the provisions of the code of conduct."[144]

The government of the Philippines under Duterte's presidency has displayed a notorious antagonism toward mandate holders. In December 2017, the Special Rapporteurs on the rights of indigenous peoples, Victoria Tauli-Corpuz, and on internally displaced persons, Cecilia Jimenez-Damary, issued a press statement condemning human rights abuses of the Lumad communities, attracting a backlash from Duterte's administration.[145] Two months later, Tauli-Corpuz was included in a terrorist list under Philippines security legislation, alleging she had links with the Communist Party of the Philippines' Ilocos-Cordillera Regional Committee.[146] The president and his entourage have also devoted verbal attacks and threats of physical violence to the Special Rapporteur on extrajudicial, summary, or arbitrary executions Agnès Callamard. Her impartiality was formally questioned with calls for strict adherence to the Code of Conduct.[147] Following a press release, expressing grave concerns about judicial independence in the

142 As explained by the then Special Rapporteur, Philip Alston, in (2011) (n. 129): 561, 596–7. The statement can be found in UN Doc. 8/PRST/2, *Terms of office of the special procedure mandate-holders*, 18 June 2008.

143 *See Report of the Special Rapporteur on Extrajudicial, Summary or Arbitrary Executions: Mission to Kenya*, UN Doc. A/HRC/11/2/Add.6 (2009), *esp.* para. 93; *see also* Alston (2011) (n. 129): 561, 597.

144 *System of Special Procedures* HRC Res 11/11, 18 June 2009, para. 2.

145 OHCHR Press Release, Philippines warned over "massive" impact of military operations on Mindanao indigenous peoples, 27 December 2017.

146 Under international pressure, the Duterte's administration removed her from the list on July 26, 2018. *See* Diane Louys, *"I'll kill you along with drug addicts"—President Duterte's war on human rights defenders in the Philippines* (The Observatory for the Protection of Human rights Defenders, 2019): 28; *see also* Victoria Tauli-Corpus, "A silent war is being waged on Philippine indigenous communities," *Financial Times*, March 29, 2018.

147 Department of Foreign Affairs, PH Tells Human Rights Council: Do Not Politicize, Weaponize Human Rights, February 27, 2018. *See* Louys (2019) (n. 146): 28–9.

Philippines,[148] the Special Rapporteur on the independence of judges and lawyers, Diego García-Sayán, was accused of breaching Articles 8 and 13 of the Code of Conduct for failing to include the state's view. The president of the Philippines told the expert "to go to hell" for interfering in domestic affairs and stated that he did not recognize the status of the Special Rapporteur as a UN expert.[149] Other public attacks have consisted on alleged breaches of the Code of Conduct without providing details on the provisions violated.[150]

iii. Withdrawing for Reform: United States of America and the Council

The pressure exercised by the United States and other Western countries to introduce criteria for membership to the Human Rights Council yielded some positive results. Candidates to membership are required to make voluntary pledges and commitments on the promotion and protection and human rights that are used as benchmarks during the Universal Periodic Review.[151] The General Assembly can also suspend the membership to the Council by a two-third majority vote based on the commission of persistent gross and systematic violations of human rights. Unlike previous practice, that contributed to providing a virtually permanent seat in the Commission on Human Rights to permanent members of the Security Council, states members of the Council are not eligible for re-election after two consecutive terms.

Shortly after losing its seat for the first time in 2001, the United States considered these reforms insufficient, and much attention was paid to the lack of criteria for becoming a member of the Council.[152] Explaining his country's opposing vote to the resolution establishing the Human Rights Council, the then Permanent Representative to the United Nations, John Bolton, highlighted the adherence of the United States to an election system that

[148] OHCHR Press Release, *Judicial Independence in Philippines is under Threat, Says UN Human Rights Expert* (Geneva, June 1, 2018).

[149] *See* Atty Dodo Dulay, "UN rapporteur Garcia-Sayán violated UN code of conduct," *Manila Times*, June 8, 2018; Jim Gomez, "Duerte tells UN expert 'to go to hell' over criticism" *AP News*, June 3, 2018, available at: https://apnews.com/a49791b446d84db79e163b8fa27b5031.

[150] *See, e.g.*, the response of the Iranian government during the interactive dialogue with the SR on human rights in Iran, 27th Meeting, 4th regular session of the Human Rights Council (11 March 2019) (minute 18), available at: http://webtv.un.org/watch/id-sr-on-human-rights-in-iran-27th-meeting-40th-regular-session-human-rights-council/6012601609001/.

[151] Elvira Domínguez-Redondo, "The Universal Periodic Review of the UN Human Rights Council: an assessment of the first session" 7(3) *Chinese Journal of International Law* (2008): 721. On the role of civil society monitoring pledges, *see* Joosten (2006) (n. 89): 7–9.

[152] *See* Conall Mallory, "Membership and the UN Human Rights Council" 2(1) *Canadian Journal of Human Rights* (2013): 1; *see also* Lyal Sunga, "What Effect if any will the UN Human Rights Council have on Special Procedures?" in *International human rights monitoring mechanisms* (Brill Nijhoff, 2009): 169, 276–7.

would have required a two-thirds majority of the Council, excluding from membership eligibility, states against which measures under Chapter VII of the UN Charter were in effect, when they related to human rights abuses or terrorism.[153] Practical, political, and ethical obstacles are associated with adopting any criteria to distinguish between states deserving a seat at the Human Rights Council and the rest.[154] In terms of coherence with the rationale presented, the United States contradicts its own policy. Promoting the exclusion from membership to states affected by a negative Chapter VII resolution—mostly characterized by the absence of an implementation timeframe—is at odds with the traditional position of this country against a closer institutional relationship between the peace and security agenda and the human rights agenda.[155] As veto-wielding powers, the permanent members of the Security Council would never be affected by this requirement; its approval would have strengthened the perception of unfairness and inequality that is eroding the legitimacy of the Security Council.

One day after the UN High Commissioner for Human Rights criticized the United States' policies of separating children from their parents at its border,[156] the country decided to withdraw again from the Human Rights Council in 2018, fulfilling the promise to quit if the reforms it sought to implement were not achieved, including the deletion of the Agenda Item 7—on Palestine and other occupied Arab territories—from the Human Rights Council' program of work.[157] Addressing the Council in June 2018, Secretary of State Pompeo characterized the body as "an exercise in shameless hypocrisy—with many of the world's worst human rights abuses going

[153] Ambassador John R. Bolton, U.S. Permanent Representative to the United Nations, Explanation of Vote on the Human Rights Council Draft Resolution (Statement in the General Assembly, New York City, March 15, 2006), available at: https://2001-2009.state.gov/p/io/rls/rm/63143.htm.

[154] *See* Philip Alston, "Richard Lillich Memorial Lecture: Promoting the Accountability of Members of the New UN Human Rights Council" 15(1) *Journal of Transnational Law and Policy* (2005–6): 49. *See also* Alston (2006) (n. 54): 191.

[155] *See* Elvira Domínguez-Redondo, "Making the connection: security and human rights" in Cherif Bassiouni and William Schabas (eds.), *New Challenges for the UN Human Rights Machinery: What Future for the UN Treaty Body System and the Human Rights Council Procedures* (Intersentia, 2011): 255, and Sandrine Turgis, "Les moyen d'alerte du Counseil de sécurité des Nations Unies en cas de violation des droits de l'homme," 2 *Civitas Europa* (2018): 33.

[156] *Opening statement and global update of human rights concerns by UN High Commissioner for Human Rights Zeid Ra'ad Al Hussein at 38th session of the Human Rights Council* (18 June 2018), available at: https://www.ohchr.org/EN/NewsEvents/Pages/DisplayNews.aspx?NewsID=23206&LangID=E.

[157] Marc Limon, "US departure from the Human Rights Council: what really happened and what will happen next?" *Universal Rights Group Blog* (June 27, 2018), available at: https://www.universal-rights.org/blog/us-departure-from-the-human-rights-council-what-really-happened-and-what-will-happen-next/.

ignored, and some of the world's most serious offenders sitting on the council itself."[158] On the same occasion, US Ambassador to the United Nations, Haley, referred to the Council as "a cesspool of political bias."[159] Shortly after, National Security Adviser Bolton threatened to defund the Office of the Office of the High Commissioner for Human Rights and the Human Rights Council.[160] Contrary to the Organization disallowing targeted funding for the regular budget, Bolton advocated for calculating the amount of the US annual budget devoted to these bodies and to reduce its outlays proportionally.[161]

The United States, a key player in creating the United Nations and its human rights apparatus historically, is widely perceived as a fundamental leader in sustaining the human rights agenda, reinforced by its strong leverage over other countries and its continuous status as the largest financial contributor to the UN regular budget.[162] However, its protracted criticism of, and detachment from, the Human Rights Council may have diminished its weight. Other states from Europe and Latin America seem to have been able to fill the perceived leadership vacuum, and it has been claimed that the year 2018 was the most positive term for the body in terms of atmosphere, cooperation, and results.[163]

4. Conclusions

Those who opposed well-established working methods developed by Special Procedures mandate holders have been successful in introducing limitations to their autonomy because the legal basis for some of the self-attributed competences were weak. The political process at the core of open mandates resulting in the great level of autonomy enjoyed by mandate holders in establishing their methods of work, compared to other international

158 US Department of State Press Briefing, "Remarks on the UN Human Rights Council" (June 19, 2018), available at: https://www.state.gov/remarks-on-the-un-human-rights-council/.

159 Ibid.

160 Jean Galbraith, "United States withdraws from the un human rights council, shortly after receiving criticism about its border policy" 112(4) *American Journal of International Law* (2018): 745.

161 "US to cut funding for UN human rights office" *AP News*, August 23, 2018.

162 The United States pays for 22 percent of the regular budget. For the latest figures on the "Assessment of Member States" contributions to the United Nations regular budget for the year 2019," *see* UN Doc. ST/ADM/SER.B/992 (24 December 2018).

163 *See The Human Rights Council in 2018. Leadership, resolve and cooperation at the UN's main human rights body* (yourHRC.org, 2019): 7–8, available at: http://yourhrc.org/wp-content/uploads/2018/12/yourHrc_end_of_year_report_2018.pdf.

monitoring mechanisms, is the same factor that facilitates blurred boundaries, when states wish to modify practices. It has been difficult for mandate holders to rebut arguments highlighting flaws in the normative basis for their work, precisely because they were never firmly established to start with. This could be viewed as an inherent characteristic of Special Procedures. The legal foundations have been particularly week in justifying the development of working methods to handle individual communications of human rights violations, since it represents an extraordinary limitation to the sovereignty of states that has traditionally required a UN-level specific consent of the state concerned. The unavoidable failure to provide a sound legal basis acceptable to member states of the Council for some working methods of mandate holders of Special Procedures has resulted in forced change of practices.

As eloquently summarized by Philip Alston, the political nature of the interests that determine the creation of new mandates, or the selective support received by different Special Procedures along with the complex nature of the interest of other stakeholders involved, explains the obstacles that have prevented meaningful and structural reforms necessary to consolidate the myriad of Special Procedures into a fully fledged system.[164] The increased number of seats held by the African and Asian Group, first in the Commission and now in the Human Rights Council, have pushed for specific agendas through different waves of reforms, which have facilitated a revival on emphasizing cooperative and constructive approaches to human rights implementation instead of more adversarial strategies naming and shaming states. This outcome has been widely perceived as a negative development, but, in practice, the fears expressed by scholars and other commentators have not materialized. The number of Special Rapporteur mandates have increased, and thematic mandates have greater security of tenure of three years. In addition a greater standardization of terminologies has emerged (Special Rapporteurs and independent experts) accompanied by a sounder legal basis for their activities.

While the rules articulated in the Code of Conduct have introduced some limits to the work of Special Procedure mandate holders, most merely codified existing practice, providing a better foundation for working methods that were already followed without clear legal basis in the resolutions establishing the scope of mandates. The Code of Conduct is itself a political mechanism without real teeth beyond its use by particular states on

[164] Alston (2011) (n. 129): 561, 581–2.

exceptional occasions that have had little negative impact in the way in which Special Procedures operate. The processes of reform strengthened consideration of Special Procedures as a distinct category of mechanisms and forced greater clarity in identifying the mechanisms belonging to the group, although other factors had a greater influence in this outcome, as will be analyzed in the next chapter.

Three
Growing Organically
A "System" of Special Procedures

1. Introduction: Building a System by Coordinating Mandates

As the previous chapters have demonstrated, the UN Special Procedures were created in response to specific situations or phenomena of human rights violations. They were disconnected from each other, depending more on consensus and a variety of extenuating political factors rather than the need to create a coherent configuration or a distinct category of monitoring bodies. As a consequence, they did not share common methods of work and objectives, which was also a contributing factor to the lack of research and writings on the theme.

While the previous chapter addressed the indirect impact of intergovernmental initiatives of reform to this outcome, the following sections focus on more direct factors that impacted the formation and development of the Special Procedures, including the role of political decisions, viewed particularly through the approval of collective mandates on cross-cutting issues. The chapter highlights how, despite the impact of such factors, the resourcefulness of many experts in charge of Special Procedures has been significant in the systematization of Special Procedures.

Two particular initiatives stand out for their effect in harmonizing practices. First, mandate holders introduced and developed joint actions that today constitute a significant part of their activities; second, their articulation and publication of pioneering methods of work have shaped a wide range of activities undertaken by Special Procedures, which have been implemented by successive experts, contributing to the emergence of an overarching system of global human rights protection. The administrative support received by Special Procedures from the Office of the High Commissioner for Human Rights has also adapted accordingly, contributing

In Defense of Politicization of Human Rights. Elvira Domínguez-Redondo, Oxford University Press (2020).
 DOI: 10.1093/oso/9780197516706.001.0001

to the consolidation of the system through reforms that have ensured distinct institutional support and better coordination among mechanisms.

2. Political Decisions: Collective Mandates

Since the late 1980s but mainly from 1993, the Commission on Human Rights adopted resolutions containing collective and cross-cutting mandates aimed at all Special Procedures, notably expanding their scope of competences while encompassing overlaps between mandates. Since then and to date, the endless list includes:

Administration of justice. For more than thirty years, Special Procedures have been called upon to pay special attention to the effective protection of human rights in the administration of justice, including juvenile justice, and to provide, wherever appropriate, specific recommendations in this regard, including proposals for advisory services and technical assistance measures.[1]

Intimidation and reprisals against those cooperating with the United Nations mechanisms in the field of human rights. Since 1990, Special Procedures mandate holders must report to the Council or the General Assembly any actions taken in relation to credible allegations of intimidation or reprisal and the hampering of access to UN human rights mechanisms.[2]

Right to freedom of opinion and expression. Between 1992 and 2004, the former Commission invited working groups, representatives, and special rapporteurs to pay attention, within the framework of their mandates, to the situation of persons detained, subjected to violence, ill-treated, or discriminated against for having exercised the right to freedom of opinion and expression, as affirmed in the Universal Declaration of Human Rights and, where applicable, the International Covenant on Civil and Political Rights. The inclusion of "hate speech" as an issue to be covered by the Special Rapporteur on this specific

[1] CHR Res. 1987/33, 10 March 1987, a mandate periodically renewed to date with its latest manifestation in HRC Res. HRC Res. 36/16, 29 September 2017.

[2] CHR Res. 1990/76, 7 March 1990, a repeated annual request that finds its latest articulation in HRC Res. 12/2, 12 October 2009, reaffirmed in subsequent resolutions in the issue, such as HRC Res. 36/21, 29 September 2017, and 41/17, 12 July 2019.

human right was controversial and resolutions relating to this mandate had to be adopted by a vote, since consensus proved impossible.[3] Additionally, the Human Rights Council has not included a call directed to all Special Procedures to address freedom of opinion or expression within the scope of their mandates since 2008.[4]

Rights of the child. All Special Procedures mandate holders are required to integrate a child-rights perspective while implementing their mandates. They are also encouraged "to include in their reports information, qualitative analysis and recommendations on the rights of the child, paying particular attention to the rights of children with disabilities."[5]

Elimination of violence and discrimination against women and girls. Since 1993, mandate holders have been called to consider, within their respective mandates, the question of discrimination faced by, and violence against, women and girls, including indigenous women and girls, while cooperating with and assisting the Special Rapporteur on violence against women and its causes and consequences.[6] This collective call has disappeared in resolutions addressing the issues of discrimination and violence against women adopted by the Human Rights Council from 2017 onward.[7]

Terrorism. Mandate holders are expected to pay due attention to the negative impact of terrorism on the enjoyment of all human rights and on alleged violations of human rights associated with counterterrorism and violent extremism conducive to terrorism, reporting their findings to the Council and General Assembly. One of the oldest collective

[3] *See* Toby Mendel, "The UN special rapporteur on freedom of opinion and expression: Progressive development of international standards relating to freedom of expression" in Tarlach McGonagle and Yvonne Donders (eds.), *The United Nations and freedom of expression and information: Critical perspectives* (Cambridge University Press, 2015): *235*, 239–42.

[4] CHR Res. 1992/22, 28 February 1992, 1994/33, 4 March 1994; 1995/40, 3 March 1995; 1996/53,19 April 1995; 1997/54, 11 April 1997; 1998/42, 17 April 1998; 1999/36, 26 April 1999; 2000/38, 20 April 2000; 2001/47, 23 April 2001, 2002/48, 23 April 2002; 2003/42, 23 April 2003 and 2004/42, 19 April 2004 and HRC Res. 7/36, 28 March 2008.

[5] CHR Res. 1993/8, 10 March 1993, a repeated mandate that finds its latest expression in HRC Res. 40/14, 22 March 2019.

[6] *See* CHR Res. 1993/46 of 8 March 1993, a mandate repeated annually in other resolutions titled "Elimination of violence against women" and "Accelerating efforts to eliminate violence against women" being the most recent in time HRC Res. 32/19, 1 July 2016 (including the latest relevant CHR Res. 2005/41 of 19 April 2005).

[7] *See* HRC Res. 35/18, 22 June 2017; 35/10, 22 June 2017; 38/1, 5 July 2018; 38/5, 5 July 2018.

mandates, this specific mandate has included the impact of other armed groups and drug traffickers within its scope. [8]

Climate change. The Human Rights Council has invited mandate holders to contribute to its panel discussion addressing the adverse impact of climate change on states' effort to realize a range of rights. Additionally, they are encouraged to consider the issue within their mandates, while calling for focused commentary on specific topics decided for the panel discussion.[9]

The Human Rights Council and/or its predecessor, the Commission on Human Rights, have also invited Special Procedures mandate holders to consider a number of other cross-cutting issues within their mandates, including: the human rights of persons with disabilities;[10] the consequences of hostage-taking;[11] internally displaced persons;[12] the rights of persons belonging to national or ethnic, religious, and linguistic minorities;[13] economic, social, and cultural rights;[14] development;[15] effects of globalization in the enjoyment of human rights;[16] fostering popular participation;[17] impact of HIV/AIDS on the enjoyment of human rights;[18] the issue of the promotion, protection, and enjoyment of human rights on the internet;[19] the right to education;[20] the regulation of civilian acquisition, possession, and

[8] CHR. Res. 1990/75, 7 March 1990, a repeated mandate over the years, recently articulated in HRC Res. 37/27, 23 March 2018.

[9] The collective mandate is introduced for the first time by HRC Res. 10/4 25 March 2009 and repeated yearly since. For the latest relevant resolutions, *see* HRC Res. 38/34, 16 July 2018 and 41/21, 12 July 2019.

[10] The mandate appears for the first time in CHR Res. 1998/31, 17 April 1998 (with latest relevant CHR decision on this issue being Res. 2005/65, 20 April 2005). Its most recent articulation can be found in HRC Res. 40/14, 8 April 2019.

[11] CHR Res. 1996/62, 23 April 1996, repeated annually until its latest articulation on CHR Res. 2005/31, 19 April 2005. The topic of hostage-taking has been subsequently subsumed under the issue of the protection of human rights while countering terrorism.

[12] *See* CHR Res. 1994/68, 9 March 1994, followed by periodic reminders that find its latest expression in HRC Res. 32/11, 1 July 2016.

[13] *See* CHR Res. 1993/24, 5 March 1993 and subsequent annual resolutions addressing the topic, including its latest articulation in HRC Res. 34/6, 23 March 2017—reproducing the mandate contained in HRC 25/15, 27 March 2014.

[14] *See* CHR Resolutions on the topic adopted. between 1997 (Res. 1997/17, 11 April 1997) and 2005 (2005/22, 15 April 2005).

[15] CHR Res.41/19, 12 July 2019.

[16] *See, e.g.*, CHR Res. 1999/59; 28 April 1999 and HRC 4/5 Res. 30 March 2007.

[17] CHR Res. 2000/40, 20 April 2000; 2001/36, 23 April 2001; 2001/43, 23 April 2001; 2002/34, 22 April 2002; 2003/47, 23 April 2003; 2004/31, 19 April 2004 and 2005/29, 19 April 2005.

[18] CHR Res. 1994/49, 4 March 1994, followed by periodic reminders of the collective mandate until its latest articulation in HRC Res. 12/27, 22 October 2009.

[19] Collective mandate introduced on 26 June 2014 by HRC Res. 26/13 and latest reaffirmed by HRC Res. 38/7, 5 July 2018.

[20] Latest included in HRC Res. 38/9, 5 July 2018 and 41/16, 11 July 2019.

use of firearms;[21] arms transfers;[22] relevant aspects concerning the shrinking of civil society space in their engagement with international and regional organizations;[23] and the negative impact of corruption on the enjoyment of human rights.[24] Mandate holders are expected to engage with other regularly held events, such as participating in seminars related to cross-cutting issues,[25] while cooperating and holding consultations with advisory and technical cooperation services.[26] On occasion, Special Procedures have also been called upon as a group to focus on a particular territory in the face of the escalation of gross violations of human rights.[27]

Between 1991 and 2002, the Commission on Human Rights adopted a resolution addressed to all thematic mandates under the rubric *Human rights and thematic procedures*,[28] requesting, among others, the inclusion in their reports of: (1) information provided by governments on follow-up actions, as well as their observations; (2) gender-disaggregated data, addressing the characteristics and practice of human rights violations specifically or primarily directed against women, or to which women are particularly vulnerable; (3) similar information in relation to children; (4) comments on how to carry out their functions more effectively, including suggestions as to areas where governments might request relevant assistance through the program of advisory services and technical cooperation. The title of these resolutions changed in 2004 to embrace all Special Procedures, including geographic mandates.[29] The content of the 2004 resolution addressing human rights and special procedures was similar to those addressed to thematic procedures.

[21] *See, e.g.*, HRC Res. 38/10, 5 July 2018.

[22] HRC Res. 41/20, 12 July 2019.

[23] HRC Res. 38/12, 16 July 2018.

[24] HRC. Res.41/9, 11 July 2019.

[25] For instance, the implementation of the Sustainable Development Goals (HRC Res. 37/6, 22 March 2018), the administration of justice through military tribunals (HRC Res. 25/4, 27 March 2014) or panel discussion on the impacts, opportunities and challenges of new and emerging digital technologies with regard to the promotion and protection of human rights (HRC Res.41/11, 22 July 2019).

[26] *See, e.g.*, CHR Res. 1987/37, 10 March 1987 and HRC Res. 8/18, 29 September 2011.

[27] *See, e.g.*, CHR Res. 1983/61, 10 March 1983, 1997/58, 15 April 1997, 1999/56, 27 April, 2000/15, 18 April 2000; 2001/19, 20 April 2001 in relation to Zaire; CHR Res. 1996/79, 23 April 1996 regarding Sudan; CHR Res. 1996/79, 23 April 1996 in relation to Nigeria; CHR Res. 2004/13, 15 April on the Democratic People's Republic of Korea; CHR Res. 2004/14, 15 April 2004 on Belarus; or more recently, referring to Libya, HRC Res. 37/41, 23 March 2018 and 40/27, 22 March 2019.

[28] *See* CHR Res. 1991/31, 5 March 1991; 1992/4, 28 February 1992; 1993/47, 9 March 1993; 1994/53, 4 March 1994; 1995/87, 8 March 1995; 1996/46, 6 April 1996; 1996/78, 23 April 1996; 1997/37, 17 April 1997; 1998/74, 22 April 1998; 2000/86, 28 April 2000; 2002/84, 26 April 2002; 2002/84, 26 April 2002. *See also* CHR Res. 1989/48, 7 March 1989, aimed at "Special rapporteurs and representatives and other mechanisms established by the Commission on Human Rights."

[29] CHR Res. 2004/76, 21 April 2004.

A notable difference is the specific addition of the express competence endowed to all special procedures to issue urgent appeals. This resolution also included more detailed recommendations for governments, civil society, the High Commissioner, the Secretary General, and mandate holders.[30]

While the list above is not exhaustive, it illustrates how the politicized mandates received by mandate holders has contributed to their cohesion as a uniform category. It also reveals the unrealistic range of mandates, in terms of resources, knowledge, and capability, entrusted to experts in charge of Special Procedures.

3. Mandate Holder Initiatives

Prior to the establishment of annual meetings of Special Procedures and the creation of the High Commissioner for Human Rights and its Office in 1993, some level of administrative coherence was provided to mandate holders by staff members of the Secretariat belonging to the Centre of Human Rights (1982–1993) and its predecessor, the Division for Human Rights.[31] The coordination of Special Procedures and meetings between mandate holders were mostly limited to those propitiated by the annual sessions of the Commission on Human Rights or, when applicable, the General Assembly. References to occasional meetings and communication with other mandate holders can be found in several reports, but the practice was not generalized or systematic, lacking continuity. Therefore, mandate holders' consideration of the work of other Special Procedures happened on an ad hoc basis. Gradually, some individual and collective initiatives paved the way for the need to act as a group and to coordinate and standardize working methods. To date, this is a work in progress with flaws that negatively affect stakeholders involved with these mechanisms and the operativity and image of the Special Procedures as a whole.

[30] *See also* Marc Limon and Ted Piccone, "Human Rights Special Procedures: Determinants of Influence" in *Brookings Institutions & Universal Rights Group Policy Report* (Universal Rights Group, 2014): 8, 19, 35, and 37.

[31] *See* GA Dec. 37/437, 21 December 1982, *Resolutions and decisions adopted by the General Assembly during its 37th session, 21 September–21 December 1982 and 10–13 May 1983*, UN Doc. A/37/51 (supp) (1 January 1983): 290. *See also* Ian Guest, *Behind the Disappearances. Argentina's Dirty war against human rights and the United Nations* (University of Pennsylvania Press, 1990): 321–2; Egon Schwelb and Philip Alston, "The Principal Institutions and Other Bodies Founded Under the Charter" in Karel Vasak (ed.), *The International Dimensions of Human Rights* (UNESCO, 1982, *vol. 1*): 232, 264–5.

A. Joint Activities and Coordination between Mandate Holders

Very early after the first Special Procedures were created, mandate holders made unilateral decisions on how they would coordinate their activities with other Special Procedures and relevant UN human rights bodies. The collective mandates of the Commission on Human Rights listed earlier, including periodic reminders to consider the work of other Special Procedures, served as an impetus to this development, but the main promoters of such activities were the mandate holders themselves. The joint hearings held by the Special Rapporteur on summary and arbitrary executions and the Chairman of the Working Group on southern Africa in 1985 are the first examples of a joint country visit by Special Procedures.[32] The Special Rapporteur on extrajudicial execution was also the first mandate holder to establish rules of coexistence with other Special Procedures, using his own (and changeable) criteria.[33] The Commission did not respond when he requested guidelines to coordinate his work with the Working Group in Enforced Disappearances in 1989.[34] Motivated by the need to delimit its scope of action in relation to the newly created UN Committee Against Torture, the 1988 Special Rapporteur on torture's report, included an extensive explanation of the terms of reference governing its mandate and operations.[35] Throughout the years, joint

[32] "Summary or arbitrary executions: Report by the Special Rapporteur, S. Amos Wako, appointed pursuant to Economic and Social Council Resolution 1985/40 of 30 May 1985," UN Doc. E/CN.4/1986/21 (7 February 1986), paras. 56, 179–83, and 192–5; the experience was repeated in subsequent years, *see, e.g.*, "Summary or arbitrary executions: Report by the Special Rapporteur, s. Amos Wako, appointed pursuant to Economic and Social Council Resolution 1986/36 of 23 May 1986," UN Doc. E/CN.4/1987/20 (22 January 1987), para. 236 and Annex I; "Summary or arbitrary executions: Report by the Special Rapporteur, S. Amos Wako, appointed pursuant to Economic and Social Council Resolution 1987/60," UN Doc. E/CN.4/1988/22 (19 January 1988), paras. 21, 236–48; "Summary or arbitrary executions: Report by the Special Rapporteur, s. Amos Wako, appointed pursuant to Economic and Social Council Resolution 1988/38," UN Doc. E/CN.4/1990/22 (23 January 1990), para. 20; and "Summary or arbitrary executions: Report by the Special Rapporteur, s. Amos Wako, appointed pursuant to Economic and Social Council Resolution 1990/51," UN Doc. E/CN.4/1991/36 (1 February 1991), paras. 20, 440–64.

[33] The Special Rapporteur initially decided not to study allegations regarding countries examined under geographic procedures, UN Doc. E/CN.4/1983/16, para. 71; *see also* UN Doc. E/CN.4/1984/29, para. 17 and 'Question of the violation of human rights and fundamental freedoms in any part of the world, with particular reference to colonial and other dependent countries and territories. Summary or arbitrary executions: Report, UN Doc. E/CN.4/1985/17 (12 February 1985), para. 64 (1985). In 1986, the Special Rapporteur removed this restriction from his methods of work and considered allegations without justifying the change of position UN Doc. E/CN/4/1986/21 (n. 32).

[34] UN Doc. E/CN.4/1989/25, paras. 300–1.

[35] "Question of the human rights of all persons subjected to any form of detention or imprisonment: torture and other cruel, inhuman or degrading treatment or punishment. Report," UN Doc. E/CN.4/1988/17 (12 January 1988), paras. 4–13. *See also* "Question of the human rights of all persons subjected to any form of detention or imprisonment: torture and other cruel, inhuman or degrading

activities have permeated all facets of the work of Special Procedures, especially in relation to the study of situations of gross violations of human rights, the treatment of urgent and nonurgent communications, and visits on the ground.

The greater political weight of a joint action warranted some animosity from states, at least until they became standard practice. In 1996, the Cuban government's representative claimed that the Working Group on Arbitrary Detention overstepped its competence by transmitting communications to the Special Rapporteur on torture and to the Special Rapporteur on the right to freedom of expression and opinion, triggering multiple interventions from several Special Procedures on the same case.[36] The Cuban representative also condemned the Working Group's decision to coordinate closely with the geographic mandate on the situation of human rights in Cuba.[37]

For many years, urgent appeals were the main object of joint actions by mandate holders. Experts in charge of Special Procedures were more reluctant to coordinate efforts with their peers when it came to sending allegation letters to states. However, this pattern has changed rapidly in recent times, and joint allegation letters and joint urgent appeals are now the norm for the treatment of all communications.[38] A comparison between the "Facts and Figures" about the activity of Special Procedures, published since 2005 on the website of the Office of the High Commissioner for Human Rights, reveals that in 2005, 53 percent of communications sent by mandate holders were signed by more than one Special Procedure. Of those, 38 percent constituted joint urgent appeals and 15 percent were joint allegation letters. Urgent appeals sent by a single Special Procedure made up 19 percent of total communications, with the remaining 28 percent consisting of allegation letters signed by a single Special Procedure.[39] By the end of 2018, allegation letters represented 74.5 percent of the communications sent that year, of which 56.9 percent were joint actions. Urgent appeals constituted the other

treatment or punishment: Report of the Special Rapporteur, P. Kooijmans, pursuant to Commission on Human Rights Resolution 1989/33," UN Doc. E/CN.4/1990/17 (18 December 1989), paras. 6–18.

[36] *Summary Record of the 29th Meeting, held at Palais de Nations, Geneva, on Tuesday, 9 April 1996: Commission on Human Rights, 52nd session*, UN Doc. E/CN.4/1996/SR.29 (17 May 1996), para. 5.

[37] Ibid. para. 6.

[38] "Facts and Figures" publications for the years 2005–2013 can be found at: https://www.ohchr.org/EN/HRBodies/SP/Pages/Publications.aspx#annual. From 2014 to date, the documents are distributed with UN nomenclature at: https://www.ohchr.org/EN/HRBodies/SP/Pages/Annualreports.aspx.

[39] Ibid.

25.5 percent, and only 1.4 percent were signed by a mandate holder acting alone.[40]

Joint missions on the ground, however, have remained exceptional since they require the concerned state to accept them. The limited number of visits undertaken by mandate holders depending on time and resources, remains a deterrent against joint missions.

Mandate holders' allusions to the work carried out by other experts in charge of Special Procedures has increased significantly over time, and some have adopted working methods that ensure the regular and systematic exchange of information. The Working Group on Enforced Disappearances pioneered the practice of transmitting allegations it received to concerned geographic and thematic mandates when they were considered as fitting within their scope of competence.[41] Since 1992, it has extended this measure to cases of disappearance when the missing person has been found dead and/or if other human rights violations that can be investigated by alternative thematic mandates in the context of enforced disappearances.[42] Except for generic references to their coordination efforts with other mechanisms, very few mandate holders have included comprehensive cooperation criteria with other Special Procedures in their published methods of work. For instance, the Special Rapporteur on torture decided to use the criteria of "dominant violation" in 1990, to assess which UN organ was better equipped to deal with allegations containing a combination of human rights violations,[43] although the latest version of this mandate's methods of work do not mention this criterion.[44] The former Special Representative on human rights defenders also decided to follow the "dominant violation" criteria as a basis to assess which Special Procedure should take the lead role in joint actions. In addition, she explained the guidelines that guided her relationship with the country offices of the High Commissioner for Human Rights.[45]

[40] *Facts and figures with regard to the special procedures in 2018*, UN Doc. A/HRC/40/38/Add.1 (18 March 2019): 36.

[41] *Report of the Working Group on Enforced or Involuntary Disappearances*, UN Doc. E/CN.4/1986/18 (24 January 1986), para. 33.

[42] *Report of the Working Group on Enforced or Involuntary Disappearances*, UN Doc. E/CN.4/1992/18 (30 December 1991), para. 33.

[43] UN Doc. E/CN.4/1990/17 (18 December 1989), para. 9. *See also* "Towards a more effective and integrated system of human rights protection by the United Nations," UN Doc. A/CONF.157/PC/60/Add. 6 (1 April 1993), paras. 30–1 and *Note of the Secretariat* (15th annual meeting of Special Procedures, OHCHR 2008) available at: http://www.ohchr.org/Documents/HRBodies/SP/AMeetings/15thsession/Comunicationsof_SPs_Discussions_Secretariat.pdf.

[44] UN Doc. E/CN.4/1997/7, Annex (10 January 1997).

[45] UN Docs. E/CN.4/2001/94 (26 January 2001), paras. 17, 51 and 30–7 and E/CN.4/2002/14 (11 September 2001), para. 48.

Those explanations are missing from the latest published version of this mandate's methods of work.[46]

The criteria framed by the Working Group on Arbitrary Detention are exemplar for their level of detail. In summary, the Working Group will refer allegations that can be more appropriately addressed by another working group or special rapporteur to the concerned Special Procedure. If the allegations fall within its competence as well as that of another thematic or geographic mechanism, it will consider the possibility of a joint action. When the Working Group considers a communication for which another body has already taken an action, the Group retains its competence to analyze the case if that body deals with the general development of human rights within its area of competence; the Working Group considers most Special Procedures to fit this category. However, if the communication has been dealt with by a body with the function of dealing with individual cases, such as the Human Rights Committee and other treaty bodies, the Working Group will transmit the case to that other body if the persons or facts involved are the same. Finally, the Working Group operates under the principle of not carrying out visits to territories for which a geographic Special Procedure exists, unless the concerned mandate holder considers the visit useful to the overall investigation, monitoring, and reporting on the human rights situation in that country.[47]

For all those mandates that have not adopted working methods in this regard, the exchange of information with other special public procedures has traditionally depended on the tenacity of their assistants in the Secretariat and on the internal guidelines and practices that the Office of the High Commissioner (and former divisions of the Secretariat) have established for this purpose. Currently, the coordination of Special Procedures is mainly operated by staff of the Office, thanks to the significant progress made in centralizing the administrative structures supporting Special Procedures, the computerization of the information, and the use of shared databases, heightened since the creation of the Quick Response Desk in 2002.

[46] Available at: https://www.ohchr.org/EN/Issues/SRHRDefenders/Pages/MethodsWork.aspx.

[47] *Methods of Work of the Working Group on Arbitrary Detention*, UN Doc. A/HRC/36/38 (13 July 2017), paras. 33 and 34.

B. Attempt to Codify Model Rules for Fact-Finding Mechanisms

In contrast with the efforts made to address this gap, tgere are bi iffucuak gyudekubes giverbubg Special Procedures' operations, The first attempts to codify general rules applicable to ad hoc bodies of the United Nations entrusted with studies of particular situations revealing a consistent pattern of violation of human rights are as old as the Special Procedures themselves.[48] Taking into account the competence contained in ECOSOC Resolution 1235 (XLII) and the Commission on Human Rights resolutions appointing the first ad hoc working groups,[49] the Teheran International Conference on Human Rights (1968) recommended the adoption of "Model rules for bodies dealing with violations of human rights."[50] The Secretary General suggested a Draft Model in 1970,[51] and, in 1974, the Economic and Social Council requested it to be drawn to the attention of all potential fact-finding bodies, although it did not approve or adopt the Draft Model as such.[52] The Draft Model informed a memorandum agreed between the Working Group on Chile and the Chilean government in 1978,[53] but this has not been widely used (if at all known) by mandate holders since. Neither Special Procedures' reports nor their Manual of Operations[54] refer to the Draft Model. It does not appear that other private initiatives such as *The Belgrade Minimum Rules*

[48] Only preceded by a 1964 general study of the Secretary General, on "Methods of Fact-finding," published in UN Doc. A/5694 (1 May 1964).

[49] *See* chapter one.

[50] Resolution X (12 May 1968) contained in the "Final Act of the 1968 Teheran International Conference on Human Rights," UN Doc. A/CONF.32/41 (1968): 12. *See also* Thomas Franck and Scott H. Fairley, "Procedural due process in human rights fact-finding by International Agencies" *74* AJIL (1980): 308.

[51] *See* "Draft model rules of procedure for the Ad Hoc bodies of the United Nations entrusted with studies of particular situations alleged to reveal a consistent pattern of violations of human rights," UN Doc. E/CN.4/1021/Rev.1 (1970) and CHR Res. 8(XXV) (4 March 1969). The Commission established a working group to revise the Draft Model. The final Draft Models are contained in UN Docs. E/CN.4/1086 (1973) and E/CN.4/1134 (1974).

[52] The ECOSOC only took note of them rather than endorsing them, ECOSOC Res. 1870 (LVI) (17 May 1974). *See also* the "Declaration on Fact-finding by the UN in the Field of the Maintenance of International Peace and Security" U.N. Doc. A/RES/46/59, Annex (1992).

[53] *See* Philip Alston and Sarah Knuckey, "The Transformation of Human Rights Fact-Finding. Challenges and Opportunities" in P. Alston and S. Knuckey, *The Transformation of Human Rights Fact-Finding* (Kindle ed., Oxford University Press, 2015): ch. 1, part III, text *supra* n. 49.

[54] Manual of Operations of the Special Procedures of the Human Rights Council (August 2008) in "Report of the 15th meeting of special procedures assumed by the Human Rights Council, from 23 to 27 June 2008," UN Doc. A/HRC/10/24, November 2008. Also available at OHCHR website: http://www.ohchr.org/Documents/HRBodies/SP/Manual_Operations2008.pdf.

of Procedures for International Human Rights Fact-Finding Missions (1981)[55] or, more recently, the *Siracusa Guidelines* (2013)[56] have had a significant impact on Special Procedures' implementation of their mandates either.[57] As eloquently articulated by Cherif Bassiouni, decades of fact-finding missions by Special Procedures and other UN bodies have not been supported by any standard operating procedure, negatively impacting data collection, continuity of mandates, and comparability of results. Every monitoring body or mission created by political bodies has had to "reinvent the wheel," undermining their performance, consistency, and predictability of methods of work and outcomes.[58]

Inexistent rules for UN monitoring bodies and mandates rooted in intergovernmental resolutions have been decisive in forcing mandate holders to create their own methods of works without predetermined restrictions. In the first years of existence of Special Procedures, only a minority of mandate holders published their methods of work. Potential users of Special Procedures had to infer what to expect from these mechanisms by reading the summaries of the activities included in their reports. To date, there is no rule compelling Special Procedures to publish their methods of work nor is any guidance available from their parental bodies, the Human Rights Council, or the General Assembly. Nonetheless, the efforts of the mandate holders who have articulated and published their working methods have served as a model followed by subsequent experts, contributing significantly to the systematization of Special Procedures.

[55] The formulation of these standards came from the initiative of the International Association of Jurists and are published in 75(1) American Journal of International Law (1981): 163–75. On the attempts to codify rules explained here and more current initiatives, *see* Alston and Knuckey (2015) (n. 53): ch. 1, part III, text *supra* nn. 40–60.

[56] M.C. Bassiouni and C. Abraham (eds.), *Siracusa Guidelines for International, Regional and National Fact-Finding Bodies* (Intersentia, 2013).

[57] However, the Special Rapporteur on extrajudicial, summary or arbitrary executions lists the "Siracusa Guidelines" as one of the instruments to bear in mind in the context of the *Revision of the UN Manual on the Effective Prevention and Investigation of Extra-Legal, Arbitrary and Summary Executions*, Annex 2, Consultation document, available at the OHCHR website at: http://www.ohchr.org/EN/Issues/Executions/Pages/RevisionoftheUNManualPreventionExtraLegalArbitrary.aspx. *See also* OHCHR, *Training Manual on Human Rights Monitoring* (Professional Training Series, No. 7, United Nations, 2001) On the attempts to codify rules explained here and more current initiatives, *see* Alston and Kuckney (2015) (n. 53): ch. 1, part III, text *supra* nn. 40–60.

[58] M. Cherif Bassiouni, "Appraising UN Justice-related fact-finding missions" 5 Washington University Journal of Law and Policy (2001): 35, 40–1.

C. Filling the Gap: Publication and Standardization of Methods of Work

Especially since the second half of the 1990s, the vagueness of resolutions outlining the competence of Special Procedures has been mitigated by the elaboration and publication of methods of work by mandate holders. Thematic procedures are less vulnerable to political fluctuations and less likely to disappear once created, with some Special Procedures having a track record dating back to the 1980s. Compared to their country-focused counterparts, this continuity has resulted in more elaborated methods of work that clarify the scope of their mandate, international standards used as the regulatory framework, and how they process information, including allegations of human rights.

For many years, the only means for a new mandate holder to obtain information about the methods of work used by her or his peers was to become familiar with their reports—as illustrated by a study published by the Secretary General that analyzed the norms, criteria, and practices established by Special Procedures in 1994. This report, commissioned by the Commission on Human Rights, could not synthetize inexistent uniform practices and instead reproduced relevant paragraphs of Special Procedures' reports.[59] At the time, only the Working Group on Enforced and Involuntary Disappearances and the Working Group on Arbitrary Detention had submitted full working methods that were expressly acknowledged in the resolutions referred to those mandates.[60]

[59] *Effective functioning of the various mechanisms established for supervision, investigation and monitoring of the implementation of the treaty obligations entered into by States in regards to human rights and of the existing international standards in this regard*, UN Doc. E/CN.4/1994/42 (14 February 1994), paras. 77–9.

[60] The WGAD submitted full methods of work from its first report in 1992 (UN Doc. E/CN.4/1992/20, paras. 12–16) as well as revised versions in subsequent years. *See* UN Docs. E/CN.4/1993/24, Annex IV (1993); E/CN.4/1994/27, Annex I (1994); E/CN.4/1996/40, Annex I (1996); E/CN.4/1997/5, Annex I (1997); E/CN.4/1998/44, Annex I (1998); E/CN.4/2001/14, (2001), paras. 81–2; A/HRC/16/47 and Corr.1, Annex (2011); A/HRC/30/69 (2015); A/HRC/33/66 (2016); and A/HRC/36/38 (2017). The WGEID explained sources used from its first report (UN Doc. E/CN.4/1435, 1981, paras. 10, 30, and 43, adding statistical data from its third report in 1983 (UN Doc. E/CN.4/1983/14; *see also* UN Doc. E/CN.4/1985/15, paras. 73–90). The Group has modified its methods of work in subsequent years as shown in the following reports: UN Docs. E/CN.4/1986/18 (1986); E/CN.4/1988/19 (1988), paras. 16–30; E/CN.4/1989/18 (1989), para. 23; E/CN.4/1990/13 (1990), paras. 25–8; E/CN.4/1991/20 (1991), paras. 402–4; E/CN.4/1992/18 (1992), para. 34; E/CN.4/1995/36, Annex (1995); E/CN.4/1996/38, Annex I (1996); E/CN.4/1998/43 (1998), para.17; E/CN.4/2000/64 (2000), para. 23; E/CN.4/2002/79, Annex I (2002); and HRC/WGEID/102/2 (2014).

Other early examples of sophisticated methods of work were produced and published by the Special Rapporteurs on extrajudicial, summary or arbitrary executions,[61] religion,[62] and the Special Rapporteur on torture, with the latter particularly motivated by distinguishing his role from the functions of the Committee Against Torture.[63]

While less elaborated and detailed, most thematic Special Procedures mandate holders have published methods of work on their landing pages within the website of the OHCHR and/or within specific sections of their reports. Publishing methods of work on official documentation with a distinct nomenclature has the obvious advantage of transparency, trackability, and permanence beyond the fluctuations on website content. Special Procedures with published working methods in sections of their reports include the mandates on freedom of opinion,[64] independence of judges and lawyers,[65] internally displaced people,[66] migrants,[67] violence against women,[68] sale of children,[69] racism,[70] hazardous substances,[71] housing,[72] mercenaries,[73] extreme poverty,[74] human rights defenders,[75] indigenous

[61] *See* UN Docs. E/CN.4/1989/25 (1989), paras. 6–25; E/CN.4/1991/36 (1991), paras. 568–74; and E/CN.4/1992/30 (1992), paras. 19–36. These methods of work were slightly modified to include follow-up activities in the 2004 report, UN Doc. E/CN.4/2004/3 (2003), paras. 10–3. *See also* UN Docs. E/CN.4/2005/7 (2005), paras. 5–12; and A/HRC/14/24 (2010), para. 60. Since 2010 the outline of methods of work appears on the website of this mandate rather than official UN documents.

[62] UN Doc. E/CN.4/1989/44 (1989), paras. 10–18 and 82–7. *See also* UN Docs. E/CN.4/1991/56 (1991), paras. 9–15; E/CN.4/1992/52 (1992), paras. 10–6; E/CN.4/1993/62 (1993), paras. 9–14; E/CN.4/1994/79 (1994), paras. 6–18; E/CN.4/1995/91 (1995), paras. 9–30 and Annex.

[63] *See* UN Docs. E/CN/4/1986/15 (1986), para. 20; E/CN.4/1988/17, paras. 4–13; E/CN.4/1990/17 (1990), paras. 6–18; E/CN.4/1993/26 (1993), paras. 6–30.

[64] *See* UN Docs. E/CN.4/1994/33, Annex (1994), paras. 24–33; E/CN.4/1995/32 (1995) 56–70; E/CN.4/1999/64, Annex (1999); E/CN.4/2002/75 (2002), para. 2; E/CN.4/2003/67, Annex II (2003); and A/HRC/11/4 (2009), paras. 32–7.

[65] UN Docs. E/CN.4/1995/39 (1995), paras. 63–93; E/CN.4/2004/60 (2004), paras. 4–14. The latest reference in an annual report to methods of work directing to those developed by predecessors and other mandate holders can be found in UN Doc. A/HRC/35/31(2017), para. 12.

[66] UN Docs. E/CN.4/1993/35 (1993), paras. 4–31, 20–3, 278–9 and 285–7; E/CN.4/1994/44 (1994), paras. 14, 40–4, and 63; E/CN.4/2004/77 (2004); A/HRC/35/31 (2017), paras. 24–9.

[67] UN Docs. E/CN.4/2001/83 (2001), paras. 16–70; and E/CN.4/2006/73 (2006), paras. 17–72.

[68] UN Docs. E/CN.4/1995/42 (1995), paras. 7–45; E/CN.4/2003/75 (2003), para. 4; E/CN.4/2004/66 (2004), paras. 3–6; and A/HRC/32/42 (2016), paras. 73–8.

[69] UN Docs. E/CN.4/1992/55 (1992), paras. 28–36 and Annex I; A/50/456 (1995), paras. 15–34; A/52/482 (1997), paras. 3–10; A/53/311 (1998), paras. 3–10; A/54/411 (1999), paras. 2–5; A/55/297 (2000), paras. 6–16; E/CN.4/1994/84 (1994), paras. 259; E/CN.4/1996/100 (1996), paras. 5–11; E/CN.4/1997/95 (1997), paras. 3–9; E/CN.4/1998/101 (1998), paras. 4–6; E/CN.4/1999/71 (1999), paras. 3–16; E/CN.4/2000/73 (2000), paras. 4–8; E/CN.4/2001/78 (2001), paras. 2–9; E/CN.4/2002/88 (2002), paras. 5–31; E/CN.4/2003/79 (2003), paras. 3–7.

[70] UN Docs. A/49/677 (1994), paras. 18–50; and E/CN.4/1994/66 (1994) 32–45.

[71] UN Docs. E/CN.4/1997/19 (1997), paras. 11–25; E/CN.4/1996/17 (1996), paras. 6–21.

[72] UN Doc. E/CN.4/2001/51 (2001) 87–107.

[73] UN Docs. E/CN.4/2004/15 (2004); and A/61/341 (2006), paras. 7–24.

[74] UN Doc. E/CN.4/2001/54 (2001), paras. 17–45 and Annex I–IV.

[75] UN Docs. E/CN.4/2001/94 (2001), paras. 39–52; and A/69/259 (2014), paras. 17–34.

people,[76] albinism,[77] development,[78] disabilities,[79] international order,[80] international solidarity,[81] leprosy,[82] and sexual orientation.[83] However, the same Special Procedure may follow these methods of work or others that may not be published in the same format, depending on decisions of subsequent mandate holders. All the Working Groups have published their working methods in UN documents.[84]

Some Special Procedures' website landing pages refer to dissimilar versions of generic information. For instance, the mandates on the right to food, leprosy, and international solidarity refer to Fact Sheet 27 on *Frequently asked questions about UN Special Procedures*, published in 2001 before the demise of the Commission, leading to confusion to those unfamiliar with UN institutional history.[85] The websites for the business and human rights and for cultural rights' mandates link to general information on how to submit information regarding allegations to any Special Procedures.[86] Others, such as the Special Procedures on development, hazardous waste, sexual orientation, and foreign debt, link to a different version of the same generic topic.[87] Yet another online submission version is linked by the mandate holder on disability, water and sanitation, and extreme poverty.[88] The Special Rapporteur on the environment refers to the leaflet on Special Procedures communications.[89] There are no indications on the dates of publication of the Fact Sheet 27 or the different versions associated with what ought to be the same information. The Special Rapporteur on internally displaced persons as well as the independent experts on a democratic and equitable international order, on

76 UN Docs. E/CN.4/2004/80/Add.1 (2004), paras. 78–101; A/HRC/12/34 (2009), paras. 6–35.
77 UN Doc. A/HRC/31/63 (2016), paras. 7–11.
78 UN Doc. A/HRC/36/49 (2017), para. 38.
79 UN Doc. A/HRC/28/58 (2015), paras. 20–1.
80 UN Doc. A/HRC/39/47 (2018), paras. 36–45.
81 UN Docs. A/68/176 (2013), paras. 7–28; and A/HRC/38/40 (2018), paras. 21–32.
82 UN Doc. A/HRC/38/42 (2018), paras. 85–93.
83 UN Doc. A/HRC/35/36 (2017), paras. 4–12.
84 In addition to those already cited on n. 60, *see* for the WG on African Descent, UN Doc. A/HRC/WG.14/12/2 (2013); for the WG transnational corporations and other business, UN Doc. A/HRC/WG.12/10/1, Annex (March 2015); and for the WG on women and girls, UN Doc. A/HRC/20/28 (April 2012), paras. 36–48.
85 Available at: http://www.ohchr.org/Documents/Publications/FactSheet27en.pdf.
86 *See* OHCHR page on the "Communication Procedure" available at: https://www.ohchr.org/EN/Issues/CulturalRights/Pages/ComplaintsSubmission.aspx.
87 *See* OHCHR page on "Communications": https://www.ohchr.org/EN/HRBodies/SP/Pages/Communications.aspx.
88 https://spsubmission.ohchr.org/.
89 https://www.ohchr.org/Documents/HRBodies/SP/SPP_PresentationFlyer.pdf.

international solidarity, and on older persons do not include information on submission of communications before them on their relevant websites.

Among geographic Special Procedures, the Working Group on Chile paved the way for other experts by publishing its working methods from its first report in 1975.[90] These were contested by the Chilean government but endorsed by the General Assembly and the Commission.[91] The Ad Hoc Working Group of Experts on the situation of human rights in southern Africa devoted a section of its reports to the "organisation of its work," but its content was limited to summarizing the activities of the Group during the examined period and the international legal framework of reference. From 1971, the Group added the procedure and formalities followed when recording testimonies.[92] More recently, the Special Procedures on Iraq,[93] Myanmar,[94] and Iran[95] have included information about their working methods in their reports.

Contrary to thematic Special Procedures, their geographically focused counterparts do not summarize their methods of work on the landing page of the website devoted to their mandate. The pertinent online link for geographic mandates directs readers to general information about the country in relation to human rights rather than the landing page of the concerned Special Procedure. For instance, after locating the online address of geographic Special Procedures,[96] clicking on the link for the Special Rapporteur on Belarus sends the reader to the country profile maintained for this country by the Office[97] where it is only the eighth listed entry that finally directs readers to specific information about this mandate. At the time of writing, only the independent expert on the situation of human rights in the Central African Republic and the Special Rapporteur on Eritrea were directly associated with

[90] "Protection of Human Rights in Chile: Note by the Secretary-General," UN Doc. A/10285 (7 October1975), Annex, paras. 13–39.

[91] On this discussion, *see* the fourth report of the Working Group in "Report of the Ad Hoc Working Group established under Resolution 8 (XXXI) of the Commission on Human Rights to inquire into the present situation of human rights in Chile," UN Doc. E/CN.4/1221 (10 February1977), paras. 29–41.

[92] UN Doc. E/CN.4/1050 and Corr. 1 (1971), para. 26. For a critique of the lack of methods of work, *see* Felix Ermacora, "International Enquiry Commission in the Field of Human Rights" *I*(2) Revue de Droits de l'Homme/Human Rights Journal (1968): 180–217, 192–3, and 205; *see also* John Carey, "United Nations Scrutiny of South African Prisons," *I*(4) Revue de Droits de l'Homme/Human Rights Journal (1968): 531–43.

[93] *See* UN Doc. E/CN.4/1993/45 (1993), paras. 164–79; and A/56/340 (2001), paras. 1–17.

[94] UN Doc. A/53/364 (1998), section II.

[95] UN Doc. A/73/398 (27 September 2018), paras. 6–14.

[96] https://spinternet.ohchr.org/_layouts/15/SpecialProceduresInternet/ViewAllCountryMandates.aspx.

[97] https://www.ohchr.org/EN/Countries/ENACARegion/Pages/BYIndex.aspx.

the information pertaining to the concerned Special Procedure. The convoluted process to access the significant landing page is a confusing, tedious, and time-consuming process requiring significant understanding of the system. Most country-related landing pages contain a short biography of the mandate holder accompanied by a brief summary of the assigned mandate. The pages do not include guidelines on how to submit information to mandate holders, with readers reverted back to general information about Special Procedures. The independent expert on Eritrea once again constitutes an exception to this rule, providing a specific form (in English, Arabic, and Tigrinya) to facilitate the submission of information addressed to her.

Historically, many mandate holders have seen their working methods acknowledged or welcomed by their parent body, yet only those articulated by the Special Rapporteur on torture have been expressly approved by states in 1994 and 1997. After the Rapporteur submitted a full version of his working methods to both the Commission on Human Rights, and the General Assembly.[98] The approval was reproduced in subsequent resolutions addressing the mandate on torture until 2001. While the expressed approval of the methods of works was maintained, it was controversial and subjected to vote because the mandate holder at that time, Nigel Rodley, had not attempted to visit the occupied Palestinian territories as requested by the Commission in its Resolution 2001/62.[99] When Theo van Boven took over the mandate in 2003, he introduced slight modifications to the working methods,[100] but the Commission ignored these and reminded the Rapporteur of the methods of work outlined in 1997 as approved in 2001.[101] The exceptional intergovernmental endorsement bestowed on these methods of work explain why they continue to be in force to date and linked to the relevant mandate's website page, although they have not been enshrined in resolutions renewing the mandate since 2004.

In summary, the articulation and publication of methods of works by Special Procedures since the early 1970s has been determinant for the standardization

[98] CHR Res. 1994/37, 4 March 1994, further endorsed by AG Res. 51/86, 12 December 1996, and CHR Res. 1997/38, 11 April 1998.

[99] CHR Res. 2001/62, 25 April 2001, para. 30. The discussions are reproduced in *Summary of the 77th meeting of the 57th session of the Commission on Human Rights, held on 25 April 2001*, UN Doc. E/CN.4/2001/SR.77 (12 December 2001), paras. 28–44. *See also* Michael J. Dennis, "The Fifty-Seventh Session of the UN Commission on Human Rights" 96 (1) American Journal of International Law (2002): 181, 188, and *Summary record of the 75th meeting of the 57th session of the Commission on Human Rights, held on 24 April 2001*, UN Doc. E/CN.4/2001/SR.75 (30 April 2001).

[100] UN Doc. E/CN.4/2003/68 (2003), paras. 12–21.

[101] CHR Res. 2004/41, 29 April 2004, para. 29.

of working methods across mandate holders. This is an outcome noticeable to those already familiar with Special Procedures rather than a feature that will likely prove useful to those engaging with them for the first time. Potential users of Special Procedures, including first and foremost victims of human rights violations that can benefit from their intervention, must navigate a metaphorical and literal web of reports, online links, and forms to familiarize themselves with basic information concerning their modus operandi. The quantity and quality of information provided and the format used to present information vary significantly between mandate holders with no correlation to divergences in the practical implementation of methods of work.

Individual efforts to compensate this state of affairs can backfire, as illustrated by the added confusion introduced by mandate holders who have decided to develop alternative websites to complement the information made available through the Office of the High Commissioner for Human Rights. Websites disconnected from the institutional framework of the United Nations, such as the one created by the former Special Rapporteur on Iran, Ahmed Shaheed—with a wealth of information that sharply contrasts with the official landing page[102]—or the latest mandate holder on extreme poverty, Philip Alston, are not particularly problematic.[103] It is relatively clear to stakeholders that these are personal initiatives with a limited shelf life. Greater confusion is generated by information posted on other online home pages linked to the official site of the Special Procedure concerned.[104] The former Special Rapporteur on water and sanitation, Catarina de Albuquerque, developed a different but official UN website, which restricts the information available to her tenure.[105] The online address set up by the former Special Rapporteur on indigenous peoples, James Anaya, has been inherited by the current mandate holder, Victoria Tauli-Corpuz, which has ensured some continuity for the time being, though this may prove difficult to sustain for future mandate holders, since these websites depend on the ability of specific mandate holders to secure funds for this purpose.[106] For instance, when Christof Heyns was Special Rapporteur on summary and arbitrary executions, he created a website that he repeatedly cited in reports

[102] Available at: http://www.shaheedoniran.org/.

[103] Available at: https://srpoverty.org.

[104] This was the case of the former Special Rapporteurs on the right to food and on indigenous people that can be still be found, respectively, at: http://www.srfood.org/ and n. 106.

[105] Available at: https://sr-watersanitation.ohchr.org/en/about_1.html.

[106] *See* http://unsr.vtaulicorpuz.org/site/ and http://unsr.jamesanaya.org/. *See also* for the mandate on environment: http://www.srenvironment.org/.

and press releases and was also linked to the page attributed to his tenure at the mandate hosted by the Office of the High Commissioners. The website (https://www.use-of-force.info/) hosted the database of legislation used to support his study examining 146 states' compliance with international standards regulating the use of force. The Special Rapporteur was committed to updating the website in the future, but it has since disappeared. Therefore, it is impossible to get hold of the documents referred to by Heyns's reports.[107] More troubling is the address—https://albinism.ohchr.org/—used by the Expert on albinism, for a website linked to her official landing page, which erroneously suggests it is hosted by the United Nations.

Contrary to others, these initiatives undermine the progressive consolidation of Special Procedures as a coherent system. Instead they reinforce the profile of individual independent experts disconnected from the United Nations and other mechanisms within the same category. While chapter six elaborates on the unsettled question of the institutional position of Special Procedures, a more significant problem that arises in this context is the creation of unnecessary barriers to access Special Procedures that add multiple sources of information about the same mandate, depending on fragmented understandings of the mandates and resources as interpreted by individual mandate holders. It is worth remembering that this occurs in the context of an already complex web of mechanisms in which unity has largely depended on mandate holders' willingness to coordinate activities among themselves.

4. Collective Initiatives: Annual Meetings and Coordination Committee

The first meeting of Special Procedures mandate holders took place in 1993. This significant delay, considering the proliferation of these mechanisms, is remarkable and reflects a lack of group awareness, taking into account that annual meetings of Chairpersons of human rights treaty bodies, established significantly later than the first Special Procedures, had started a decade

[107] *See*, for instance, *Report of the Special Rapporteur on the use of information and communications technologies to secure the right to life*, UN Doc. A/HRC/29/37 (24 April 2015) fn. 9; *see also* A/HRC/26/36 (1 April 2014), para. 40, or OHCHR Press Release, *Laws on the Use of Force by the Police Require Urgent Global Reform, UN Human Rights Expert Says* (Geneva, June 13, 2014) at: https://www.ohchr.org/en/NewsEvents/Pages/DisplayNews.aspx?NewsID=14700&LangID=E.

earlier.[108] Although the Commission on Human Rights had already considered convening a meeting of Special Procedures in 1989,[109] the need for periodic meetings arose from the conviction of the experts themselves on realization and acknowledgment of the similarities of their work.[110] The first informal meeting took place on June 14–16, 1993, during the preparatory process of the World Conference on Human Rights, resulting in a "joint declaration" by which mandate holders recommended, inter alia, the facilitation of periodic meetings to harmonize their work.[111] Since 1994, these annual meeting have been formalized and result in the adoption of a final report. The content of the first annual meeting report reveals that, almost three decades after the creation of the first Special Procedure, experts responsible for these mechanisms were lacking "basic information about the system of special procedures, its history, examples of previous work accomplished, and practical details relating to administrative matters."[112] The paucity of published works investigating and analyzing this area of human rights has been a contributing factor to this deficit.

Nothing demonstrates the superficial coherence of the mechanisms conforming the system of Special Procedures better than the impossibility of clearly ascertaining, during many years, which mechanism could be included within such category, leading to diverging conclusions by the few scholars invested in this subfield.[113] Within this reality, it is hardly surprising

[108] The origins, development and relevant documentation on these meetings is available at: https://www.ohchr.org/EN/HRBodies/AnnualMeeting/Pages/MeetingChairpersons.aspx.

[109] CHR Res. 1989/48, 7 March 1989.

[110] *Report on the meeting of special rapporteurs/representatives/experts and chairpersons of working groups of the special procedures of the Commission on Human Rights and of the advisory services programme*, UN Doc. E/CN.4/1995/5 (14 June 1994), para. 3.

[111] *Joint declaration of the independent experts responsible for the special procedures for the protection of human rights*, UN Doc. A/CONF.157/9 (18 June 1993).

[112] UN Doc. E/CN.4/1995/5 (14 June 1994) (n. 110), para. 8.

[113] *See, e.g.*, the divergences between those listed during similar period of time, by Olivier de Frouville, *Les procédures thématiques: une contribution efficace des Nations Unies à la protection des droits de l'homme* (A. Pedone, 1996): 17 and 19; Carmelo Faleh Pérez, "El Grupo de Trabajo sobre la Detención Arbitraria de la Comisión de Derechos Humanos de las Naciones Unidas" *0* Revista de la Facultad de Ciencias Jurídicas de la Universidad de Las Palmas (1995): 103, 105; Anne Gallagher, "The human rights protection system of the United Nations and of its specialized Agencies" in *Recueil des Cours* (Strasbourg: Institut International des Droits de l'Homme, 1998): 197, 236; Beate Rudolf, "The Thematic Rapporteurs and Working Groups of the United Nations Commission on Human Rights" (*4*) Max Planck Yearbook on UN Law (2000): 289, 295–6; Lyal Sunga, "The Special Procedures of the UN Commission on Human Rights" in Alfredson, Gudmundur, "Concluding Remarks: More Law and Less Politics" in Alfredson et al. (eds.), *International Human Rights Monitoring Mechanisms* (Martinus Nijhoff, 2001): 233, 271–3; José A. Pastor Ridruejo, "Les procédures publique spéciales de la Commission des Droit de l'Homme des Nations Unies," *III-228* Recueil de Cours de l'Académie de Droit International (1991): 183, 216; and Miko Lempinen, *Challenges Facing the System of*

that mandate holders and the administrative teams supporting them were slow in institutionalizing a forum for coordinating their activities, despite attempts to identify the contours of the Special Procedures themselves. Between 1996 and 2006, the Secretary General included an annex to its provisional annotated agenda, listing the persons mandated to carry out Special Procedures.[114] This information is currently published as part of the communication report of Special Procedures and was also included in their annual meeting reports until 2013.[115] Still, some of the efforts to clarify the category of mechanisms belonging to Special Procedures added further confusion. For instance, the report of the first official meeting of Special Procedures explains that participants to the meeting included experts from the advisory services program, whose work had essential similarities to that of the Special Procedures. This statement involved a fictional distinction, maintained until 2008, between country mandates examined under the agenda item focusing on advisory services and "real" Special Procedures as reflected in the titles of the reports.[116] In 1998, the Representative of the Secretary General for children and armed conflicts, a mandate created by the General Assembly in 1996, was included in the annotated agenda of the Commission of Human Rights as a Special Procedure, disappearing in subsequent years.[117] However, it continued to be listed as such in the annual meeting reports of mandate holders, on the website of the Office of the High Commissioner, and in the compilation of recommendations and conclusions of Special Procedures elaborated by the Secretary General until 2001.[118] On the other hand, the Fact Sheet 27 to which some mandate holders continue to refer as a relevant source of information, mentions the Representative for children and armed conflicts as the sole Special Procedure created by the General Assembly.[119]

Special Procedures of the United Nations Commission on Human Rights (Åbo Akademi University, 2001): 298–9.

[114] This list appears for the first time in UN Doc. E/CN.4/1996/1/Add. 1, Annex, responding to the mandate contained in the CHR Res. 1995/87, 8 March 1995.

[115] For the latest examples, *see*, respectively, UN Docs. A/HRC/41/56, Appendix (17 June 2019); and A/HRC/24/55 (22 July 2013).

[116] *See* UN Doc. E/CN.4/1995/5 (n. 110), para. 4. From 2008, the annual meeting reports refer to Special Procedures of the Human Rights Council, including country mandates examined under the Agenda Item 10.

[117] *See* GA Res. 51/77, 12 December 1996, and UN Doc. E/CN.4/1998/1/Add.1, Annex (1998).

[118] *See* UN Docs. E/CN.4/1994/35 (1994); E/CN.4/1995/47(1995); E/CN.4/1996/47 (1996); E/CN.4/1997/38 (1997); E/CN.4/1998/46 (1998); E/CN.4/1999/96 (1999); E/CN.4/2000/124 (2000); and E/CN.4/2001/101 (2001).

[119] *Fact Sheet 27* (August 2001): question 4.

Finally, the Annual Appeal of the Office of the High Commissioner included this mandate among Special Procedures in 2000, removing it subsequently.

Similar confusion has surrounded the categorization of other ad hoc mechanisms without monitoring powers that have been randomly listed as Special Procedures in the annual meeting reports or the website of the Office of the High Commissioner for Human Rights at different periods of time. The examples include the former independent expert on examining the question of a draft Optional Protocol to the International Covenant on Economic Social and Cultural Rights, the independent expert charged with examining the international criminal and human rights framework for the protection of persons from enforced or involuntary disappearances, and the independent expert on the right to restitution, compensation, and rehabilitation for victims of grave violations of human rights and fundamental freedoms.

The concerted efforts of the Secretariat and mandate holders through the celebration of annual meetings have been fundamental to resolving this situation, culminating in the clarification of mandate holders categorized as Special Procedures by themselves and the Office of the High Commissioner on Human Rights. This development has clearly been a necessary condition both for a meaningful standardization and harmonization of practices as well as for the development of effective collective actions. Annual meetings that have also included the participation of mandate holders of confidential Special Procedures have yielded multiple positive results for this purpose. Since their inception, these meetings have served as an invaluable channel of communication and coordination with other organs of the United Nations, to promote actions protecting mandate holders from external political pressure, and to raise collective concerns. Annual meetings have also played a key role in harmonizing methods of work, thereby contributing to greater coherence. From the celebration of the first meeting, mandate holders worked on drafting a Manual of Operations that was finally adopted in 1999, outlining the "Terms of Reference for Fact-Finding Missions by Special Rapporteurs/Representatives of the Commission on Human Rights" adopted as a working practice a year earlier.[120] Yet the Manual, updated in 2008, has been kept purposely vague, reflecting the constant tension between the acknowledged need to achieve greater consistency, while emphasizing the necessity

[120] On early proposals, *see* UN Docs. E/CN.4/1995/5 (1005), para. 26; E/CN.4/1996/50 (1996), para. 62; and E/CN.4/1998/45 (1998), paras. 59–60; *see also* Calos Villán Durán, *Curso de Derecho internacional de los derechos humanos* (Trotta, 2002): 761–5.

of maintaining the specificities of each mandate and highlighting that, as independent mechanisms, mandate holders remain the "owners" of their methods of work. This specific element constitutes a continuing issue that explains why the Manual was not published or distributed beyond the realm of annual meetings until 2006, as well as the resistance of mandate holders to submit the Manual to formal intergovernmental approval.[121]

The cohesion attained through the annual meetings has led to the submission of periodic reports compiling summaries of communications and statistical information in order to prevent duplications and inconsistencies among mandate holders, which has, in turn, facilitated the follow-up of communications, an analysis of cross-cutting human rights issues and a more effective input into the universal periodic review process.[122]

The most remarkable product of annual meetings is the establishment of a Coordination Committee in 2005.[123] Composed of six members elected during annual meetings of Special Procedures,[124] it provides a unified voice to Special Procedures, increasing their visibility and facilitating collective actions on behalf of all Special Procedures through open letters, press releases, and/or statements.[125] Since its creation, the Committee has enacted actions to strengthening the position of mandate holders against undue interference with their independence,[126] enhanced the coordination among mandate holders,[127] and acted as a bridge between them and other

[121] *See* Alston and Knuckey (2015) (n. 53): ch. 1, part III. The first draft of the Manual circulated under nomenclature HR/NONE/98/93 (in author's files). *See also* reports of annual meetings in UN Docs. E/CN.4/2000/5; E/CN.4/2001/143; E/CN.4/2002/14, Annex, paras. 15 and 76(v); E/CN.4/2003/6, Annex, para. 17; E/CN.4/2004/4, Annex, paras. 64–5; and E/CN.4/2005/5, para. 21.

[122] *See Reports of the fifteenth, sixteenth and seventeenth meeting of Special Procedures mandate-holders*, UN Docs. A/HRC/10/24 (17 November 2008), paras. 34–5; A/HRC/12/47 (22 July 2009), paras. 24–6; and A/HRC/15/44 (19 July 2010), paras. 26–7.

[123] *Report of the Twelfth meeting of Special Rapporteurs/Representatives, Independent Experts and Chairs of Working Groups of the Special Procedures of the Commission on Human Rights and of the Advisory Services Programme*, UN Doc. E/CN.4/2006/4 (3 August 2006), section B.

[124] *See* Najat M'jid, "The UN Special Procedures System: The Role of the Coordination Committee of Special Procedures" in Aoife Nolan, Rosa Freedman, and Thérèse Murphy (eds.), *The United Nations Special Procedures System* (Brill, 2017): 131, 133.

[125] Reproduced at: https://www.ohchr.org/EN/HRBodies/SP/CoordinationCommittee/Pages/CCSpecialProceduresIndex.aspx.

[126] *See, e.g.*, Press Release, *Accusations Against UN Expert a Retaliation by Philippines, Say Fellow Rapporteurs* (Geneva, March 8, 2018), available at: https://www.ohchr.org/EN/NewsEvents/Pages/DisplayNews.aspx?NewsID=22783&LangID=E.

[127] *See, e.g.*, Statement of the Coordination Committee at the 27th Special Session on the human rights situation of the minority Rohingya Muslim population and other minorities in the Rakhine State of Myanmar, 5 December 2017 (Geneva, December 5, 2017), available at: https://www.ohchr.org/EN/NewsEvents/Pages/DisplayNews.aspx?NewsID=22499&LangID=E.

organs of the United Nations, governments, and civil society.[128] Through the Coordination Committee, mandate holders have ensured the consideration of their perspective in different processes of reform affecting their work while also articulating the technical qualifications and skills they deem necessary for the election of new mandate holders. Despite protracted resistance from some states, frustrating several attempts to gather and publish this data, the strength gained through collective action has facilitated inclusion of information on the issue of state cooperation with Special Procedures.[129] The "Facts and Figures" generated as addenda of annual meeting reports now contain information about the number of standing invitations, visits carried out in the relevant year, states never visited, and communications by countries and responses received.[130]

The Coordination Committee has also played an important role in relation to the application of the Code of Conduct and has established an "Internal Advisory Procedure to Review Practices and Working Methods" of Special Procedures as a self-regulatory mechanism, allowing the Committee to intervene when issues are raised regarding the performance of mandate holders in relation to agreed standards.[131] Since 2012, mandate holders voluntarily disclose external financial support they may receive for the fulfillment of their duties that is published as part of their annual meeting reports.[132] Overall, the Committee has played a key role in crystallizing a sense of belonging to an expert community among mandate holders that has had a significant impact in redressing the deficit that existed in the early history of the creation of the Special Procedures.[133]

[128] *See, e.g.*, the information shared with the Security Council, through the government of the Netherlands, about the work of special procedures mandate holders pertinent to the work of the Council, UN Doc. S/2018/280 (2 April 2018).

[129] Jane Connors, "Special Procedures: Independence and Impartiality" in Nolan, Freedman, and Murphy (n. 124): 52, 69.

[130] *See, e.g., Facts and figures with regard to the special procedures in 2018*, UN Doc. A/HRC/40/38/Add.1 (18 March 2019) chs. X and XV.

[131] *See* M'jid (2017) (n. 124): 131, 136. Information about the procedure is available at: https://www.ohchr.org/EN/HRBodies/SP/CoordinationCommittee/Pages/InternalAdvisoryProcedure.aspx.

[132] Connors (2017) (n. 129): 52, 83.

[133] Surya P. Subedi, "Human rights experts in the United Nations: a review of the role of United Nations Special Procedures" in Monika Ambrus, Karin Arts, Ellen Hey, and Helena Raulus (eds.), *The Role of "Experts" in International and European Decision-Making Processes* (Cambridge University Press, 2014): 241, 250–1.

5. Institutional Coherence: Role of the Office of the High Commissioner for Human Rights

One of the least visible factors that has decisively impacted the functioning of Special Procedures is the structure of the administrative apparatus of the Secretariat that supports them. In 1997, the administrative support to the High Commissioner and the former Centre for Human Rights—which had been the main body of the Secretariat supporting human rights activities since 1982[134]—were consolidated into a single Office of the UN High Commissioner for Human Rights.[135] Different reforms of the administrative divisions comprising the Office of the High Commissioner have improved the support provided to Special Procedures, particularly with the creation of a "Special Procedures Branch" in May 2003,[136] currently under the "Thematic Engagement, Special Procedures and Right to Development Division," of the Office.[137] However, not all mandate holders have been historically supported by the Special Procedures Branch. This has affected how mandate holders have performed their work and also the extent to which coordination among them is possible, since mandate holders rely heavily on the administrative unit to which they have been assigned. The number of Special Procedures assigned to each branch was made public in the 2005 Annual Report of the High Commissioner. It explained that seventeen thematic Special Procedures were assisted by the Special Procedures Branch, and twelve—those focusing on economic, social, and cultural rights—by staff in the Research and Right to Development Branch.[138] The twelve country mandates were assisted by

[134] The Centre replaced the former Division for Human Rights following GA Res. 37/237 of 21 December 1982, section XII. On the change of structures and tensions deriving from the coexistence of the Centre co-existed with the Office of the High Commissioner between 1993–1997, *see* Philip Alston, "Neither Fish nor Fowl: The Quest to Define the Role of the UN High Commissioner for Human Rights" 8 European Journal of International Law (1997): 321, 324–5, and Eric Berman, *Bringing a New Life to the UN Human Rights Operations* (United Nations Association of the United States, 1998): 14–5.

[135] *See Renewing the United Nations: A Programme of Reform,* UN Doc. A/51/950 (1997), *esp.* paras. 79 and 197–8.

[136] *See Secretary-General's Bulletin—Organization of the office of the United Nations High Commissioner for Human Rights,* UN Doc. ST/SGB/1997/10 (15 September 1997), and *Re-structuring the Centre for Human Rights UN,* UN Doc. A/C.5/50/71 (17 June 1996). The Special Procedure Branch is created in 2004 following proposals of the OHCHR, *see* "Report of the Joint Inspection Unit on the management review of the Office of the United Nations High Commissioner for Human Rights," UN Doc. A/59/65-E/2004/48 (12 March 2004).

[137] Formerly under the "Human Rights Council and Special Procedures Division," *see* "Organizational Chart" in *OHCHR Management Plan 2014–2017—Working for Your Rights* (OHCHR, 2014): 15.

[138] Annual Report of the High Commissioner for Human Rights 2005 (OHCHR, 2005): 43, at: http://www.ohchr.org/Documents/AboutUs/annualreport2005.pdf.

the Capacity Building and Field Operations Branch.[139] A year later, the OHCHR reported its decision to transfer eight thematic mandates from the Research and Right to Development Branch to the Special Procedures Branch, "bringing to 25 the number of thematic mandates directly supported by the latter."[140] There were twenty-eight thematic Special Procedures at the time, thus three were still not supported by the Special Procedure Branch, but the OHCHR never specified which mandates were assigned to different sections nor the rationale for these decisions.[141] In practice, the Special Procedures Branch was responsible for mandates dealing with civil and political rights as well as "groups in focus" issues.[142] After several restructures of the Office of the High Commissioner, the support to all mandate holders has now been centralized through the Special Procedures Branch.[143] This move should strengthen synergies among Special Procedures, and achieve greater transparency in resource management.[144]

The relationship between Special Procedures and the OHCHR is fraught at times, with tension and mutual mistrust.[145] This strain is partially inevitable due to the singular relationship between experts, lacking an institutional link with the United Nations and its staff members.[146] Nonetheless, significant progress has been made in terms of supporting Special Procedures. Besides a greater centralization of the administrative support received by the Secretariat through the creation of the Office of the High Commissioner for Human Rights and the Special Procedures Branch, the computerization of the information and the use of shared databases have greatly improved the access to information about Special Procedures, while facilitating coordination among mandate holders.

The "Special Procedure Branch's Quick Response Desk" was established in 2000 to centralize data concerning urgent appeals by Special Procedures and extended to the work of all mandate holders in 2003.[147] Databases on

[139] Ibid.

[140] Annual Report of the High Commissioner for Human Rights 2006 (OHCHR, 2006) 118, at: http://www.ohchr.org/Documents/AboutUs/annualreport2006.pdf.

[141] Ibid.

[142] Connors (2017) (n. 129): *52*, 61.

[143] On the current structure, *see* UN Human Rights Report—2018 (OHCHR, May 2019): 372.

[144] Connors (2017) (n. 129): *52*, 62–3.

[145] *See* Ted Piccone, *Catalysts for Change: How the UN's Independent Experts Promote Human Rights* (Brookings Institute Press, 2012): 57–60; *see also* Elvira Domínguez-Redondo, *Los procedimientos Públicos Especiales de la Comisión de Derechos Humanos* (Tirant lo Blanc, 2005): 428–36.

[146] *See* chapter six.

[147] *See* OHCHR Annual Report 2001: 147, OHCHR Annual Report 2003: 106–10 and OHCHR Annual Report 2004: 40. *See also* OHCHR Strategic Management Plan 2014–2017: 105. All reports

communications sent and received by Special Procedures, as well as the response received by states or other relevant stakeholders cover, at the time of writing, all communications processed since December 1, 2010.[148] The "Universal Human Rights Index" also hosted and maintained by the Office provides access to human rights recommendations issued by treaty bodies, Special Procedures, and the Universal Periodic Review.[149] The "Facts and Figures on Special Procedures" published as separate reports since 2005 have generated greater transparency and availability of information concerning activities carried out by Special Procedures, including statistical graphics. [150]

6. Conclusions

The successive approval of collective mandates aimed at all Special Procedures has contributed to the coherence of the mandates assigned to them, yet has also opened the door to indirect and an unaccounted—in terms of resources—multiplication of tasks.

Over the years, Special Procedures mandate holders have developed practices that have abetted their progressive configuration as belonging to a "system" of human rights mechanisms. This process has evolved through two main categories of initiatives. First, mandate holders implemented and subsequently increased the practice of undertaking joint activities, coordinating their work among several other mandate holders. The first joint activity was held in 1985, when the Special Rapporteur on summary or arbitrary executions and the Chairman of the Working Group of Experts on southern Africa met in Namibia for joint hearings focusing on allegations of violations of the right to life. The mandate holders repeated the experience in the following years, and joint activities have become the rule rather than the exception particularly in the treatment of communications on human rights violations. Secondly, it is possible to observe a trend toward the formalization and standardization of methods of work, providing a further sense

are available at OHCHR website at: http://www.ohchr.org/EN/PublicationsResources/Pages/AnnualReportAppeal.aspx.

148 Available at: https://spcommreports.ohchr.org/Tmsearch/TMDocuments.
149 Available at: https://uhri.ohchr.org/en/.
150 *See* n. 38. .

of unity and coordination among Special Procedures. Special Procedures follow similar processes to submit reports to the Human Rights Council and the General Assembly about their activities and undertake visits on the ground for which terms of references have since been drafted and included as part of their Manual of Operations. Yet some differences remain, as explored in the next chapter, particularly in the handling of allegations concerning human rights violations. The particular geographic or thematic contexts in the nature of the mandate also dictates different approaches to their methods of work.

Special Procedures mandate holders have insisted that the need of greater consistency in methods of work should not undermine the necessity of maintaining their autonomy and the specificities of each mandate. Correspondingly, the working methods outlined in the Manual of Operations of Special Procedures avoid in-depth detail or examples of good practices. However, the need for flexibility and respect for the independence and autonomy of mandate holders, or particular political sensitivities associated to thematic or country mandates, does not justify the unnecessary difficulties in accessing basic information about their methods of work. With the support of the Secretariat, all mandate holders should ensure they present this information in a standard user-friendly format that ought to include reports where the latest methods of work are published, the scope of their mandate, how to submit information to bring to their attention, clear criteria of admissibility, how the information will be processed, and expected outcomes for states and those submitting complaints or other information about human rights violations.

The celebration of annual meetings since 1993, alongside the creation of a Coordination Committee in 2005[151] have contributed to greater standardized methods of work and, perhaps more importantly, to a group awareness that has facilitated a unified voice. In this process, the support received by the Office of the High Commissioner for Human Rights is a key determinant in their perception as a coherent human rights mechanism, rather than as a collection of disjointed monitoring bodies under the sole charge of independent experts.

[151] Information about its membership, activities, statements, and reports of the Coordination Committee are available on the OHCHR website at: http://www.ohchr.org/EN/HRBodies/SP/CoordinationCommittee/Pages/CCSpecialProceduresIndex.aspx.

Four
Shuttling between Diplomacy and Expertise in Developing Methods of Work

1. Introduction

Mandate holders have developed methods of work that have consolidated the Special Procedures as direct interlocutors with governments, intergovernmental, non-governmental organizations and other stakeholders. Contemporary Special Procedures constitute a regular system of monitoring state behavior through the treatment of alleged cases of human rights violations under their competence; visits on the grounds; analytical studies of specific issues influencing the situation of human rights in a concerned territory or worldwide; and the generation of an enormous volume of data on recorded violations over time. They shed light, clarify, and at times contribute to the applicable international and national legal frameworks. They play an activist role beyond the realm of individual cases, using their expertise to mediate or intervene in legal and political disagreements within and outside formal mechanisms of dispute settlement. They raise awareness of, highlight, and promote best practices to improve the situation of human rights around the globe, as well as the circumstances that propitiate human rights violations, including their link with the development and security agendas.

The first section of this chapter engages with two opposite phenomena resulting from intergovernmental influence wielded over the operations of Special Procedures. On one hand, mandate holders have enjoyed an extraordinary autonomy in the development of methods of work derived from the historical coordinates characterizing their creation and development, the political nature of the decisions creating or renewing Special Procedures following negotiations based on specific circumstances and national interests, the personality of the mandate holders appointed, and the absence of standardized frameworks of reference. Additionally, the autonomy of mandate holders has delayed the consolidation of Special Procedures as a system and generated a wide margin for inconsistency and fragmented approaches to

In Defense of Politicization of Human Rights. Elvira Domínguez-Redondo, Oxford University Press (2020).
 DOI: 10.1093/oso/9780197516706.001.0001

similar issues. On the other hand, political interference and the attempt to counter this has had a significant impact in influencing Special Procedures in a particular direction in implementing methods of work, depending on their thematic or geographic nature, and on whether they focus on civil and political rights or economic, social, and cultural rights.

After analyzing the influence of political factors in providing both freedom for diverse approaches to implementation of methods of work and explicit or implicit limits determining the operationalization of mandates, this chapter focuses on the challenges associated with the public nature of the activities of Special Procedures. A separate chapter (chapter five) will address the question of the manner in which their methods of work have contributed to the normative development of international human rights law, their flexible processes to investigate communications of alleged violations of human rights, and the prolific use of country visits with privileged access to sources of information operating on the ground.

2. The Lights and Shadows of Improvising Methods of Work

Special Procedures have acquired the importance they enjoy today because mandate holders have developed pioneering methods of work that would have been difficult to envisage from the tone and content of the resolutions creating and/or renewing these mandates. The first individuals appointed as mandate holders of Special Procedures had few precedents to use as guidelines. The attempts to codify rules for fact-finding monitoring bodies were not successful, and they had to operate in line with the vague compromise language contained in what were political decisions. The creation of a substantial number of geographic Special Procedures and the evolution of thematic mandates occurred in a short period of time. Between 1980 and 1987, new thematic Special Rapporteurs were appointed on the issues of summary and arbitrary executions,[1] torture,[2] religious intolerance,[3] and the use

[1] Following a Commission's recommendation (CHR Res. 1982/29, 11 March 1982) the ECOSOC created this mandate by Res. 1982/35 (7 May 1982). In 1992, the Commission extended the scope of the mandate, adding the word "extrajudicial" to its name, CHR Res. 1992/72 (5 March 1992).

[2] CHR Res. 1985/33 (13 March 1985). On the origin of the mandate, *see* Nigel Rodley, *The Treatment of Prisoners Under International Law* (2nd ed. Clarendon Press, 1999): 18–45 and 134–46.

[3] CHR Res. 1986/20 (10 March 1986). Its mandate was different from others at the time, since it was the first one focused on a specific international instrument, that is, the Declaration on the Elimination of All Forms of Intolerance and of Discrimination Based on Religion or Belief (UNGA

of mercenaries as a means of violating human rights and of impeding the exercise of the right of peoples to self-determination.[4] During the same period, geographic Special Procedures were entrusted to a Special Representative on El Salvador,[5] a Special Envoy on Bolivia,[6] a Special Rapporteur on Guatemala,[7] a Representative of the Secretary General on Poland,[8] a Special Representative on Iran,[9] and a Special Rapporteur on Afghanistan.[10] Free from clear rules to follow, Special Procedures' mandate holders introduced a range of practices to promote and protect human rights that have been progressively adopted by most Special Procedures, contributing to the standardization of methods of work over time.

A. Doing It All: Multidimensional Approach to Mandates

The list of tasks endorsed to mandate holders keeps growing. Joint mandates emanating from the Human Rights Council are added to personal and collective initiatives to fulfill mandates, encompassing the need to adopt different roles in different contexts by the same mandate holders. In publicly identifying and condemning states and non-state actors for their participation in human rights violations that mandate holders have investigated, they function as fact-finding bodies that may reach quasi-adjudicatory decisions regarding the perpetration of human rights violations, particularly in the

Res. 36/55, 25 November 1981). On the background concerning its creation, *see* "Implementation of the Declaration of the Elimination of All Forms of Intolerance and of Discrimination based on Religion or Belief," UN Doc. E/CN.4/1987/35 (24 December 1986), paras. 1–11. The Special Rapporteur was renamed Special Rapporteur on freedom of religion or belief by CHR Res. 2001/42 (23 April 2001), para. 11.

4 CHR Res. 1987/16 (9 March 1987). On the political alliances linking the mandate on religious intolerance and mercenaries—as late symbols of the Cold War—*see* Theo van Boven, "'Political' and 'Legal' Control Mechanisms: Their Competition and Coexistence" in Asbjørn Eide and Bern Hagtvet (eds.), *Human Rights in Perspective. A Global Assessment* (Basil Blackwell Ltd., 1992): 36, 45 and Olivier de Frouville, *Les procédures thématiques: une contribution efficace des Nations Unies à la protection des droits de l'homme* (A. Pedone, 1996): 25–7.

5 CHR Res. 32 (XXXVII) (11 March 1981).

6 CHR Res. 34 (XXXVII) (11 March 1981).

7 CHR Res. 1982/31 (11 March 1982).

8 CHR Res. 1982/26 (10 March 1982).

9 CHR Res. 1984/54 (14 March 1984).

10 It is again the ECOSOC that created the mandate by Res. 1984/37 (24 May 1984) following the Commission's proposal (CHR Res. 1984/55, 15 March 1984). A summary of the precedents leading to the creation of this Special Procedure can be found in the first report of the Special Rapporteur, Felix Ermacora, "Question of Human Rights in Chile," UN Doc. E/CN.4/1985/21 (1 February 1985), paras. 8–40.

treatment of individual cases. Special Procedures mandate holders engage in advocacy work directed, for instance, to the explicit recognition of new rights or to protect possible victims of violations, without prejudging the behavior of the state concerned, for example, through "urgent actions." Through the analysis and public reporting of the situation of human rights in countries or the thematic issue under their competence, they keep the international community informed about pressing human rights issues around the globe, while forcing debate by states under the agendas of the Human Rights Council and the General Assembly. They provide technical and advisory services issuing recommendations to states and other stakeholders based on their experience of keeping a record of violations and the circumstances and measures that propitiate their occurrence or prevention. Special Procedures have also acted as early warning mechanisms that have alerted other UN bodies and the international community to issues that required attention to prevent gross violations of human rights and even threats to peace and security.

Mandate holders must encompass those functions with the diplomatic skills needed to secure the state cooperation required to fulfill their mandates effectively. In direct contact with victims and civil society without many rules governing their interaction with them, the experts in charge of Special Procedures must master the art of being perceived as objective and reliable, while implementing the necessary caution in protecting their sources of information from reprisals or other negative consequences for their engagement with mandate holders. A mandate holders is thus "expected to be a human rights activist, a rallying point for human rights, an international diplomat, a human rights lawyer, a media specialist, a human rights academic and/or a government advisor."[11] The length of the never-ending list of tasks to be accomplished leads many mandate holders to engage in another time-consuming and independence-endangering task: fundraising.[12]

[11] Surya P. Subedi, "Human rights experts in the United Nations: a review of the role of United Nations Special Procedures" in Monika Ambrus, Karin Arts, Ellen Hey, and Helena Raulus (eds.), *The Role of "Experts" in International and European Decision-Making Processes* (Cambridge University Press, 2014): 241, 249.

[12] Inga T. Winkler and Catarina de Albuquerque, "Doing It All and Doing It Well? A Mandate's Challenges in Terms of Cooperation, Fundraising and Maintaining Independence," Aoife Nolan, Rosa Freedman, and Thérèse Murphy (eds.), *The United Nations Special Procedures System* (Brill, 2017): 188.

B. Autonomy and Fragmentation

Since the establishment of the first Special Procedures, every mandate holder has had to decide the material and temporal scope of their mandate within the—usually very few—parameters outlined in the resolutions creating or renewing mandates. As a result, mandate holders have been able to develop unprecedented methods of work that have been consolidated over the years, enjoying the explicit or implicit endorsement of states. However, the political ambiguity of their mandates has also enabled different approaches to similar mandates. For instance, ignoring other elements of the Commission's original definition of the scope of its work, the Working Group on Disappearances decided to focus on individual cases of disappearances, prioritizing those considered urgent;[13] the Special Envoy on Bolivia decided to limit his analysis to civil and political rights, while acknowledging the relevance of economic, social, and cultural rights violations in the country;[14] the Special Representative of the Secretary General on Poland concluded that the refusal of the Polish government to grant him a visit meant he had "no other choice than to limit [his] analysis of the situation to the normative aspects of the question relating to the application of the relevant international instruments ratified by Poland."[15] Some mandate holders understood they had competence to study allegations and events predating their appointment, while others took the opposite view.[16] These early disparities have been

[13] For more details on this, *see* David Weissbrodt, "The Three 'Theme' Special Rapporteurs of the UN Commission on Human Rights" 80 *American Journal of International Law* (1986): 685, 685–7, and Ilka Bailey-Wiebecke, "The UN Working Group on Disappearances: After 15 Years, Focus on Asia" V Human Rights Forum (1995): 51.

[14] "Study on the human rights situation in Bolivia by the Special Envoy, Hector Gross Espiell, appointed pursuant to Resolution 34 (XXXVII) of the Commission on Human Rights of 11 March 1981," UN Doc. E/CN.4/1500 (31 December 1981), para. 125, although he included a small section on the topic in his second report, UN Doc. E/CN.4/1983/22 (13 December 1982), paras. 32–7.

[15] Report on the situation in Poland presented by Under Secretary-General Hugo Gobbi, UN Doc. E/CN.4/1983/18 (21 February 1983), *esp.* para. 52.

[16] The Special Rapporteur on executions decided that 1980 was the critical date to study allegations (although his mandate was created in 1982), *see* "Summary or arbitrary executions: Report by the Special Rapporteur, Mr. S. Amo Wako, Appointed pursuant to Resolution 1982/35 of 7 May 1982 of the Economic and Social Council," UN Doc. E/CN.4/1983/16 (30 January 1983), paras. 71, 125–216; and "Summary or arbitrary executions: Report by the Special Rapporteur, Mr. S. Amo Wako, Appointed pursuant to Resolution 1983/26 of 27 May 1983 of the Economic and Social Council," UN Doc. E/CN.4/1984/29 (21 February 1984), Annex 4. The Working Group on Enforced Disappearances could not decide on a date and studied cases largely predating its creation, *see* UN Doc. E/CN.4/1988/19 (31 December 1987), para. 14; the Special Rapporteur on Religious Intolerance gave priority to the use of "recent information" with exceptions, "Implementation of the Declaration on the Elimination of all forms of Intolerance and of Discrimination based on Religion or Belief: Report of the Secretary-General prepared pursuant to paragraph 11 of Commission on Human Rights Resolution 1987/15," UN Doc. E/CN.4/1988/44 (23 November 1987), para. 13.

mitigated by standardization of practices through individual, collective, and institutional initiatives, but have not disappeared. Two particular fields have been the object of significant discrepancies in working methods of Special Procedures: pre-conflict, conflict, and post-conflict situations; and the treatment of non-state actors.

i. Armed Conflicts and Applicability of International Humanitarian Law

During the first forty-five years of existence of the United Nations, the majority of states were reluctant to consider questions of compliance with international humanitarian law as relevant within the human rights agenda of the United Nations. Coinciding with the end of the Cold War, several factors contributed to a change of direction.[17] Iraq's invasion of Kuwait in 1990 and the surge of regional conflicts that followed were crucial to ignite progressive consensus around the question of the applicability and complementarity of international humanitarian law and human rights law, despite objections of a minority of states.[18]

More recently, the use of remotely piloted aircrafts, known as drones, for targeted killings has renewed interest in the controversial discussion among scholars over the applicability of international human rights law in armed-conflict situations.[19] The protracted debate about the relationship between humanitarian law and human rights law reflects a continuing existence of divergent approaches that are also reflected in the work of Special Procedures.[20] Very few resolutions addressing Special Procedures expressly

[17] *See* John R. Crook, "The Fiftieth Session of the UN Commission on Human Rights" 88(4) *American Journal of International Law* (1994): 806, 814–5; *id.*, "The Fifty-first Session of the UN Commission on Human Rights" 90(1) *American Journal of International Law* (1996): 126, 132; Michael J. Dennis, "The Fifty-Second Session of the UN Commission on Human Rights" 91(1) *American Journal of International Law* (1997): 167, 167–8; and *id.*, The Fifty-Third Session of the UN Commission on Human Rights" 92(1) *American Journal of International Law* (1998): 112, 114–5; Miko Lempinen, *Challenges Facing the System of Special Procedures of the United Nations Commission on Human Rights* (Institute for Human Rights, Åbo Akademi University, 2001): 115–21.

[18] *See* Françoise Hampson and Ibrahim Salama, *Working paper on the relationship between human rights law and international humanitarian law*, UN Doc. E/CN.4/Sub.2/2005/14 (21 June 2005), para. 69; Philip Alston, Jason Morgan, and William Abresch, "The competence of the UN Human Rights Council and Its Special Procedures in Relation to Armed Conflicts" 18(1) *European Journal of International Law* (2008): 183; and Cordula Droege, "Elective affinities? Human rights and humanitarian law" 90 *International Review of the Red Cross* (2008): 501.

[19] *See* Noam Lubell and Nathan Derejko. "A global battlefield? Drones and the geographical scope of armed conflict" 11(1) *Journal of International Criminal Justice* (2013): 65; *see also* Jeans D. Ohlin, "Is *Jus in Bello* in Crisis?" 13(1) *Journal of International Criminal Justice* (2013): 27.

[20] *See, e.g.*, Noam Lubell, "Challenges in applying human rights law to armed conflict" 87(860) *International review of the Red Cross* (2005): 737; William Schabas, "*Lex Specialis?* Belt and Suspenders? The Parallel operation of human rights law and the law of armed conflict and the conundrum of *jus ad bellum*" 40(2) *Israel Law Review* (2007): 592; Françoise Hampson, "The relationship

endow mandate holders with specific competence to investigate situations that may involve violations of international humanitarian law, as is the case with the Special Rapporteur on the situation of human rights in the occupied Arab territories.[21] Some commentators and practitioners have not welcomed the few instances where Special Procedures have received an express mandate to integrate humanitarian law to their monitoring activities, because of the inconsistency of the practice and the risk of undermining humanitarian standards if not taken seriously or if applied in a disjointed manner by human rights bodies.[22] For the most part, Special Procedures have been created without specific mention of the applicability of international humanitarian law as a legal framework of reference. Even when special rapporteurs have requested specific guidance on this question, they have not always received an answer.[23]

Therefore, as in virtually every other matter covered by Special Procedure mandates, the uncertain terms of the mandates have spawned a variety of approaches. The Special Rapporteur on extrajudicial, summary, or arbitrary executions has interpreted the scope of his mandate to cover armed conflict scenarios engaging applicable humanitarian standards.[24] The Special Representative on the situation of human rights in El Salvador devoted a specific section of his reports to the implementation of international humanitarian law.[25] When Felix Ermacora took up the mandate of Special Rapporteur on the situation of human rights in Afghanistan, he laid down the legal framework relevant to his mandate, including international humanitarian law.[26] However, others, such as the Working Group on Arbitrary

between international humanitarian law and human rights law from the perspective of a human rights treaty body" 90 *International Review of the Red Cross* (2008): 549.

[21] Despite the clear mandate, Israel had strong objections to this as reflected in the report of the Special Rapporteur, who sought further guidance on this point from the Commission: *see Report of the Special Rapporteur on the situation of human rights in the Occupied Arab Territories, including Palestine*, UN Doc. E/CN.4/2002/32 (2002), paras. 7–10.

[22] Daniel O'Donnell, "Trends in the application of international humanitarian law by United Nations human rights mechanisms" (1998): 38 *International Review of the Red Cross* 481. *See also* Theodor Meron, "The humanization of humanitarian law" 94(2) *American Journal of International Law* (2000): 239, at 269 and 270.

[23] Elvira Domínguez-Redondo, "Making the Connection: Security and Human Rights," in Cherif Bassiouni and William Schabas (eds.), *New Challenges for the Human Rights Machinery: What Future for the UN Treaty Body System and the Human Rights Council Procedures?* (Intersentia, 2011): 255.

[24] The position of the Special Rapporteur over the years is summarized in Philip Alston et al. (2008) (n. 18): 183, at 202–6.

[25] *See*, for instance, UN Doc. E/CN.4/1992/32 (1992), paras. 96–117; and UN Doc. A/47/596 (13 November 1992), paras. 105–7.

[26] UN Doc. E/CN.4/1985/121 (1985), para. 161.

Detentions, decided from the outset not to deal with situations and cases linked to the existence of an armed conflict.[27] Similarly, in light of the competence of the International Red Cross to address situations of disappearance during international armed conflicts, the Working Group on Enforced or Involuntary Disappearances has determined not to deal with situations of international armed conflict, although it does consider disappearances in internal armed conflicts when the agent perpetrating an enforced disappearance may be a representative of the state.[28] Despite the clear position outlined in their methods of work, both working groups have been inconsistent in their application.[29]

ii. Non-state Actors

Until recently, special rapporteurs have mostly adhered to uncontroversial norms of international law concerning responsibility for breaches of international law by confining their attribution of alleged human rights violations to state actors. As a consequence, they implicitly or explicitly adopted the principle that non-state actors should not be approached in the course of their investigations into cases or situations of human rights violations.[30] One of the early explicit explanations of this approach was advanced in the 1986 report of the Working Group on Enforced or Involuntary Disappearances.[31] Yet the Working Group also listed allegations of disappearances allegedly committed by non-state actors, without investigating them, in the visit report to Peru carried out that same year.[32] A minority of mandate holders were keen to engage with non-state actors under different justifications. For instance, the Special Rapporteur on the situation of human rights in El Salvador, interpreted the political nature of the mandate as a license to investigate human rights violations attributed to insurgents or guerrilla groups.[33]

[27] The Working Group established its position in its first report (UN Doc. E/CN.4/1992/20, para. 16), and it is reflected in its current working methods (see chapter three).

[28] The Working Group established its position for the first time in relation to the cases of disappearances brought to its attention during the Iran-Iraq war: *see* UN Doc. E/CN.4/1983/14 (1983), paras. 118–20. This was confirmed as a general position in the WGEID report in 1984: *see* UN Doc. E/CN.4/1984/21 (1984), paras. 20 and 21. *See also* the methods of work published in UN Doc. E/CN.4/1996/38, Annex I at para. 5; and UN Doc. A/HRC/13/31, Annex 1 at para. 11.

[29] *See* David S. Weissbrodt and Brittany Mitchell, "The United Nations Working Group on Arbitrary Detention: Procedures and Summary of Jurisprudence; 38(3) *Human Rights Quarterly* (2016): 655, 660–1; *see also* Domínguez-Redondo (2011) (n. 23): 255, 260.

[30] UN Doc. E/CN.4/1986/18 (1986) para. 34.

[31] Ibid.

[32] *See* UN Docs. E/CN.4/1986/18/Add.1 and E/CN.4/1987/15/Add.1.

[33] The mandate holder, José Antonio Pastor-Ridruejo, explained this decision, based on political and ethical considerations rather than legal principles, in "Les procédures publiques spéciales de la

Even those experts who routinely acknowledged abuses of human rights perpetrated by non-state actors, such as the Special Rapporteur on summary executions,[34] emphasized that their methods of work only permitted them "to intervene when the perpetrators are believed to be government agents or have a direct or indirect link with the state."[35]

Over the years, Special Rapporteurs have increasingly changed this position. The Manual of Operations of the Special Procedures devotes a section to the relationship between Special Procedures and non-state actors,[36] affirming that non-state actors may be held to account for human rights violations, and therefore may be relevant interlocutors "in the quest to restore respect for human rights and to establish accountability for violations."[37] Special Procedures are contributing to the emerging trend that expects common human rights standards as expressed in the Universal Declaration of Human Rights to be respected by non-state actors.[38]

Since 2011, the Office of the High Commissioner has expressly acknowledged the standardization of this practice, including in its publications on the "Facts and Figures of Special Procedures." These annual publications contain data on allegations of human rights violations sent to non-state actors, including international organizations or multinational corporations.[39] The database on communications sent by Special Procedures show that the vast majority have sent allegations of possible human rights violations to non-state actors in the past decade, particularly since 2015. The details available for communications sent between December 1, 2010, and July 15, 2019, reveal that virtually all experts in charge of thematic mandates have sent communications to non-state actors, while the practice remains exceptional among geographic Special Procedures. [40]

The range of non-state actors Special Procedures routinely engage with include de facto authorities in specific territories which confirms

Commission des Droits de l'Homme des Nations Unies" 228(3) *Recueil de Cours de l'Académie de Droit International* (1991): 183, at 214–5.

[34] For a summary of this approach with references to the case law of the International Court of Justice, the Human Rights Committee, and the Inter-American Commission on Human Rights, *see* UN Doc. E/CN.4/2005/7 (2005), paras. 65–76.

[35] UN Doc. E/CN.4/2002/74 (2002), para. 71.

[36] *Manual of Operations of Special Procedures* (2008): section E, paras. 81–3.

[37] Ibid., para. 81.

[38] *See* Andrew Clapham, "Human rights obligations of non-state actors in conflict situations" 88 *International Review of the Red Cross* (2006): 491, 504–7.

[39] For the references to these publications, *see* chapter three *esp.* n. 38.

[40] *See* tables in Annex 1.

well-established principles of state responsibility.[41] Many mandate holders have sent communications in relation to human rights cases and situations perpetrated by governments that may not have enjoyed international recognition, such as the Taliban in Afghanistan[42] or the once unrecognized government of Haiti in the early 1990s.[43] Mandate holders have also addressed alleged human rights violations committed by international authorities in territories under their jurisdiction, such as in Timor Leste between 1999 and 2002[44] and Kosovo between 1999 and 2008.[45]

After the attacks against the United States on September 11, 2001, groups labeled as "terrorist" have gained prominence among non-state actors for whom accountability for human rights abuses is sought by states. Whether this is a change of focus or merely a change of language is a matter beyond the scope of this chapter. However, the mandate holder with the closest relationship to the issue, the Special Rapporteur on the promotion and protection of human rights and fundamental freedoms while countering terrorism, has adopted a "neutral" approach to this topic. The former mandate holder, Martin Scheinin, expressed his willingness to follow the work of the (then) Commission on Human Rights on the question of whether human rights violations can be attributed to non-state actors.[46] His successor, Fionnuala Ní Aoláin, has sent communications addressed to Mark Zuckerberg, chairman and chief executive officer of Facebook, regarding the company's definitions of terrorism and terrorist organizations, recalling the importance of ensuring such definitions are compatible with international law standards, including human rights and humanitarian law.[47] Another relevant example from this mandate holder is the joint communication sent with the Special Rapporteurs on health and persons with disabilities, to the Director General

[41] Article 9, *Articles on Responsibility of States for Internationally Wrongful Acts*, GA Res. 56/83, 12 December 2001.

[42] *See*, for instance, the reports of the Special Rapporteur on freedom of religion or belief, UN Doc. A/56/253, at paras. 25–30.

[43] *See* Report of the Special Rapporteur on the situation of Haiti, UN Doc. E/CN.4/1993/47, at para. 124(c).

[44] *See* Report of the Working Group on Enforced Disappearances, UN Doc. E/CN.4/2002/79, at paras. 355–6. The communications of the Group during 2001 were sent to the UN Transitional Administration in East Timor (UNTAET) and to Indonesia.

[45] *See* the allegation letter addressed to the UN Interim Administration in Kosovo (UNMIK) by the Special Rapporteur on trafficking in persons, especially women and children, and the Special Rapporteur on extrajudicial, summary or arbitrary executions on 19 October 2011, available at: http://spdb.ohchr.org/hrdb/19th/AL_Kosovo_19.10.2011_(1.2011).pdf. *See also* the dialogue established with UNMIK during the visit to Serbia (including Kosovo) in the 2009 report of the Special Rapporteur on freedom of religion or belief, UN Doc. A/HRC/13/40/Add.3.

[46] UN Doc. E/CN.4/2006/98 (2006), paras. 67 and 70.

[47] Communication OL OTH 46/2018, 24 July 2018.

for Home Affairs of the European Commission relating to a paper published by the Radicalisation Awareness Network (RAN) Centre of Excellence and the RAN Health and Social Care Working Group on March 19, 2019, including a reminder of the human rights treaties to which the European Union is a party.[48]

The launch of a Forum on Business and Human Rights within the United Nations in 2012[49] is another milestone in the consideration of non-state actors by UN Charter bodies and marks the culmination of a process ignited by the Global Compact project launched by the former Secretary General Kofi Annan in 1999.[50] This represents a substantial change from the sporadic and fragmented consideration of the impact of trade,[51] economic aid,[52] and debt[53] as well as that of business enterprises on the enjoyment of human rights that could be found, since 1977, in the reports of different subsidiary bodies of the former Commission on Human Rights.[54] Mandate holders have also pioneered and rapidly consolidated the practice of scrutinizing the role of transnational corporations in human rights abuses. This activity has merited scant political opposition despite its contested legal basis.

The practice of engaging with corporations as actors potentially accountable for human rights violations outside the realms of traditional state responsibility is no longer confined to the few mandate holders endowed with competence to deal with violations typically involving business, such as the Special Rapporteur on toxic waste[55]

[48] Communication OL OTH 41/2019, 21 August 2019.

[49] Established by HR Council Res. 17/4 on Human rights and transnational corporations and other business enterprises, 6 July 2011, at operative para. 12.

[50] Kofi Annan, *The Global Compact* (United Nations World Economic Forum, 1999).

[51] Elvira Domínguez-Redondo and Magdalena Sepúlveda Carmona, "An Overview of Human Rights Instruments to Raise Concerns About Trade and Investment Policies," in Sophia Murphy and Armin Paasch (eds.), *The Global Food Challenge: Towards a Human Rights Approach to Trade and Investment Policies* (Brot für Alle, 2009): 92.

[52] *See* CHR Decision 1997/103, 3 April 1997, appointing an independent expert on the effects of structural adjustment policies on economic, social, and cultural rights. On the study by Cassese regarding the impact of foreign economic aid and assistance on respect for human rights in Chile, *see* Elvira Domínguez-Redondo and Magdalena Sepúlveda Carmona, "Contextualizando el Informe Cassese: La dictadura que cambió el sistema de derechos humanos de Naciones Unidas y su legado en el monitoreo de derechos económicos, sociales y culturales" in Juan P. Bohoslavsky, Karinna Fernández, and Sebastian Smart (eds.), *Un país desigual a la fuerza: Complicidad económica con la dictadura chilena* (LOM, 2019): 97; and Bertrand Ramcharan, *The Protection Roles of the UN Human Rights Special Procedures* (Martinus Nijhoff, 2009): 131.

[53] *See* CHR Res. 1998/24, 17 April 1998. The mandate on structural adjustment programs and foreign debt got consolidated as a single mandate by CHR Res. 2000/82, 26 April 2000.

[54] Ramcharan (2009) (n. 52): 131–4.

[55] It is part of the mandate of the Special Rapporteur to examine and produce a list of transnational corporations engaged in the illicit traffic of toxic and dangerous products and wastes to developing

and the Working Group on Transnational Corporations and Business Enterprises.[56]

The treatment of non-state actors as potential violators of human rights illustrates the disparity of methods of work among Special Procedures that is evolving toward harmonization, contributing to the normalization of the discussion and assessment of non-state actors as accountable for human rights abuses in political fora.

C. Political Influence Determining Disparity in Working Methods

The difference in approaches to similar issues have not always been the result of the autonomy of mandate holders. The geopolitical coordinates that have favored the development of methods of work and broad interpretation of competences have also imposed explicit and implicit restrictions on how mandate holders were expected to operate. The politicized stances on differentiated treatment of rights have had a fundamental weight on how Special Procedures dealing with country or thematic mandates, or focused on distinct categories of rights, have articulated their methods of work in practice. The prima facie freedom in developing methods of work without normative restraints have never applied to all mandates equally.

i. Country and Thematic Mandates

The differences in working methods between thematic and geographical procedures that have existed since their establishment persist at present, highlighting the greater dependence of the latter type of mandates on the Human Rights Council's political composition. While the importance of the work of thematic Special Procedures beyond the realm of regular sessions of the Council is clear, the relevance of geographic mandates remain inherently attached to their discussion within the Council. That is, their effectiveness continues to reside more in the regular scrutiny of a specific country under the agenda items of the Council and the Assembly, in a bid

countries as requested in the latest Human Rights Council resolution renewing the mandate: HR Council Res. 18/11, 29 September 2011.

[56] For the Methods of Work followed by the Working Group, *see* UN Doc. A/HRC/WG.12/3/1, Annex.

to maintain publicity and international pressure that, over time, could contribute to political or other changes to remedy a persistent human rights violations. A governmental change in a territory under scrutiny by a Special Procedure or an alteration of consensus within the Council can determine the abrupt end of a geographic mandate, adding to their sensitivity to a specific political climate. This is reflected in the tenure of mandates. While thematic mandates are established for three years, their geographic counterparts are normally created or renewed for a year, with some notable exceptions. For instance, the Commission on Human Rights renewed the mandate of Afghanistan for three years in 2002. A year later, the same extension was decided for the mandates on Somalia, Myanmar, and Liberia. The current mandate on Cambodia enjoys a two-year tenure, while the Special Procedure on the occupied Palestinian territories has been established without a deadline, subjecting its dismissal to the end of the occupation.

The nomenclature used to name different mandate holders has been streamlined over the years, with former denominations such as "Special Representative" or "Special Envoy" disappearing from the Special Procedures' system.[57] All mandate holders are appointed as Working Groups, Special Rapporteurs, or independent experts. The denomination received by mandate holders is a political decision that may influence methods of work because they denote governmental expectations on the nature of the mandate as usually reflected in the language of the resolution creating the Special Procedure or the point of the agenda under which its work is debated.[58] In practice, the denomination "Special Rapporteur" is for situations considered more "serious." Only thematic Special Procedures are assigned to Working Groups, composed of five members, one from each of the five UN regional groupings. At the time of writing, there were working groups in force on people of African descent; arbitrary detention; human rights and transnational corporations and other business enterprises; enforced or involuntary disappearances; the use of mercenaries as means of violating human rights and impeding the exercise of rights of people to self-determination; and

[57] *See* HRC Res. 5/1 (2006), para. 59.

[58] On the meaning of the different denominations, *see* Helena M. Cook, "International Human Rights Mechanisms. The Role of the Special Procedures in the Protection of Human Rights. The Way Forward After Vienna" 50 *Brooklyn Law Review* (1993): 31, 43–4; Tom J. Farer and Felice Gaer, "The UN and Human Rights: At the End of the Beginning" in Adam Roberts and Benedict Kingsbury (eds.), *United Nations, Divided World. The UN's role in International Relations* (2nd ed. Clarendon Press, 1993): 240, 284; Allison Jernow, "Ad-hoc and Extra-conventional Means for Human Rights Monitoring" 28(4) *New York University Journal of International Law & Policy* (1996): 785, 791–2.

the issue of discrimination against women in law and in practice. The remaining thirty-nine thematic Special Procedures were assigned to a Special Rapporteur except for six independent experts on persons with albinism; the effect of foreign debt and other related financial obligations of states on the full enjoyment of all human rights; the promotion of a democratic and equitable international order; human rights and international solidarity; and the enjoyment of human rights by older persons. In September 2019, four out of ten geographic mandates were carried out by independent experts addressing the situation of human rights in Central African Republic, Mali, Somalia, and Sudan. More significantly, thematic Special Procedures are discussed under Item 3 of the Agenda of the Human Rights Council devoted to the "Promotion and protection of all human rights, civil, political, economic, social and cultural rights, including the right to development," while geographic mandates reports are tabled under three different agenda items. Item 7 is exclusively focused on Israel, while other geographic procedures, normally those denominated independent experts, are discussed under Item 10 (Technical assistance and capacity building) or Item 4 (Human rights situations that require the Council's attention). With exceptions, independent experts do not report to the General Assembly.[59]

Because the denomination of Special Rapporteur is perceived as more authoritative, some thematic mandate holders have successfully promoted a name change. This is the case, for instance, of the former independent experts on minority issues,[60] water and sanitation,[61] extreme poverty,[62] cultural rights,[63] and environment.[64]

The chosen denomination has had less impact on working methods than the geographic or thematic nature of the mandate. More vulnerable to political interference, mandate holders in charge of geographic mandates tend to operate without publishing their methods of work and keeping a lower public profile than their thematic counterparts.[65] The different articulation of the resolutions creating or renewing mandates has contributed to geographic mandate holders' reluctance in dealing with individual cases from

[59] The independent expert on the situation of human rights in Somalia was requested to submit a report to the General Assembly for the first time in 2017 by HRC Res. 36/37, 29 December 2017.
[60] HRC Res. 19/6, 12 December 2011.
[61] HRC Res. 16/2, 24 March 2011.
[62] HRC Res. 17/13, 17 June 2011.
[63] HRC Res. 19/6, 22 March 2012.
[64] HRC Res. 28/11, 28 March 2015.
[65] On the publication of methods of work and overall accessibility to information related to geographic mandates, *see* chapter three.

the early years of evolution of Special Procedures, a trend that continues to date.[66] Their reports identify and analyze the situation of human rights in the territory under their competence and routinely comment on relevant policies, legislative development, and administrative practices but tend to refrain from engaging with overarching thematic studies.

ii. Categories of Human Rights

Political and ideological distinctions associated with the positions of the two blocks of the Cold War resulted in the dichotomy between civil and political rights and economic, social, and cultural rights. In 1977, the Commission on Human Rights acknowledged it had concerned itself mainly with violations of civil and political rights, pledging a commitment to "also study violations of economic, social and cultural rights."[67] The same year, an additional category "solidarity or collective rights" was added when, relying on the French national motto "liberty, equality and fraternity," Karel Vasak constructed a third-generation of rights, and the "generations" typology became widely used among academics and civil society organizations.[68]

The division of human rights into different categories has always been controversial, in particular the introduction of "generations," because it conveys ideas of European and North American hierarchies of rights, temporal sequence, a straight compartmentalization of rights, and the defeat of their professed indivisibility.[69] Nonetheless, this division still permeates political debates associated with "North" or "South" positions, another pernicious and artificially constructed dichotomy, in addition to its geographically nonsensical character. Well-respected scholars have kept the categorization of rights alive, fueled through academic arguments over the years. For instance, in 1975, Marc Bossuyt defended the need to distinguish social and

[66] *See* Annex 1.

[67] *See* Res. 5(XXXIII) 28 February 1977, UN Doc. E/5927(supp)-E/CN.4/1257, *Question of the violation of human rights and fundamental freedoms in any part of the world, with particular reference to colonial and other dependent countries and territories*, operative para. 2.

[68] *See* Karel Vasak, "A 30-year struggle. The sustained efforts to give force of law to the Universal Declaration of Human Rights" 30 *The UNESCO COURIER* (November 1977): 29. He further developed this later, *see* Karel Vasak, "Pour une troisième generation des droits de l'homme," *Studies and essays on international humanitarian law and Red Cross principles* (Martinus Nijhoff Publishers, 1984): 837–850.

[69] A concise overview of the origins and the criticisms can be found in Steven L.B. Jensen "Putting to rest the Three Generations Theory of Human Rights," *Open Global Rights* (November 15, 2017), available at: https://www.openglobalrights.org/putting-to-rest-the-three-generations-theory-of-human-rights/.

civil rights based on their different nature and characteristics.[70] He argued that the different treatment of different categories of rights was not a conscious political or ideological decision but an inevitable and necessary consequence linked to their intrinsic differences.[71] Prestigious scholars have kept using this problematic categorization for decades, even when theoretically refuting "Western-only" views of human rights.[72] Human rights activists and mainstream civil society organizations supported this view. In 2004, Ken Roth, Executive Director of Human Rights Watch, stated that shaming strategies were not the most suitable in dealing with violations of economic, social, and cultural rights. While this was an attempt to justify the approach of Human Rights Watch in not addressing violations of economic, social, and cultural rights based on strategic grounds, it exacerbated the artificial distinction.[73] This mindset excludes discussion on certain human rights–related concerns within any international forum. Topics intrinsically intertwined with the enjoyment of human rights are sided off by denying their "human rights" nature within human rights bodies, while it continues to be difficult, if not impossible, to raise them before other international mechanism.[74] This approach has had a long-lasting impact on Special Procedures.

The optimism generated by the end of the Cold War is reflected in the creation of new thematic mandates. Between 1990 and 1994, new thematic Special Procedures were created on the question of sale of children and child prostitution and child pornography (CHR Res. 1990/68, 7 March 1990); arbitrary detention (CHR Res. 1991/42, March 5, 1991); internally displaced persons (CHR Res. 1992/73, March 5, 1992); freedom of opinion and expression (CHR Res. 1993/45, March 5, 1993); racism (CHR Res. 1993/20, March 2, 1993); violence against women (CHR Res. 1994/45, March 4, 1994); and independence of judges and lawyers (CHR Res. 1994/41, March 1, 1994). The euphoria of the early 1990s did not last, with calls for rationalization of the mechanism dominating endless discussion of reform they have been

[70] Marc Bossuyt, "La distinction juridique entre les droits civil et politiques et les droits économiques, sociaux et culturels" VIII(4) *Revues des droits de l'Homme/Human Rights Journal* (1975): 783.0.

[71] Ibid., 813.

[72] Jason Morgan-Foster, "Third Generation Rights: What Islamic Law Can Teach the International Human Rights Movement" *Yale Human Rights and Development Law Journal* 8 (2005): 67.

[73] Ken Roth, "Defending Economic, Social and Cultural Rights: Practical Issues Faced by an International Human Rights Organization" 26 *Human Rights Quarterly* (2004): 63. For a response, *see* Leonard S Rubenstein "How International Human Rights Organizations Can Advance Economic, Social, and Cultural Rights: A Response to Kenneth Roth" 26 *Human Rights Quarterly* (2004): 845.

[74] Philip Alston, "Extreme inequality as the antithesis of human rights" *Open Global Rights* (August 27, 2015).

subjected to since.[75] The attempt to balance the attention paid to civil and political rights with economic, social, and cultural rights as well as "third-generation rights" involved the creation of new Special Procedures but encompassed substantial changes in the language chosen for the relevant resolutions creating them.

After 1997, several thematic Special Procedures covering topics belonging to the categories of economic, social, and cultural rights or collective rights were born with the function of "undertaking studies" of phenomena related to human rights rather than to "investigate" or "respond" to human rights violations, which had become standardized for previous Special Procedures.[76] The language of many of these resolutions further reinforces the categorization of rights. For example, the original mandate of the independent expert on the effects of structural adjustment policies was born as an auxiliary body to the Working Group on the same issue and was requested to focus its work on studying the consequences of structural adjustment policies on economic, social, and cultural rights, updating previous work on the subject.[77] As part of the Commission's "efforts to impart a higher visibility to economic, social and cultural rights," the Special Procedure on the right to education was established to report on the progressive realization of the right to education as laid down in the Universal Declaration of Human Rights and relevant provisions of the Covenant on Economic, Social and Cultural Rights, as well as to promote assistance to governments in the elaboration of plans of actions to achieve the gradual application of the principle of compulsory education.[78] The competences attributed to the rapporteurs on housing[79] and health[80] were similar in content. The mandate on extreme poverty was focused on the study of the relationship between this phenomenon and the promotion and protection of human rights, offering suggestions on a possible declaration on human rights and extreme poverty, as well as recommendations on technical cooperation.[81] The independent expert on the issue of human rights obligations related to access to safe drinking water and sanitation was given competence to prepare a compendium of best practices, as well as to develop a study to clarify the content of human rights

[75] *See* chapter two.
[76] On the handling of individual communications, *see* chapter five.
[77] CHR Res. 1997/103 of 3 April 1997.
[78] CHR Res. 1998/33 of 17 April 1998.
[79] CHR Res. 2000/9 of 17 April 2000.
[80] CHR Res. 2000/31 of 21 April 2000.
[81] CHR Res. 1998/25 of 17 April 1998 (approved by vote 52 against 1).

obligations in relation to its mandate. Additionally, the expert had to make recommendations to help the realization of the Millennium Development Goals, in particular Goal 7.[82] Likewise, the independent expert in the field of cultural rights' original mandate demanded a focus on the identification of good practices and challenges, cooperating with states to foster the adoption of measures aimed at the promotion and protection of cultural rights.[83] The creation of the Special Representative of the Secretary General on the issue of human rights and transnational corporations (replaced by a Working Group on the same topic in 2011) further illustrates the difference in treatment of Special Procedures' mandates. His main competence consisted in identifying and clarifying standards of corporate responsibility and accountability for transnational corporations and other business enterprises concerning human rights and to develop methodologies for undertaking human rights impact assessments.[84] Having completed his codifying mandate by drafting the "Guiding Principles on Business and Human Rights," the Working Group replacing the Special Representative is in charge of promoting its dissemination and to identify, exchange, and promote good practices in the field,[85] while also considering the implementation of the Guiding Principles in the context of the 2030 Agenda for Sustainable Development. While the Working Group has the express competence to undertake visits on the grounds, successive resolutions have not included the power to investigate relevant human rights violations.[86]

The support received by mandate holders from the Office of the High Commissioner for Human Rights in earlier times contributed to the consolidation of different approaches between Special Procedures, since different institutional structures supported mandates focusing on economic, social, and cultural rights from others. These were considered "soft mandates" and were assigned different nomenclature to "Special Rapporteur." They were designed without the explicit or implicit mandate to investigate cases of human rights violations and separated from the daily activities of other Special Procedures through a different institutional framework of operations. Consequently, many published reports were akin to academic studies, not daring to step outside of the confines of their mandates.

[82] HRC Res. 7/22 of 28 March 2008 (adopted without a vote).
[83] HRC Res. 10/23 of 26 March 2009 (adopted without a vote).
[84] CHR Res. 2005/69 of 20 April 2005 (adopted by a recorded vote of 49 votes to 3, with 1 abstention).
[85] HRC Res. 17/4 of 16 June 2011 (adopted without a vote).
[86] HRC Res. 35/7 of 22 June 2017 (adopted without a vote).

The impact of the political decisions conferring different mandates is illustrated by the resolution establishing the Special Procedure on the right to food. Unlike other Special Procedures on economic, social, and cultural rights, it contained a similar albeit more restricted version of the standard mandate to "respond effectively" to information on all aspects of the realization of the right to food. This was enough for the Special Rapporteur appointed, to adopt from its inception, a similar approach in his methods of work to that of other Special Procedures on civil and political rights, including the handling of individual communications.[87] The eventual standardization of methods of work and mainstreaming of institutional support has had a tangible effect, with all mandate holders considering handling of individual communications part of their competences.

The protracted dissimilar treatment of thematic Special Procedures is partly because states had not even considered several of the topics covered as belonging to the catalogue of internationally recognized rights. This is illustrated by the discussions leading to the appointment of a Special Rapporteur on adequate housing,[88] which prompted the Special Rapporteur to recommend to the Commission on Human Rights, the provision of "unequivocal recognition to the human right to adequate housing,"[89] and the competence to deal with communications of human rights violations.[90] Similar discussions marked the birth of the Special Rapporteur on the right to health.[91]

It is important to highlight that, with the exception of the Special Procedure on the right to education, many of the contested mandates relate to themes not included in the Universal Declaration on Human Rights, the International Covenant on Economic, Social and Cultural Rights, or any

[87] CHR Res. 2000/10 of 17 April 2000 (adopted by 49 votes to 1, with 2 abstentions).

[88] Some of these discussions are reflected in "Summary record of the 52nd meeting, held at the Palais des Nations, Geneva, on Monday, 71 April 2000: Commission on Human Rights, 56th Session," UN Doc. E/CN.4/2000/SR.52 (1 May 2000). *See* Michael Dennis, "The Fifty-Sixth Session of the UN Commission on Human Rights" 95 *American Journal of International Law* (2001): 213, 216–7, "The Fifty-Seventh Session of the UN Commission on Human Rights" 96 *American Journal of International Law* (2002): 181, 189–91; on the background of the discussion and the position of the United States, contrary to the recognition of right to adequate housing as an international human right, *see* Philip Alston, "The U.S. and the Right to Housing: A Funny Thing Happened on the Way to the Forum" 1 *E.H.R.L.R.* (1996): 120.

[89] "Report of the Special Rapporteur on adequate housing as a component of the right to an adequate standard of living, and on the right to non-discrimination, Miloon Kothari, submitted in accordance with Commission Resolution 2002/21," UN Doc. E/CN.4/2003/5 (3 March 2003), para. 65(A).

[90] Ibid para. 65(b).

[91] *See* "Summary Records of the 56th meeting of the 59th Session of the Commission on Human Rights, 22 April 2003," UN Doc. E/CN.4/2003/SR.56 (18 May 2003).

other codifying instrument. As will be examined in the next chapter, the contribution of Special Procedures to the normative development of human rights has been decisive for the acceptance by states of the inclusion of a wide variety of human rights in the Human Rights Council agenda. Nowadays, Special Procedures on economic, social, and cultural rights face a different threat. Their mandates seem more prone to the addition of cross-cutting and global issues that may dilute their consideration as equivalent rights to civil and political rights. For instance, most resolutions addressing these Special Procedures include references and appeals to cover consideration of the sustainable development goals. The Council has also urged Special Rapporteurs and other thematic mechanisms in the field of economic, social, and cultural rights to address the impact and consequences of unilateral coercive measures on the enjoyment of human rights.[92]

The divergences in methods of work and content of mandates influenced the doctrinal approaches to Special Procedures. Frouville advanced the concept of "reactive" thematic procedures (*procedure thematic de reaction*) to distinguish Special Procedures operating similarly to treaty-based mechanisms from those without the mandate to "respond" to allegations of human rights violations.[93] Rudolf sustained that only thematic mandates dealing with cases of human rights violations could be considered "authentic" Special Procedures, which at the time of writing meant that most Special Procedures focusing on economic, social, and cultural rights were not part of the category Special Procedures. He named them "study rapporteurs," whose task would be circumscribed to study a specific problem at a theoretical level (although most of these mandates studied actual violations rather than theories).[94]

These distinctions were never sustained by strong arguments. The concerned mandate holders have participated in annual meetings and have been considered Special Procedures by the Office of the High Commissioner for

[92] The latest mandate can be found in HRC Res. 40/3 of 21 March 2019, which was approved by vote. Resolution 40/3 of 21 March 2019 was approved with 27 votes in favor by Angola, Bahamas, Bahrain, Bangladesh, Burkina Faso, Cameroon, Chile, China, Cuba, Democratic Republic of the Congo, Egypt, Eritrea, Fiji, India, Iraq, Nepal, Nigeria, Pakistan, Philippines, Qatar, Rwanda, Saudi Arabia, Somalia, South Africa, Togo, Tunisia, and Uruguay; 15 votes against casted by Australia, Austria, Brazil, Bulgaria, Croatia, Czechia, Denmark, Hungary, Iceland, Italy, Japan, Slovakia, Spain, Ukraine, and United Kingdom of Great Britain and Northern Ireland; and 5 abstentions (Afghanistan, Argentina, Mexico, Peru, Senegal). *See also* similar mandates contained in HRC Res. 24/14, 27 September 2013, 27/21; 26 September 2014; 30/2, 1 October 2015; 34/13, 24 March 2017 and 37/21, 23 March 2018.

[93] Frouville (n. 4): 16–7.

[94] Rudolf Beate, "The Thematic Rapporteurs and Working Groups of the United Nations Commission on Human Rights" 4 *Max Planck Yearbook on UN Law* (2000): 289, 290–1.

Human Rights and themselves. The mainstreamed cross-cutting themes, such as those requesting every mandate holder to include a gender perspective, do not discriminate between different categories of Special Procedures. In any case, the methods of work have progressively become more standardized, independent of the original resolution creating the mandate. The Human Rights Council has also sought to balance attention paid to all human rights issues. In 2018, there was almost the same number of resolutions focused on civil and political rights (16); economic, social, and cultural rights (15); and cross-cutting human rights concerns (16).[95]

3. Publicity Governing the Activities of Special Procedures

The importance acquired by Special Procedures is rooted in the publicity of their work under the stamp of the United Nations. All mandate holders submit annual reports to the Human Rights Council that include a summary of their activities, such as field missions and investigations on individual cases. The reports of the Working Group on Arbitrary Detention and the Working Group on Enforced Disappeared, concerned primarily with the outcome of individual cases, routinely include statistical summaries of the year's cases as well as their deliberations/general comments.[96] Most Special Procedures also report to the General Assembly, and some reports have been drawn to the attention of the Security Council. All debates, resolutions, and decisions undertaken within the ambit of the Human Rights Council are public. More decisively, publicity is not confined to the intergovernmental and non-governmental discussions taking place during the regular sessions of the Council where their reports are debated. Mandate holders use publicity not only as a channel of information at any point in time but also as a tool to exercise direct pressure over states and other concerned actors. Because mandate holders combine approaches to human rights implementation that seek the trust of states and their cooperation with other approaches aiming at shedding light on human rights abuses, they must remain attentive to publicity attendant to their work, avoiding, to the extent possible,

[95] *The Human Rights Council in 2018. Leadership, resolve and cooperation at the UN's main human rights body* (yourHRC.org, 2019): 21.
[96] *See* chapter five.

individual decisions that may compromise the credibility of the system of Special Procedures as a whole.

A. The Annual Report

A summary of mandate holders' activities is submitted annually to the Human Rights Council. Annual reports are public and distributed by the Office of the High Commissioner among all state members of the Council and Observers as well as non-governmental organizations with consultative status before the Economic and Social Council. They are also available to the press. The reports of Special Procedures have become the basis of most points of the agenda of the Human Rights Council. Experts open the debate on the topic under the competence with an oral presentation of their report, followed by an interactive dialogue with states and other stakeholders. Annual reports follow a similar structure; they are preceded by a summary that is normally followed by an introduction, the main body of analysis, conclusions, and recommendations. Some Special Procedures add a section clarifying the scope of their mandate and methods of work, although such information is increasingly absent from reports and published instead on the website of the relevant mandate. A significant number of thematic mandates devote an important part of their reports to recording individual communications, ordered by country, with a summary of the allegations, alleged violation of rights, and the replies received by governments. The full text of the communications sent since December 2009 are now available online.[97] Annual reports are currently restricted to twenty pages to ensure their translation in all official UN languages. As a result, reports on country visits, specific thematic reports, and reports on individual communications are often found as addendums to the main report.

The vast majority of mandate holders must also submit a report to the General Assembly. Those reports tend to summarize the information submitted to the Council, and many contain thematic analysis of issues under the focus of the Special Procedure. The Working Group on African Descent submits a single consolidated report to both the General Assembly and the Human Rights Council. In 2019, the geographical Special Procedures on the Central African Republic, Mali, and Somalia did not report to the General

[97] Available at: https://spcommreports.ohchr.org/.

Assembly. Among thematic Special Procedures, the mandates on arbitrary detention, enforced disappearances, leprosy, older persons, and discrimination against women and girls, did not report to the General Assembly.

The findings and recommendations contained in Special Procedures' annual reports are an essential component of one of the three documents constituting the basis for Universal Periodic Review. Hence, they can receive further attention by the governments of the Human Rights Council when they contain relevant information concerning the state under review.[98]

B. Beyond the Annual Report: The Challenges of Publicity

Contrary to other international human rights mechanisms, the publicity of the activities of Special Procedures is not confined to the public nature of their reports and their public debate. Mandate holders are free to publicize their actions between sessions by any means available to them. The potential to cause external reputational cost remains even if states manage to control or eliminate the impact of unwelcome assessments within the Human Rights Council. Publicity is the cornerstone of Special Procedures on which the significance and effectiveness of the system relies. It is essential that neither the introduction of limits to publicity through the Code of Conduct nor their occasional invocation undermines the availability of their findings or their relationship with the press and/or the multiple channels they use to disseminate their work.

The continuity of publicity is guaranteed by press releases and their interaction through social media. The personal prominence of the mandate holder becomes relevant in this context. Some Special Rapporteurs' actions frequently attract mass media attention, and they also enjoy influential profiles on social media platforms, while others remain virtually invisible despite the efforts of the Secretariat to provide equal publicity to all mandate holders through its official channels. The manner in which Special Procedures' methods of work has developed involves plenty of room for individual initiatives and hence for the importance of individual profiles. The interactions of mandate holders with the press have been the origin of significant conflict with governments and the origin of occasional calls for the application of the Code of Conduct.[99]

[98] HRC Res. 5/1 (2006), Annex, para. 15.
[99] *See* chapter two.

The importance of transparency and public availability of Special Procedures' outcomes also requires responsible use of this powerful tool by mandate holders. Their behavior has the potential to cause significant damage to the credibility and legitimacy of the system of Special Procedures. On several occasions, the allure of the spotlight seems to have resulted in misguided decisions regarding public communications that have resulted in formal statements from the UN headquarters disassociating the Organization from the declarations of a specific mandate holder.[100]

Experts perform their role pro bono and part-time, most of them combining it with their employment. Their professional and educational background has an inevitable impact on mechanisms allowing a high degree of autonomy to individuals, who are experts in their field of competence but not necessarily familiar with many unwritten rules governing relationships with the many actors they interact with. Mandate holders perform different roles and are unique in combining fact-finding functions, technical assistance, investigation of allegations of human rights violations, or the production of analytical reports, transcending barriers that normally compartmentalize the intergovernmental world of the United Nations, the work of human rights activist at grassroots level, and the direct interaction with state's organs as well as other local, national, and international stakeholders. In their more cooperative, diplomatic role, a sympathetic statement toward a positive advance regarding a particular state's policy may disappoint the expectations of those eager to have the flaws highlighted. A different stance, naming and shaming relevant governments for their failures at complying with human rights standards, may hinder further necessary cooperation with states when it is most needed. Striking a balance is inherently difficult, and questions arise about the possibility of adopting these roles simultaneously, particularly under public scrutiny. This situation is inevitable and intrinsic to the multiple facets of the methods of work developed by Special Procedures.

However, experts should also be aware of their own agendas and how their other professional and activist interests, no matter how legitimate, can undermine Special Procedures. Mandate holders have ample discretion in deciding the countries they visit, the individual cases they take up, or the follow-up of recommendations they pursue. The scarcity of resources and the characteristics of Special Procedures necessitate selectivity and potential for questioning the wisdom of choosing one objective over others. Expert holders should

[100] *See* chapter six.

always carefully consider the confines of their independence as organs that carry the authority of the United Nations, when opting for one particular avenue, especially if they promote the public profile of some of their actions instead of others. The weight of their decisions and authority depends on their belonging to the institutional umbrella of Special Procedures' system. The reaction to the Working Group of Arbitrary Detention and the Special Rapporteur on torture's focus on the Assange case illustrate this point. After publishing a controversial opinion declaring the incarceration of Assange constituted a form of arbitrary detention in December 2015 (Opinion 54/2015),[101] the Working Group made a significant effort to keep this case under public scrutiny using multiple press releases.[102] One of its members followed the decision with a TV appearance, signaling the high profile of this case.[103] The mandates on extrajudicial executions, human rights defenders, and privacy also issued press releases endorsing the view of the Working Group.[104]

The involvement of the Special Rapporteur on Torture in the case has been more problematic, bearing in mind the obstacles of arguing the prevalence of torture or ill treatment in Mr. Assange's situation. His widely self-publicized decision to travel to the United Kingdom to visit Mr. Assange in a high-security prison on May 9, 2019, accompanied by two medical experts was unprecedented.[105] Never before had an official visit of a Special Procedure been used to assess the case of a single individual. The visit coincided with the denunciation of inhumane conditions in UK prisons, probably a more suitable object of investigation during a country visit.[106] On the occasion of the International Day on Support of Torture Victims, Melzer published an article that he sought to disseminate as widely as possible.[107] The content of

[101] *See*, for instance, Joshua Rozenberg, *How did the UN got it so wrong on Julian Assange*, The Guardian (February 5, 2016)) or Liora Lazarus, "The United Nations Working Group on Arbitrary Detention decision on Assange: 'ridiculous' or 'justifiable'?" *Ejil: Talk* (February 9, 2016), available at: http://www.ejiltalk.org/the-united-nations-working-group-on-arbitrary-detention-decision-on-assange-ridiculous-or-justifiable/.

[102] *See* UN Press Releases, *United Kingdom: Working Group on Arbitrary Detention expresses concern about Assange proceedings* (Geneva, May 3, 2019); *UN experts urge UK to honour rights obligations and let Mr. Julian Assange leave Ecuador embassy in London freely* (Geneva, December 21, 2018); *Julian Assange arbitrarily detained by Sweden and the UK, UN expert panel finds* (Geneva, February 5, 2016).

[103] *Julian Assange: UN panel member defends ruling*, BBC Newsnight (February 5, 2016).

[104] These are summarized in UN News, *UN experts warn Assange arrest exposes him to risk of serious human rights violations* (April 11, 2019).

[105] Press Release, *UN expert says "collective persecution" of Julian Assange must end now* (Geneva, May 31, 2019).

[106] *Dutch court blocks extradition of man to "inhumane" UK prisons*, The Guardian (May 10, 2019).

[107] Nils Melzer, "Demasking the Torture of Julian Assange," *Medium* (June 26, 2019) available at: https://medium.com/@njmelzer/demasking-the-torture-of-julian-assange-b252ffdcb768.

the statement, signed by him in his official capacity as Special Rapporteur, dismissed the allegations of rape against Mr. Assange using a sarcastic tone rather than sound legal arguments, motivating a critical response endorsed by dozens of academics and lawyers.[108]

4. Conclusions

Different processes of reform and coordination among mandate holders have contributed to the harmonization of practices and the understanding of Special Procedures as a distinct group of human rights mechanisms. However, the political dynamics informing the creation of different categories of mandates remain a stimulus for disparity, based on the expectations and controversies informing their creation and renewal. Efforts to ensure uniform practices, fail under governmental pressures to maintain different approaches depending on the geographical or thematic nature of the Special Procedures and whether their thematic mandate tackles civil and political rights, economic, social, and cultural rights, phenomena impacting human rights or solidarity rights. These obstacles continue to stand in the way of standardization despite significant progress.

The flexibility and autonomy characterizing Special Procedures have resulted in an accumulation of functions within the UN human rights system which requires a range of skills and expertise that cannot be always displayed simultaneously. Mandate holders must decide whether more cooperative/diplomatic or confrontational/legalistic approaches are better suited to achieve a specific objective or whether their role lies more in communicating more effectively with the relevant interlocutor. Certain expectations are entrenched in the dynamics governing relationships with diverse stakeholders and in fulfilling different functions. Engaging as representatives of the United Nations with governmental delegations normally requires diplomatic skills associated with the expectation of discretion, if not confidentiality. However, when mandate holders appraise the behavior of states, collecting and examining facts to reach conclusions based on human rights standards, they are expected to disseminate their findings widely, providing an authoritative voice to those far from sites of power, unafraid of endorsing strategies

[108] Marie Davoise, "Open letter in response to UN Special Rapporteur's op-ed on Julian Assange," *Medium* (July 1, 2019) available at: https://medium.com/@mariedavoise/response-to-un-special-rapporteurs-op-ed-on-julian-assange-e911e0684182.

that are confrontational toward those considered accountable. The limited resources act as a further restriction for decisions that can be perceived by others as unjustifiably biased. Despite these circumstances, mandate holders are expected to use the authority that accompanies their position with caution, ensuring to the maximum degree possible that their actions further the human rights underpinning their specific mandate while not undermining the work of the system of Special Procedures to which they belong.

Five
Implementation of Methods of Work

1. Introduction

Having explored the historic, institutional, and political factors that explained the distinct characteristics of Special Procedures and their organic growth, this chapter will address the primary methods of work used to monitor, report, and advise on the thematic or geographic issue under their competence. Human rights monitoring mechanisms operating at international level are institutionally linked to international organizations and submit a public report summarizing their activities, conclusions, and recommendations to that intergovernmental body. They ensure human rights issues under their competence are engaged in international fora by the representatives of the states that must cooperate for their implementation. They provide a voice to disempowered communities, identify practices and circumstances that negatively or positively impact the enjoyment of human rights, and issue conclusions and recommendations accordingly. In accomplishing their mission, they draw upon multiple governmental and non-governmental sources.

In addition to these functions that Special Procedures share with other human rights bodies, they have developed unique methods of work for their interference with the sovereignty of states, for their adaptability to multiple scenarios, and for their accessibility. This chapter focuses on the three most salient among these methods of work: (1) the handling of communications; (2) visits on the ground; and (3) development of normative standards in the field of human rights.

2. Communications

The lack of rigid normative frameworks governing the methods of work, coexistence and coordination of different UN mechanisms have been key

In Defense of Politicization of Human Rights. Elvira Domínguez-Redondo, Oxford University Press (2020).
 DOI: 10.1093/oso/9780197516706.001.0001

factors in facilitating the expansion of the accessibility of Special Procedures to victims of human rights violations. Well-established practice, subsequently endorsed by the Code of Conduct and other reforms experienced by Special Procedures, have consolidated the normative foundations for the competence to investigate cases of human rights violations, whether or not this power was expressly in the original decisions establishing the material scope of their mandate.[1] The level of engagement with individual cases varies significantly between different Special Rapporteurs and Working Groups, but there is clear understanding and consensus that all of them have competence to investigate cases of human rights abuses. Communications to the Special Procedures may deal with cases concerning human rights of individuals or groups with the aim of protecting possible victims or preventing an immediate or imminent violation. They may be considered, instead or simultaneously, as a useful source of information to delimit the situation of human rights in a particular territory. They may have a humanitarian nature or may seek to assess the compliance of international standards by the state concerned. Communications may raise issues unrelated to specific individuals and could focus instead on a change of legislation or policies.

A. Pioneering the Intervention of UN Bodies on Behalf of Individual Cases of Violations

Between 1967 and 1980, Special Procedures were mainly governed by the mandate of examining "information relevant to gross violations of human rights and fundamental freedoms" as stated in the 1967 ECOSOC Resolution 1235 (XLII), *Question of the violation of human rights and fundamental freedoms, including policies of racial discrimination and segregation and of apartheid, in all countries, with particular reference to colonial and other dependent countries and territories*. Individual allegations of human rights were normally considered as possible evidence of patterns of human rights violations, but did not receive specific responses.

There were a few, but significant, exceptional actions on behalf of individuals during the final years of the 1970s.[2] Dealing with a situation that was not considered part of the domestic affairs of a state, and referred to

[1] *See* chapter two.

[2] Examples of responses to individual cases by the Security Council, the General Assembly, and the Commission on Human Rights during this period are provided in Menno T. Kamminga, *Inter-State Accountability for Violations of Human Rights* (University of Pennsylvania Press, 1992): 103–9.

specifically in the title of Resolution 1235 (XLII), the Group of Experts on the Situation of Human Rights in Southern Africa was born in 1967, with the specific mandate of receiving and investigating communications as well as hearing witnesses.[3] The Working Group on the Situation of Human Rights in Chile, created in 1973, intervened on behalf of alleged victims of torture, arbitrary arrest, and forced disappearances.[4] The Commission on Human Rights publicly debated the assassination of Guatemalan Congressman Alberto Fuentes Mohr in 1979 and the case of the Soviet nuclear physicist Andrei Sakharov in 1980.[5] The practice of sending "urgent appeals" to governments when there is an imminent risk to the life or physical integrity of the victim also originated in this period. The Commission on Human Rights decided urgent interventions regarding situations of alleged human rights violations in 1968 and 1969. In 1974, following a model pioneered by the NGO Amnesty International, the Commission sent the first of a series of telegrams requesting the government concerned for expeditious actions regarding named individuals.[6] Five years later in 1979, the Commission on Human Rights partially delegated the competence to decide on the need of urgent appeals to the Ad Hoc Working Group of Experts on Violations of Human Rights in Southern Africa.[7] However, the final decision remained the prerogative of the Chairman of the Commission.[8]

The first ever thematic Special Procedure created in 1980, the Working Group on Enforced and Involuntary Disappearances, understood its mandate "to bear in mind the need to be able to respond effectively to information" coming before the Group,[9] as dealing with individual cases. From its first report, the Group reported upon the procedure it would follow to process urgent appeals.[10] In the following years, experts with thematic mandates

[3] CHR Res. 2 (XXIII) 6 March 1967, para. 3.

[4] *See Report of the* Ad Hoc *Working Group to inquire into the situation of human rights in Chile*, UN Doc. A/33/331, 25 July 1978, *esp.* paras. 312–33; 337–52; 389–407.

[5] *See* (regarding Andrei Sakharov) Bertrand G. Ramcharan, *The Concept and Present Status of the International Protection of Human Rights* (Martinus Nijhoff, 1989): 80–2; *see also* Concepción Escobar-Hernández, *La Comisión de Derechos Humanos de Naciones Unidas y la violación de los derechos humanos y libertades fundamentales: un estudio de los procedimientos especiales.* Doctoral Thesis (3 volumes) (Universidad Complutense de Madrid, 1988), at vol. II, 724 (Fuentes-Mohr); and 893, 894 (Andrei Sakharov).

[6] On the content and beneficiaries of these actions, *see* Kamminga (1992) (n. 2): 105–7. The telegrams are reproduced in Ramcharan (1989) (n. 5): 84–104.

[7] CHR Res. 12 (XXXV) 6 March 1969.

[8] On the urgent appeals suggested to the Commission by the Group and the actions undertaken, *see* reports UN Docs. E/CN.4/1429 (1981), para. 21; E/CN.4/1984/8, paras. 17–19; and E/CN.4/1986/9, para. 12.

[9] CHR Res. 20 (XXXVI) of 29 February 1980, para. 6.

[10] UN Doc. E/CN.4/1435 (1981), para. 10.

followed the steps of the Working Group and established procedures to receive allegations, processing them as "letter of allegations" or "urgent appeals" when there was a possibility to prevent serious human rights violations by acting expeditiously, even when they had not received an express mandate from the Commission. During the 1980s, only the thematic mandate holder on the use of mercenaries as a means of impeding the exercise of the right of peoples to self-determination did not deal with individual communications.

Conversely, geographic mandate holders were less keen on individual communications. Reports of geographic Special Procedures during the 1980s contain, at most, summaries of cases, and from the available record it is not always clear whether these were sent to the concerned governments or whether such communications were treated as letters of allegations or urgent appeals. If the state provided an answer to the allegations, the answer was not always reproduced, making it difficult to know the full extent of the intervention by Special Rapporteurs from the reports alone. From the geographic mandates' report at the time, it is possible to conclude that most actions on behalf of individuals occurred within the context of field visits.[11]

B. Mainstreaming Communications as Standard Practice of All Special Procedures

The legal basis for intervention on behalf of individuals was weak for most Special Procedures operating under the Commission on Human Rights. The Working Group on Arbitrary Detention, created in 1991, was the first Special Procedure to receive a clear mandate of "investigating cases."[12] During that period, only two other Special Procedures had such competence from their conception: the Special Rapporteur on the independence of judges and lawyers created in 1994[13] and the Special Rapporteur on the implications for human rights of the environmentally sound management and disposal of hazardous substances and wastes established in 1995.[14] For

[11] Providing more detail than the average are the reports on the situation of human rights in Chile both from the Working Group and the Special Rapporteur that replaced it. *See* Report of the Working Group A/33/331 (1978) (n. 4) and reports from the Special Rapporteur UN Docs. E/CN.4/1986/2 (1986) paras. 88–9; E/CN.4/1987/7 (1987) paras. 20–2, 24–5; *see also* second report and subsequent of the Special Representative on the situation of human rights in Iran, UN Doc. E/CN.4/1987/23 (1987).

[12] CHR Res. 1991/42, 5 March 1991, para. 2.

[13] CHR Res. 1994/41, 4 March 1994, para. 3.a.

[14] CHR Res. 1995, 8 March 1995, para. 7.c.

other Special Procedures, the Commission endorsed practices post facto. For instance, it requested the Special Rapporteur on extrajudicial, summary, and arbitrary executions to "continue to examine situations of summary or arbitrary executions and to pay special attention to cases in which a summary or arbitrary execution is imminent or threatened."[15] The Working Group on Enforced Disappearances was reminded of its primary role as a "channel of communications between families of disappeared persons and the Governments concerned."[16] However, most Special Procedures had, at most, a mandate to "respond effectively" to information coming before them using all available sources of information (including individual allegations of human rights violations)[17] as the basis of their power to investigate communications.

In practice, many mandate holders of thematic Special Procedures made individual cases a central part of their monitoring activities. The following statement of the Special Representative (today Special Rapporteur) of the Secretary General on human rights defenders explains the combined approach to situations and cases adopted by a growing number of mandate holders at the start of the twenty-first century:

> The mandate of the Special Representative implies a combined approach that considers the general situation of human rights defenders around the world as well as concrete incidents and individual cases. Therefore, the work of the Special Representative will involve both the study of phenomena related to human rights defenders and action on concrete incidents and cases.[18]

The Special Rapporteur on summary executions has also been among the earliest mechanisms to clearly state the difference between its work regarding

[15] ECOSOC Res. 1984/35, 24 May 1984 and GA Res. 39/110, 14 December 1984. Notice this mandate was created and renewed by the Economic and Social Council instead of the Commission on Human Rights for its first few years of existence.

[16] CHR Res. 1997/26, 11 April 1997, para. 2.

[17] While many mandates were born with a limitation of the range of sources they could use, these limitations slowly disappear for all mandates in the decade of the 1990s. The following mandates and Commission on Human Rights resolutions mark the end of limitations in the sources: religious intolerance (1990/27 of 2 March 1990); executions (1990/49 of 6 March 1990); torture (1995/37 of 3 March); violence against women (1995/85 of 8 March); arbitrary detention (1998/41 of 17 April); right to education (1999/25 of 17 April). However a specific list of sources was maintained for the Representative of the Secretary General on internally displaced people and the Special Rapporteur on toxic waste.

[18] UN Doc. E/CN/4/2001/94 (2001), para. 41. *See also* UN Doc. E/CN.4/2002/14, para. 48.

situations and cases of human rights violations, emphasizing that general responses of state, while useful to understand the situation in a given country, were inadequate in relation to specific allegations.[19] The working groups on arbitrary detention and disappearances went a step further by establishing methods of work focused on the investigation of individual cases, arguing that they had no capacity to deal with situations of human rights violations unless exceptional circumstances justified it.[20]

During the Commission years, a significant number of Special Rapporteurs decided not to consider individual cases of alleged human rights violations. Previous chapters have addressed the main factors behind these decisions in relation to the influence of governmental interest in distinguishing between categories of rights and geographic and thematic mandates. The standardization of practice accompanied by the provision of clear grounds for the treatment of individual cases to all Special Procedures changed this state of affairs. As illustrated in the table reproduced in Annex 1, all mandate holders (except for the mandate on Mali) send communications to states and other relevant stakeholders, with the majority of them handled jointly by several Special Procedures. It is also apparent that some Special Procedures are more focused on the treatment of individual cases than others. The most prolific Special Procedures continue to belong to those monitoring civil and political rights, with geographic mandates more reluctant to engage in this facet of their activities.

Given the autonomy enjoyed by mandate holders and the wide interpretation over their original mandate, decisions on making communications a central part of their activities also depends on the judgement of the relevant expert. For instance, the experts who have acted as Special Rapporteur on mercenaries (today a Working Group) did not address cases during the twenty years this mandate reported to the Commission. The first Special Rapporteur on the sale of children and the use of children in pornography dealt with individual cases,[21] while the second expert's approach focused on a yearly topic of study with individual communications disappearing from reports.[22] When Jean Manuel Petit took up the post in 2001 he went back

[19] UN Doc. E/CN.4/1994/7 (1994), para. 37.a).

[20] *See* UN Doc. E/CN.4/1995/31 (1995), para. 53 (arbitrary detention), and UN Doc. E/CN.4/1993/25 (1993), para. 41.

[21] *See* UN Docs. E/CN.4/1992/55 (1992), para. 31; E/CN/41993/67, paras. 22, 214–26; and A/49/478, para. 7.

[22] Former reference to individual cases disappear from the methods of work of the mandate holder as visible in UN Doc. A/50/456, paras. 15–34. While willingness to use urgent appeals is stated in subsequent reports (UN Docs. A/52/482, para. 9; and E/CN.4/1996/100, para. 151), there is no

to the practice of intervening on behalf of individual cases. During his first years as mandate holder, the Special Rapporteur on the right to health decided to approach the mandate without investigation of individual cases, despite the indirect request of the Commission.[23]

C. Methods of Work to Handle Communications of Human Rights Violations

Special procedures receive allegations of human rights violations from all available sources, including civil society organizations, activists, or victims of human rights violations. When there is a risk to the life or physical integrity or other circumstances requiring an expedited response to prevent serious human rights violations of the person or group to which the appeals refers to, mandate holders issue an "urgent appeal." In other cases they handle the communication as an "allegation letter." The introduction of a database on communications, in 2011, has facilitated the accessibility of information about communications sent to governments. Until then, sources of information and victims had to wait to the publication of the final report to know whether their case had been handled by a Special Procedure.

The Working Group on Arbitrary Detention and the Working Group on Enforced or Involuntary Disappearance continue to be the Special Procedures with the most detailed methods of work on their handling of communications. Both mechanisms are concentrated on resolving individual cases, although through different approaches. The Working Group on Disappearances aims to assist, in a humanitarian capacity, the families of reported disappeared persons in determining their fates or whereabouts of the victim.[24] Conversely, the Working Group on Arbitrary Detention follows what is commonly categorized as a "quasi-judicial" process. All the

evidence of the Rapporteur using this kind of actions. The Commission had included the mandate to "respond effectively" to information on the original mandate of the Rapporteur (Res. 1990/68 of 7 March 1990), but limited itself to welcome her reports from 1994.

[23] *See* CHR Res. 2002/31 of 22 April 2002, 2003/28 of 22 April 2003, and 2004/27 of 16 April 2004, where the Commission called upon governments to respond promptly to her or his communications. From the reports of the expert it seems he intervened in isolated cases, but no names or countries are named. *See* UN Doc. E/CN.4/2004/49, paras. 5 and 6.

[24] On the pragmatic reasons for such approach, *see* Olivier de Frouville, "Working Out a Working Group: A View from a Former Working Group Member" in Aoife Nolan, Rosa Freedman, and Thérèse Murphy (eds.), *The United Nations Special Procedures System* (Brill, 2017): 223, 225–8.

communications considered admissible are assessed examining the information provided by (or on behalf of) the alleged victim and the state, after which the Group issues an "Opinion" declaring whether it deems to be a violation of the international standards of reference decided by the Group. Both Working Groups have also developed a methodology to follow up individual cases until they consider them resolved.

The financial and human resources available to Special Procedures are insufficient to fulfill the ambitious scope of their mandates. Open to all sources of information without admissibility criteria, this is particularly true for individual communications. Lacking real capacity to investigate the facts, mandate holders' decisions on admissibility and treatment of the information available depends on the credibility they associate with the source and their human capacity to deal with a limited number of cases. The introduction of databases has helped immensely to improve the consistency in the handling of communications. However, most Special Procedures are not able to assess the existence of a violation under their competence for every communication received, based on the information received. As a result, they tend to include a summary of the allegations sent to the states concerned and the reply received, if any, in their reports. While some mandate holders have also engaged in the assessment of the replies provided by states to determine the existence of breaches of human rights obligations, there is no consistency over time, and the practice depends on the will and resources of the expert in charge of the procedure. For instance, emulating the practice of the Working Group on Arbitrary Detention, the Special Rapporteur on freedom of religion established different categories of violations of human rights relevant to his mandate in 1996 and then named some of the states fitting one of the categories in 1997, without referring to the specific cases the violation referred to.[25] Later reports contain individual statements about specific violations related to communications under the rubric "observations."[26] Since 2011, the new mandate holders continues to be prolific in communicating allegations to states but only provides statistical data about them in reports, having clarified that such information merely serves as indicators of the extent of the violations related to his mandate, due to the limitations of the system of communications under Special Procedures.[27] The Special

[25] *See* UN Docs. A/51/542 (1996), paras. 31–7; and E/CN.4/1997/91 (1997).

[26] *See, e.g.*, UN Docs. A/56/253 (2001), para. 30; E/CN.4/2004/63 (2004) paras. 115–22; and A/HRC/13/40/Add.1 (2010).

[27] UN Doc A/HRC/40/58 (2019), para. 12.

Rapporteur on human rights defenders includes "observations" assessing individual communications when enough information is available.[28] The former Special Rapporteur on Iraq, Andreas Mavrommatis, divided his report by categories of violations, including within them the details of relevant individual cases and the governmental response received.[29] His predecessor, Max van der Stoel, was among the most active geographic mandate holders in handling individual cases.[30] In any case, the Working Groups on arbitrary detentions and disappearance remain exceptional in their consistency over time for the treatment of individual cases, and only the former formulates final opinions based in law regarding all cases considered admissible. For the Special Procedures that provide more detail about the content of the allegations and the reply received, any assessment about a possible violation by the state concerned must be deduced by the reader. Since this information has become available through the database on communications of the Office of the High Commissioner, repeating the same details in the reports seems redundant. However, Special Procedures should resist the temptation to remove those details from their reports since they are the documents submitted to the Council and, therefore, debated by states. In addition, the documents recorded in the electronic database are not considered official and are published without UN nomenclature. In practice, it means they tend to disappear from the system and become untracktable when the system of recording or archiving information is updated.

Many Special Procedures have published forms and questionnaires that victims should use to facilitate the submission of communications. Some are generic models provided by the Office of the High Commissioner, but available in different versions. Others are specific to the relevant Special Procedure. Section 3.C of chapter three outlines the different formats that mandate holders use to publish their methods of work. Even the most accessible human rights mechanisms of the world remain difficult to access for those not familiar with the system of Special Procedures as a whole and/or the specific mechanism they want to approach.

Victims of human rights violations not only need to know how to access the system but also what kind of remedy may be forthcoming, what kind of response can be expected, and the estimated timeline for any potential

[28] *See, e.g.*, UN Docs. A/HRC/28/63/Add.1 (2015) and A/HRC/34/52/Add. 1 (2017).

[29] *See, e.g.*, UN Doc. E/CN.4/2001/42 (2001).

[30] *See, e.g.*, UN Docs. E/CN.4/1992/31 (1992), paras. 137–45; and E/CN.4/1993/45 (1993) paras. 140–68.

action. This will depend on the interpretation, variable over time, that mandate holders have of their role in processing individual communications. Some try to provide some redress to individual grievance by identifying human rights violations published in annual reports, while others consider communications part of the sources contributing to understanding the magnitude and characteristics of violations pertinent to their mandates. In those cases, communications lose their individuality and are instead merged into another potential source of data.

D. The Lights and Shadows of the Communications System

The universal scope of Special Procedures' coverage and their easy accessibility are particularly valuable in a world where many states are not covered by specific regional systems of human rights protection, may not have ratified all the core UN international human rights instruments, or may have ratified them while accepting limited monitoring procedures. In addition, many Special Procedures cover issues and rights (food, health, housing, water, or poverty) or groups (minorities, indigenous peoples) for which international channels are limited or inexistent. Access to Special Procedures is also characterized by the lack of standard formalities, not requiring the exhaustion of domestic remedies, enabling a swift and flexible response to cases of human rights violations, that are unattainable to other international human rights bodies. The possibility of using publicity to exercise pressure over states and other concerned actors has reinforced the "naming and shaming" impact to which the effectiveness of their actions depends. Special Procedures have used press releases and other media outlets to reinforce their actions in relation to selected communications. The most salient example is provided by the widely reported findings of the six-month investigation carried out by the Special Rapporteur on extrajudicial, summary, or arbitrary detention into the killing of Mr. Khashoggi at the Saudi consulate in Turkey.[31] Along with other Special Procedures, the Special Rapporteur on executions, Agnes Callamard, had called for an international investigation

[31] OHCHR Press Release, "Khashoggi killing: UN human rights expert says Saudi Arabia is responsible for 'premediated execution'" (Geneva, June 19, 2019). For a detailed oral presentation of the findings and discussion, *see* Agnes Callamard, Tamara Cofman Wiittes, and Ted Piccone, "Investigating the Khashoggi murder: Insights from UN Special Rapporteur Agnes Callamard" (Podcast, The Brookings Institute, July 2, 2019) available at: https://www.brookings.edu/events/investigating-the-khashoggi-murder-insights-from-un-special-rapporteur-agnes-callamard/.

into the case and finally decided to take up that endeavor herself.[32] The content and diffusion of the resulting one-hundred-page document, published as an Annex to the official report of the Special Rapporteur and submitted to the Human Rights Council, is testimony of the power of a single individual to force states to publicly discuss a case that would have otherwise escaped any public intergovernmental scrutiny.[33] The extraordinary engagement of the Special Rapporteur with the Khashoggi affair is justified by the even more extraordinary circumstances surrounding his murder and the seriousness of the human rights violated, including the disappearances and killing of a journalist in the hands of a state. The case raises far-reaching issues of international responsibility, criminal and financial accountability, including those concerning the role of third parties in the commission of crimes or their remedy.

Most Special Procedures make daily decisions about what decisions will be handled without following clear rationale or informing the sources of the allegations. This is compounded by the fact that the overwhelming majority of communications are handled jointly with other Special Procedures. Therefore, it remains difficult to assess why particular communications may be acted upon: whether it is lack of resources or substantial merits of a particular case.[34] The communications' database has mitigated this problem by publishing details of all allegations sent to states, providing guidance to those approaching the system about the format and content of communications expected or more likely to yield positive outcomes. This information is further completed by the specific databases held by the Working Group on Arbitrary Detention.[35]

The better coordination among Special Procedures and the practice of handling communications jointly also, however, brings delays in processing them. Empirical data suggests that each additional mandate joining an urgent appeal delays it more than a week on average.[36]

[32] OHCHR Press Release, *Mandates of the Special Rapporteur on the promotion and protection of the right to freedom of opinion and expression, the Special Rapporteur on extrajudicial, summary, or arbitrary executions, and the Working Group on enforced or involuntary disappearances 20 November 2018 Excellency, It has now been six weeks since Saudi journalist Jamal Khashoggi has disappeared and was murdered in the Consulate of Saudi Arabia in Istanbul. The killing has had a profound impact on journalists and human rights defenders* (Geneva, November 20, 2018).

[33] *See* UN Doc. A/HRC/41/CRP.1 (19 June 2019).

[34] Janika Sannagel, *Chasing Shadows, A Quantitative Analysis of the Scope and Impact of UN Communications on Human Rights Defenders (2000–2016)* (Global Public Policy Institute, January 2018).

[35] Available at: https://www.unwgaddatabase.org/un/.

[36] Sannagel (2018) (n. 34): 12.

These weaknesses in the system are the inevitable cost of the flexibility and independence that has permitted the intervention of Special Procedures in individual cases in the first place. Any attempt to regulate admissibility criteria or standards to be followed by all Special Procedures will lead to treating all communications as sources of information rather than investigating and/or intervening to protect specific individuals. The absence of admissibility criteria, such as the exhaustion of domestic remedies, combined with the dependence on the credibility of the source and the demands for a prompt action by Special Procedures, can result in ill-founded or premature interventions and justified criticism of the work of mandate holders.

Experts should exercise extra caution when deciding to promote a particular case through media or other public platforms, including their own social media profiles, when they are acting as mandate holders of Special Procedures. Preserving their image as independent from their personal biases and agendas is vital to preventing damage to the whole system of Special Procedures. The tone and content of public statements discussed earlier, such as on the Assange case by the Special Rapporteur on torture, demonstrate the possibility of unfortunate backlash and criticism. The seriousness and urgency of the violations addressed in a public statement should be considered carefully before any condemnatory press release is issued. For instance, the statement signed by the Special Rapporteur in the field of cultural rights, the Chairperson of the Working Group on Business and Human Rights, and the Special Rapporteur on minority rights, regarding the closure of a London market as part of a gentrification project, may have been better confined to the realm of the report of activities and the databases of the Special Procedures.[37]

A freely available compilation of all internal and public as well as formal and informal rules guiding the practice of the Office of the High Commissioner for Human Rights when handling individual communications would significantly enhance the accessibility to Special Procedures. This would benefit users of human rights mechanisms and the persons charged with making them effective. Mandate holders, normally appointed for their knowledge of a particular topic, are not always familiar with treaty bodies or Charter bodies mechanisms. The same is true for the Secretariat, and even more for Junior Professional Officers and interns who contribute significantly to the

[37] OHCHR Press Release, *London market closure plan threatens "dynamic cultural centre"* (Geneva, July 27, 2017).

daily functioning of the Office. It has taken decades to introduce induction programs for new mandate holders. Newly appointed experts to treaty bodies have benefited since 2001 from technical briefings aimed at providing information about the functions to the treaty body on which they were elected to serve; on the support provided by the Secretariat; the relationship between their treaty body and the agencies and departments of the United Nations; the administrative regulations and practices of the United Nations affecting their conditions of services; and other relevant information.[38] In 2002, similar induction programs became available to mandate holders of Special Procedures.[39] Since 2009, the Coordination Committee is responsible for running the induction, facilitating the participation of former mandate holders.[40] Mandate holders are not UN employees and therefore cannot be forced to attend the induction program even when their agenda might coincide with a visit to Geneva during the annual meeting of Special Procedures.

The content of the necessary knowledge for new mandate holders should be widely available, not only to ensure access to recently appointed experts but also to those aspiring to the position. The chances are that those shortlisted for an interview as future Special Rapporteurs will engage with such material. The reprisals suffered by those cooperating with UN mechanisms on human rights as annually reported by the Secretary General suggest that such material should include, at the very least, clear guidelines that should direct interactions with those approaching Special Procedures.[41]

3. Visits

Visits provide direct knowledge of the situation under investigation as well as direct access to a variety of sources of information, including to grassroots-level organizations, individuals, groups, and communities not operating

[38] *See* UN Doc. HRI/MC/2001/2 (2001, *Review of Recent Development Relating to the Work of the Treaty Bodies—Status of the Annual Appeal 2001 of the Office of the United Nations High Commissioner for Human Rights and the Plans of Action Strengthening Support to and Enhancing the Effectiveness of the Treaty Bodies*, para. 14. On proposals to enhance skills and training regarding mandate holders of Special Procedures, *see also* UN Doc. E/CN.4/2000/5, para. 39.

[39] On the introduction of these training/induction sessions, *see* UN Doc. E/CN/4/2003/6 (2003) Annex, para. 16, and OHCHR Annual Report 2002; UN Doc. E/CN.4/2005/5 (2005) Annex, para. 22.

[40] Ted Piccone, *Catalysts for Change: How the UN's Independent Experts Promote Human Rights* (Brookings Institution Press, 2012): para. 50.

[41] Other recommendations to improve the system of communications have been put forward in Marc Limon, *Reform of the UN human rights petitions system* (URG, January 2018).

at UN level. They present a unique opportunity to assess the veracity of allegations, the reliability of governmental and non-governmental sources as well as the context in which they operate. Most visits focus on situations within a country, but international organizations such as the World Trade Organization, Food and Agriculture Organization, or the World Health Organization have also been the chosen destination for missions of mandate holders.[42] The Special Rapporteur on indigenous people has visited the traditional region of the Sami people in 2010 (unofficial visit) and in 2015, pioneered an initiative focusing on a group living across borders.[43]

The unorthodox origin of Special Procedures, as disconnected fact-finding bodies, has determined that competence to undertake visits on the ground was always considered inherent to the mechanism, although few decisions creating or renewing mandates refer explicitly to them. Both the Human Rights Council and former Commission have repeatedly called upon all states to accept visit requests from Special Procedures. Missions on the ground require the consent of the relevant state, although mandate holders have carried out alternative visits to access direct sources of information when they have not been able to secure an invitation.[44] Contrary to other Special Procedures' methods of work, the principles governing visits are fairly uniform and are set out in some details in their Manual of Operations. This section will not paraphrase them, focusing instead on features that are beyond the scope of the Manual.

The stated purpose of missions on the ground is "to assess the actual human rights situation in the country concerned, including an examination of the relevant institution, legal, judicial and administrative aspects and to make recommendations thereon in relation to issues that arise under the relevant mandate."[45] Several Special Procedures have discriminated between "types of visits," however, depending on whether the main objective sought is investigative or enhancing cooperation with the government of the concerned

[42] *See Report of the Special Rapporteur on the right to health to the World Health Organization*, UN Doc. E/CN.4/2004/49/Add.1 (4 March 2004); *Report of the Special Rapporteur on the right to food to the World Trade Organization*, UN Doc. A/HRC/10/5/Add.2 (4 February 2009); *Report of the Special Rapporteur on the right to food to the Food and Agriculture Organisation*, UN A/HRC/22/50/Add.3 (14 January 2013).

[43] This required the consent of the three states involved (Norway, Sweden, and Finland); *see* OHCHR Press Release, *UN rights expert to assess Sami people's self-determination and land and resource rights* (Geneva, August 24, 2015).

[44] *See, e.g.*, Ahmed Shaheed and Rose Parris Richter, "Coping Mechanisms for State Non-cooperation" in Nolan, Freedman, & Murphy (eds.), *The United Nations Special Procedures System* (Brill, 2017): 155, 172–5.

[45] *Manual of Operations of Special Procedures*, para. 53.

country. The first to introduce the concept was the Special Representative on human rights in El Salvador, who accepted the condition that he carry out the mission in his "personal capacity" to overcome the objections of the government to the legal nature of the mandate.[46] After announcing, in his second record, his readiness to carry out "on-site observation" to "assess the allegations transmitted by different sources on concrete cases and verify facts,"[47] the Special Rapporteur on torture proposed visits a year later, with the main aim of holding consultations with the concerned governments. In reference to a possible mission to a range of Latin-American (countries), he suggested a regional visit "with the purpose of exchanging views with governmental authorities, focusing in particular on remedial and preventive measures aimed at assisting in the eradication of the phenomenon of torture."[48] The subsequent report highlighted the consultative and preventative character of his visits and confirmed that the mission was not designed to investigate allegations on the ground.[49] This position was abandoned when the new mandate holder took over as Special Rapporteur in 1993. The Special Rapporteur on freedom of religion considered convenient "traditional visits" but also others aiming at facilitating the dialogue with governments.[50] The Expert on extreme poverty announced, in his first report, his intention to visit countries in which there was evidence of effective practices to overcome poverty.[51] The stated objective of the mission to the World Trade Organization by the Special Rapporteur on the right to health was to contribute constructively to the debate about the right to health and international trade.[52]

While visits that seek to facilitate cooperation with states may be considered better than no visit at all, they also involve breach of the terms of reference governing missions that Special Procedures expect governments to respect. The principles governing fact-finding missions by Special Procedures were drafted in 1999,[53] codifying the practice that had already been developed by mandate holders.[54] The "Terms of Reference for country

46 UN Doc. E/CN.4/1984/25 (1984), para. 10.
47 UN Doc. E/CN.4/1987/13 (1987), para. 22.
48 UN Doc. E/CN.4/1988/17 (1988), para. 22.
49 UN Doc. E/CN.4/1989/15 (1989), para. 34.
50 UN Doc. A/50/440 (1995), para. 34.
51 UN Doc. E/CN.4/2001/54 (2001) para. 35 and 41.
52 UN Doc. E/CN.4/2004/49/Add. 1 (1 March 2004), para. 2.
53 UN Doc. E/CN.4/1999/104 (1999), Annex II.
54 *See, e.g.*, report of the Special Rapporteur on Iran, UN Doc. E/CN.4/1990/24 (1990), para. 12; and Myanmar, UN A/50/568 (1995), section II.

visits by Special Procedures" were revised in 2016.[55] It has been repeatedly proven that their existence prevents conflict and misunderstanding that may arise during the visit and provide well-founded arguments to justify a denial to carry out a visit or to suspend it if these conditions are not met.[56] From a political and ethical point of view, it is sensitive and potentially damaging for the credibility of Special Procedures' to accept visits by agreeing to conditions that breach those terms of reference, particularly those referring to guarantees of freedom of movement during the visit, including to otherwise restricted areas, freedom of inquiry, including with all authorities and branches of government as well as civil society organizations and victims of human rights violations, among others. When mandate holders do not abide by their own standards, dependent on variable objectives, their work becomes more vulnerable to justified criticism.

Even more problematic are what some mandate holders have referred to as "informal visits" or "unofficial visits." The concept is intentionally obscure and has been applied to a range of missions that may or may not be funded or administratively supported by the Office of the High Commissioner and that may result (or not) in specific official reports. Official press releases have also been used to report about informal visits before and/or after they have been completed. For instance, on July 12, 2017, the Special Rapporteur on Belarus reported, through a press release, about his unofficial visit to the country, as a hopeful step forward toward the start of a dialogue on the situation of human rights in that territory.[57] Subsequent reports of the Special Rapporteur to the Council and the General Assembly do not provide further

[55] *See Revised Terms of Reference for country visits by Special Procedures mandate holders of the United Nations Human Rights Council (based on Appendix V, E/CN.4/1998/45)* (June 2016), available at: https://www.ohchr.org/EN/HRBodies/SP/Pages/TermsOfReference.aspx.

[56] *See, e.g.*, visit carried out by the mandates on executions and disappearances to the Republic Democratic of Congo, *Report of the joint mission charged with investigating allegations of massacres and other human rights violations occurring in eastern Zaire (now Democratic Republic of the Congo) since September 1996*, UN Doc. A/51/942 (1997), paras. 25–37; visit to Brazil by the Special Rapporteur on the sale of children, UN Doc. E/CN.4/1992/55/Add. 1, para. 3; or visit of the WGAD to Vietnam, UN Doc. E/CN.4/1995/31/Add. 4 (1995), para. 9. For criticism directed to the mandate on racism regarding missions, *see, e.g.*, Rudolf Beate, "The Thematic Rapporteurs and Working Groups of the United Nations Commission on Human Rights" 4 *Max Planck Yearbook on UN Law* (2000): 289, 323–4. On the conditions accepted by the Special Rapporteur on Myanmar during his first visits, *see* Jernon Allison, "Ad-hoc and extra-conventional means for human rights monitoring" in Paul C. Szasz (ed.), *Administrative and Expert Monitoring of International Treaties* (Ardsley, 1999): 21–48, 31–2, and the decision of the same mandate to halt a mission after discovering listening devices in interviews with prisoners, Dominic Whiting, *Bugged U.N. Envoy Urges Myanmar to Free Prisoners* (Reuters, March 26, 2003).

[57] OHCHR Press Release, *Back from an unofficial visit to Belarus, UN Special Rapporteur "hopeful" for dialogue on human rights* (Geneva, July 12, 2017).

details about the development or outcomes of such visit; neither is the visit listed on the website page of the Office of the High Commissioner that lists cumulative country visits since 1998.[58] Belarus has not accepted the request for a visit of this Special Rapporteur, whose mandate it does not recognize, nor have other requests for visits issued by other Special Procedures since 2009 been accepted. According to several media reports, the Special Rapporteur on human rights defenders also visited Belarus unofficially in April 2019.[59] The former mandate holder of the Special Procedure on freedom of assembly and association, Maina Kiai, reported on his personal website as Former Special Rapporteur, his unofficial visit to Cambodia, in February 2014. The press release provides information about a three-day unofficial visit involving meetings with a range of civil society, leaders, activists, and government officials (including the Secretary of State for the Ministry of Foreign Affairs) following months of massive post-election protest. During the visit, the Special Rapporteur suggested an invitation for a formal visit to call on the government to lift the ban on public assemblies.[60] Intriguingly, the report submitted to the Human Rights Council that year devotes a line to inform the Council about an "academic visit" to Cambodia organized by the Asian Forum for Human Rights and Development.[61] The Special Rapporteur on Cambodia had visited the country a few days earlier, but the press release does not refer to it, suggesting deviation of customary coordination with the geographic mandate. The joint unofficial visit to the city of Detroit by the former mandate holders on water and sanitation, Catarina de Albuquerque, and on adequate housing, Leilani Farha, is unique. Because of its unofficial nature, no report of the visit was published, a limitation the mandate holders sought to mitigate by securing wide media coverage.[62] They also used official press releases to provide information about the visit.[63] The visit to the Sami region in 2010 by the mandate on indigenous peoples also constitutes an unofficial visit, but its outcomes are published in a separate report that is

[58] Available at: https://www.ohchr.org/EN/HRBodies/SP/Pages/CountryandothervisitsSP.aspx.

[59] "UN Special Rapporteur on the Situation of Human Rights Defenders Michel Forst Advises Journalists to Contact Him Directly" (BAJ Press Service, April 17, 2019), available at: https://baj.by/en/content/un-special-rapporteur-situation-human-rights-defenders-michel-forst-advises-journalists.

[60] Maina Kai, "Kiai Makes Unofficial Visit to Cambodia, Calls on Government to Lift Ban on Public Assemblies," (February 10, 2014), available at: http://freeassembly.net/news/cambodia-unofficial-visit/.

[61] *See* UN Doc. A/HRC/26/29 (2014), para. 6.

[62] On this initiative, *see UN Special Procedures to advance human rights at home: A guide for US advocates* (The Columbia Human Entre Rights Law School Institute, July 2015).

[63] OHCHR Press Release, *Detroit: Disconnecting water from people who cannot pay—an affront to human rights, say UN experts* (June 25, 2014).

presented as containing general information on a conference attended by the Special Rapporteur in Finland.[64]

Unofficial visits raise challenges beyond the skewing of terms of reference that should guide the visits. Either experts are acting "unofficially" or as mandate holders of Special Procedures. They are not UN employees, and their immunities as "experts on mission" are functional privileges they enjoy when they are working on their mandates. As explained in different parts of this book, when addressing the application of the Code of Conduct (chapter two) and the institutional position of mandate holders (chapter six), the legal issues involved are not merely theoretical with several mandate holders having faced legal proceedings where their immunity and privileges have been contested. Also disputed is the value of visits for which no data is released. Acting independently but on behalf of the United Nations might be useful under certain circumstances, particularly when a state does not cooperate. However, it involves rewarding bad behavior by lowering standards applicable to all visits. It also undermines those standards as guidelines that can be changed depending on uncertain circumstances. Finally, it weakens the position of the mandate holders as institutionally attached to the United Nations, on which the authority of all their actions depends.

Mandate holders enjoy discretion in deciding the countries and institutions they wish to visit, unless they have received a specific mandate from the Human Rights Council or the General Assembly to visit a specific territory. Special Procedures' resources allow two or three visits per year, which means they must decide carefully which countries they will visit. Special Procedures that have published methods of work do not tend to include information on the rationale underpinning the selection of territories.[65] However, it is a well-established practice that thematic mandate holders will not seek a visit to a country for which a geographic Special Procedure is in force.[66] Some Special Procedures such as the Working Group on Arbitrary Detention replicate this rule in their methods of work. The Special Rapporteur on torture will not

[64] UN Doc. A/HRC/15/37/Add.6 (7 July 2010).

[65] An early example of explanations of criteria to decide visits is available on the 1988 report of the Special Rapporteur on summary executions, UN Doc. E/CN.4/1988/22 (1988), Annex, para. 10. *See also* conditions required to undertake a visit elaborated by the mandate on Iran, UN Doc. E/CN.4/1990/24 (1990), para. 12; and Myanmar, UN Doc. A/50/568 (1995), section II.

[66] *See Report of the annual meeting of Special Procedures*, UN Doc. E/CN.4/1998/45 (1998), para. 29.

visit countries investigated by the Committee Against Torture under its confidential procedure.[67]

By October 2019, 122 states had extended "standing invitations" to thematic mandates, a symbolic gesture of goodwill toward the system, which does not necessarily wave the requirement for the consent of the state prior to a visit in practice. The visits completed or requested since 1998, by country and by mandate, is published on the website of the Office of the High Commissioner for Human Rights and reveals that most states of the world have been visited to date.[68] However, the decisions on which countries are visited remain politically sensitive. A country receiving an invitation or a higher than average number of invitations will inevitably felt singled out. It is vital that Special Procedures seem to follow a coherent approach. This may involve rejecting direct invitations from states that are not a priority for their mandate or that may be using them for opportunistic purposes.[69]

4. Codification and Clarification of Human Rights Standards

The former UN Commission on Human Rights has been described as the International Law Commission for human rights. Special Procedures have contributed significantly to this function, now facilitated by the direct relationship between the Human Rights Council and the General Assembly.[70]

As early as 1972, the Ad Hoc Working Group of Experts on South Africa submitted a study to the Commission on the question of apartheid from the point of view of international penal law.[71] In 1976, the Commission on Human Rights ordered its Ad Hoc Working Group of Experts on

[67] *See* UN Docs. E/CN.4/1993/26 (1993), para. 17; E/CN.4/1997/7 (1997), Annex, para. 11; and E/CN.4/2003/68 (2003), Annex, para. 10.

[68] Although mandate holders were not particularly supportive of this idea. *See Implementation of recommendations of the second joint meeting of chairpersons and special mandate holders*, UN Doc. HRI/MC/2001/Misc.3 (8 June 2001).

[69] *See* Felice D. Gaer, "Picking and Choosing? Country Visits by Thematic Special Procedures" in Nolan, Freedman, and Murphy (eds.), *The United Nations Special Procedures System* (Brill, 2017).

[70] *See* David P. Forsythe and Baekkwan Park, "The Changing of the Guard: From the UN Human Rights Commission to the Council" 29(1–5) *Human Rights Law Journal* (2008): 3–14, 5; *see also* Dinah Shelton, "Standard-Setting by the United Nations Commission on Human Rights—An Overview from its Inception I 1947 until the Creation of the Human Rights Council in 2006" 29(1–5) *Human Rights Law Journal* (2008) 15–27.

[71] Egon Schwelb and Philip Alston, "The Principal Institutions and Other Bodies Founded Under the Charter" in Karel Vasak (ed.), *The International Dimensions of Human Rights* (UNESCO, 1982, vol. 1): 232–301, 290–1.

Southern Africa to evaluate the Declaration and Programme of Action of the International Seminar on the Eradication of Apartheid and in Support of the Struggle for Liberation in South Africa.[72] The contribution of Special Procedures to the codification of international human rights law since then, warrants concerted analysis on their working methods. The reports of Special Procedures have become a reference point in assessing the conceptual framework, obligations, and rights underpinning any human rights issue. They are cited by scholars, civil society organizations, and governmental and intergovernmental bodies as sources of authority and are now an important source of public international law. Their utility is also visible in opinio juris and state practice having been used by national courts and policymakers seeking to influence legislative change. Their width of coverage of issues is unmatched by any other human rights mechanism. As a consequence, it is safe to state that there is a Special Procedure for every well-established international human right but also to assert that many mandates cover issues emerging as new human rights even when openly contested by some states. The analysis of the contributions of Special Procedures to the codification of international norms further underscores how the political nature of the resolutions creating mandates has actually facilitated pioneering practices. The open-ended nature of these resolutions has allowed mandate holders to use a wide range of binding and non-binding national, regional, and international norms as normative frameworks to evaluate the information brought before them.

Some of the most salient contributions by Special Procedures to the development of international human rights standards have emerged as a direct result of the need to clarify their scope of competence. The creation of mandates with ill-defined scope in international human rights law, or that generate opposition among UN member states, have compelled mandate holders to clarify the confines of emerging areas of international human rights law that serve as the basis of their operations. The work of mandate holders has been fundamental to the acceptance of some topics as human rights. The mandates on the right to food or on water and sanitation are classic manifestations of this. Others, such as the Special Procedures on sexual orientation or unilateral coercive measures, remain actively opposed by states that consider their mandate as outside "human rights." Since several mandates focus on topics for which there is no international codification of reference and no international monitoring body, the delimitation of conceptual frameworks and

[72] *See* UNCHR Res. 8 (XXXII), 4 March 1976; and UNCHR Res. 6 (XXXIII), 4 March 1977.

content of the rights are original contributions to the field within international organizations.[73]

A. Conceptualization of Human Rights Issues through the Delimitation of Competence

Mandate holders of Special Procedures are formally required to evaluate the information they receive in the light of any internationally recognized human rights standards relevant to their mandate, as stated by the operative Paragraph 6 of their Code of Conduct, which codified a practice already well established among them. However, some mandates were created to monitor rights with no clear normative framework identified; for example, the mandates on foreign debt, the use of mercenaries as a means of impeding the right to self-determination, the right to water, and the right to food. Therefore, some mandate holders have had to focus on clarifying, and sometimes codifying, the human rights standards they are called upon to promote and implement.

i. Determining the Scope of Mandates

The oldest thematic procedure, the Working Group on Enforced or Involuntary Disappearances, has included thematic studies in its reports from its inception, relying on a wide range of international human rights instruments.[74] Its 1981 report included a study of the wide range of civil, political, economic, social, and cultural rights infringed by the practice of enforced or involuntary disappearances.[75] The Working Group based its analysis on the full range of relevant human rights instruments. These included the Universal Declaration of Human Rights (UDHR); the International Covenant on Economic, Social and Cultural Rights (ICESCR); the International Covenant on Civil and Political Rights (ICCPR); the American Declaration on the Rights and Duties of Man; the American Convention on Human Rights (ACHR); the European Convention on Human Rights

[73] A former version of this section is published in Elvira Domínguez-Redondo, "Human Rights Through the Backdoor: The Contribution of Special Procedures to the Normative Development of International Human Rights Law" in Carla Buckley, Alice Donald, and Philip Leach (eds.), *Towards Coherence in International Human Rights Law: Approaches of Regional and International Systems* (Brill, 2017): 543.

[74] For the original mandate *see* n. 9.

[75] UN Doc. E/CN.4/1435 (n. 10) paras. 184–7.

(ECHR); the Standard Minimum Rules for the Treatment of Prisoners;[76] and Additional Protocol 1 to the Geneva Convention of 12 August 1949, relating to the Protection of Victims of International Armed Conflicts. It also relied on other relevant resolutions of the General Assembly,[77] as well as the report of the Working Group on the situation of human rights in Chile.[78] In subsequent reports, the Working Group on Enforced or Involuntary Disappearances has been completing and updating its normative framework by focusing on other international human rights provisions potentially violated in relation to groups affected by disappearances such as children and mothers[79] or other relatives of the victims.[80]

The Special Rapporteur on arbitrary and summary execution is another early example of the breadth of normative standards used by Special Procedures to delimit the conceptual and legal contours of their mandates. From his first report in 1983, the then Special Rapporteur, Amos Vako, listed the international and national standards used to carry out his work, including the UDHR; ICCPR; ACHR; ECHR; the African Charter on Human and Peoples' Rights; commentaries of the Human Rights Committee; Code of Conduct of Law Enforcement Officials;[81] UN Declaration on the Protection of All Persons from Being Subjected to Torture and Other Cruel, Inhuman and Degrading Treatment;[82] Standard Minimum Rules for the Treatment of Prisoners;[83] Geneva Conventions of 1949 and their Protocols; Convention on the Prevention and Punishment of the Crime of Genocide; International Convention on the Suppression and Punishment of the Crime of Apartheid; and numerous General Assembly resolutions.[84]

In the context of delimiting the scope of his mandate, the first Special Rapporteur on torture, Peter Kooijmans, addressed the meaning of "torture" in international law in his first report, as well as the judicial and administrative measures available to prevent it and mitigate its effects.[85] The report contained an analysis of the conditions under which torture is normally

[76] ECOSOC Res. 663 C (XXIV), 31 July 1957.
[77] GA Res. 34/179, 17 December 1979; and GA Res. 35/188, 15 December 1980.
[78] Report of the Working Group A/33/331 (1978) (n. 4).
[79] *See* UN Docs. E/CN.4/1492 (1982) paras. 164–71; and E/CN.4/1984/21 (1984) paras. 151–61.
[80] UN Doc. E/CN.4/1984/21, at paras. 147–50.
[81] GA Res. 34/169, 17 December 1979.
[82] GA Res. 3452 (XXX), Annex, 9 December 1975.
[83] *See* n. 76.
[84] *See* UN Doc. E/CN.4/1983/16 (1983) at paras. 22–47. On the conceptual analysis of the scope of the mandate, *see* paras. 48–67.
[85] *See* UN Doc. E/CN.4/1986/15 (1986) paras. 22–54.

perpetrated.[86] More significantly, it introduced innovative approaches to the topic of torture. The Special Rapporteur was the first human rights monitoring body to recognize rape as a method of torture and to report on the use of gender-based torture such as rape, sexual assaults, and sexual threats.[87] Kooijmans was also ahead of his time when he examined the legal framework applicable to the trade of implements specially designed to implement torture in 1986.[88] This was a topic not properly considered by intergovernmental bodies until the twenty-first century, again by another mandate holder of the mandate on torture, Theo van Boven,[89] with the first—and still unique—set of multilateral trade controls set up by the European Union in 2005.[90]

In 2000, the Working Group on Arbitrary Detention issued its view on whether the deprivation of liberty of persons held at Al-Khaim prison in south Lebanon involved the responsibility of the government of Lebanon, Israel, or the South Lebanon Army.[91] With this opinion, the Working Group contributed to clarifying (or perhaps obscuring further) the fragmented jurisprudence regarding the need to evaluate attribution of unlawful acts of states, by endorsing the "overall test" doctrine established by the International Criminal Tribunal for Yugoslavia,[92] rather than approaches developed by other adjudicatory bodies, in particular the International Court of Justice.[93]

[86] Ibid. at paras. 112–7.

[87] UN Doc. E/CN.4/1986/15 (1986) para. 119. This has been repeatedly established by subsequent Special Rapporteurs and relevant case law. *See*, for instance, report of the Special Rapporteur on torture, UN Doc. A/HRC/7/3, at para. 36. On the significance and limitations of the recognition of rape as torture by the Special Rapporteur in 1986, *see* Deborah Blatt, "Recognizing Rape as a Method of Torture" 19(4) *New York University Review of Law and Social Change* (1992): 821, at 833 and 847. For a compilation of international jurisprudence on the topic, *see* "Redress for Rape: Using international jurisprudence on rape as a form of torture or other ill-treatment," 2013, available at: http://www.redress.org/downloads/publications/FINAL%20Rape%20as%20Torture%20(1).pdf.

[88] UN Doc. E/CN.4/1986/15 (n. 88) para. 120.

[89] *See* several studies on the situation of trade in and production of equipment that is specifically designed to inflict torture or other cruel, inhuman or degrading treatment, its origin, destinations and forms: UN Docs. E/CN/4./2005/62 (2005) paras. 12–39; E/CN.4/2004/56 (2004) 66–68; A/58/120 (2003) paras. 22–28; and E/CN.4/2003/69 (2003). Other failed attempts to codify the trade of torture equipment can be found in Abi Dymond and Joe Farha, "The trade in torture technologies," in ACAT, *A World of Torture* (ACAT-France, 2013): 243.

[90] *See* Council Regulation (EC) No. 1236/2005 of 27 June 2005 concerning trade in certain goods which could be used for capital punishment, torture or other cruel, inhuman or degrading treatment or punishment [2007] OJ L 200/1; and Regulation (EU) No. 1352/2011 of 20 December 2011 amending it (OJ L 338/31).

[91] UN Doc. E/CN.4/2000/4 (2000) paras. 11–18.

[92] Opinion of the Working Group on Arbitrary Detention 9/1998 (category III) "Handling of communications concerning detentions at the Al-Khaim prison (south Lebanon)," UN Doc. E/CN.4/2000/4, paras. 11–18.

[93] For a commentary, *see* Antonio Cassese, "The *Nicaragua* and *Tadić* Tests Revisited in Light of the ICJ Judgment on *Genocide in Bosnia*" 18(4) *European Journal of International Law* (2007): 649,

As already discussed, the debate surrounding the creation of a Special Procedure on water and sanitation highlighted the controversy over its status as a separate human right. The work of the Special Rapporteur, Catarina de Albuquerque, in explaining its substantive content was decisive in achieving its recognition through consensus via resolutions of the Human Rights Council and the General Assembly.[94]

ii. Replicating the Treaty Bodies: General Comments and Deliberations

The Working Group on Arbitrary Detention and the Working Group on Enforced or Involuntary Disappearances have drafted the equivalent of "general comments/observations" following a model pioneered by treaty bodies. The Working Group on Enforced or Involuntary Disappearances uses the same terminology as the treaty bodies[95] and devoted its first six "general comments," issued between 1996 and 2006, to the interpretation of specific Articles of the Declaration on the Protection of All Persons from Enforced Disappearance.[96] Since the creation of the Human Rights Council, such comments have addressed topics other than Articles of the Declaration, including the definition of enforced disappearance;[97] disappearance as a crime against humanity[98] and as a continuous crime;[99] the right to truth;[100] the right to recognition as a person before the law;[101] and the specificity of disappearances when affecting children[102] and women.[103]

The Working Group on Arbitrary Detention uses the terminology "deliberations." Most of its deliberations are related to particular cases that raise matters of a general nature, the aim being to provide consistent

especially at n. 19. *See also* James Crawford, *State Responsibility* (Cambridge University Press, 2013): at 141.

[94] *See* GA Res. 64/292 (2010) and 68/157 (2013); *see also* HR Council Res. 15/9 (2010) and 24/18 (2013).

[95] *See* UN Doc. E/CN.4/1997/34 (1997) paras. 20 and 21.

[96] *See* UN Docs. E/CN.4/1996/38 (1996) paras. 48–58 (Articles 3 and 4); E/CN.4/1997/34 (1997) paras. 22–30 (Article 10); E/CN.4/1998/43 (1998) paras. 68–75; E/CN.4/2001/68 (2001) paras. 25–32 (Article 17); and E/CN.4/2006/56 (2006) para. 49 (Article 18).

[97] UN Doc. A/HRC/7/2 (2 January 2008) para. 26.

[98] UN Doc. A/HRC/13/31 (21 December 2009) para. 39.

[99] UN Doc. A/HRC/16/48 (26 January 2011) para. 39.

[100] Ibid.

[101] UN Doc. A/HRC/19/8/Rev.1 (2 March 2012) para. 42.

[102] UN Docs. A/HRC/WGEID/98/1; and A/HRC/WGEID/98/1/Corr.1 (14 February 2013).

[103] UN Doc. A/HRC/WGEID/98/2 (14 February 2013).

precedents in order to assist as many states as possible to prevent the practice of arbitrary deprivation of liberty.[104]

These deliberations offer another striking example of the potential to use Special Procedures to question the practice of other bodies operating at an international level on concomitant issues. The Working Group on Arbitrary Detention accepted a complaint brought by General Duško Tadić, which challenged the legality of his detention by the International Criminal Tribunal for the Former Yugoslavia on the basis of Article 9 of the ICCPR (the right to liberty and security).[105] The Group finally accepted its lack of competence to express a view on the conformity of a decision taken by an international court within the norms of international law. It did, however, decide that this raised an interpretation problem and adopted a "deliberation" that would guide the Group in the future if other communications relating to the administration of justice by an international criminal court were brought before it.[106] The Working Group re-engaged with this topic in relation to the arrest of Joseph Kanyabashi, which raised the issue of the legality of the establishment of the International Criminal Tribunal for Rwanda.[107] This was the first time a Special Procedure had examined the legality of the practice of another UN body, in particular one established as a subsidiary organ of the Security Council.

The Special Rapporteur on the promotion and protection of human rights and fundamental freedoms while countering terrorism has since examined the question of the compliance with human rights standards by the United Nations by assessing the role of the General Assembly, the Security Council, and UN field presences in antiterrorist activities.[108] The Special Rapporteur has concluded that Chapter VII of the UN Charter does not provide a legal basis for the Security Council framework of mandatory resolutions of a quasi-legislative or quasi-judicial nature;[109] has commented on the compatibility of the mandate of the Office of the Ombudsperson of the Security Council with international human rights norms using case law from treaty bodies, the European Court of Human Rights, and British and Swiss domestic courts,

[104] A compilation of its nine deliberations—covering the issues of house arrest; rehabilitation through labor; immigrants and asylum seekers; allegations against the International Criminal Court for the former Yugoslavia; psychiatric detention; and deprivation of liberty linked to the use of the internet—is available at: https://www.ohchr.org/EN/Issues/Detention/Pages/Deliberations.aspx.

[105] UN Doc. E/CN.4/2001/14 (2001) paras. 12–33.

[106] Ibid.

[107] UN Doc. E/CN.4/2003/8 (2003) paras. 49–60.

[108] *See* UN Doc. A/65/258 (6 August 2010).

[109] Ibid. at paras. 33–58.

among others;[110] and has recommended a means of improving the accountability of the United Nations in this area.[111]

General comments and deliberations issued by the working groups use a variety of international and regional instruments as their normative framework. These include references to the American Convention on Human Rights, the Rome Statute of the International Criminal Court, the Inter-American Convention on Forced Disappearances of Persons, the Hague Convention concerning the Laws and Customs of War, and the Geneva Conventions of 1949, among others. Leading case law articulated by other treaty bodies and international and regional courts is also frequently cited.

B. Codification of New International Human Rights Instruments

Exceptionally, Special Procedures have been created with the main mandate of contributing to the codification of a particular area of law. This trend commenced with the articulation in 1986,[112] of the Special Rapporteur on freedom of religion or belief, who is mandated to examine incidents and governmental actions incompatible with the Declaration on the Elimination of All Forms of Intolerance and Discrimination Based on Religion or Belief[113] in addition to recommending remedial measures.[114] The international standards considered by the Special Rapporteur extend beyond this instrument, as laid out in the digest published by the mandate holder in 2011, on the twenty-fifth anniversary of the creation of the mandate.[115] The standards include the UDHR, most core human rights instruments, and the general comments of different treaty bodies.

This section outlines some of the most salient initiatives by Special Procedures that have been endorsed or approved by their parent bodies, therefore endowing them with special authority. These new human rights standards serve as international benchmarks in a variety of areas. They

[110] *See* UN Doc. A/67/396 (26 September 2012) paras. 12–58.

[111] Ibid. paras. 68–80.

[112] UNCHR Res. 1986/20, 10 March 1986.

[113] GA Res. 31/138, 16 December 1976.

[114] This remains a central part of its mandate, as reiterated in HR Council Res. 6/37, 14 December 2007, at para. 18(c).

[115] Rapporteur's Digest on Freedom of Religion or Belief, 2011, available at: http://www.ohchr.org/Documents/Issues/Religion/RapporteursDigestFreedomReligionBelief.pdf.

enjoy a special position among other normative contributions by Special Procedures because they have been adopted or endorsed by the Human Rights Council (or former Commission) or/and the General Assembly. In the absence of specific restrictions on the geographic scope of their mandates, or the sources they can use in the course of their work, these codification efforts have involved the consideration of a topic from a universal perspective, considering the contributions of governmental, intergovernmental and non-governmental actors worldwide. In that sense, the normative standards developed by Special Procedures function as a catalyst for efforts to conceptualize and codify human rights worldwide.

The Working Group on Enforced or Involuntary Disappearances has pioneered codification of a new international instrument among Special Procedures—the Declaration on the Protection of All Persons from Enforced Disappearance,[116] the immediate precedent for the Convention with the same name adopted fourteen years later.[117] The Working Group instigated adoption by the UN General Assembly of the Declaration[118] and contributed substantially to the final draft.[119] The Working Group oversees states' implementation of the Declaration, which constitutes the main legal framework within which it carries out its mandate.[120]

The Special Rapporteur on the human rights of internally displaced persons[121] understood that the main aim of his mandate was the elaboration of a specific norm for internally displaced people, and framed the Guiding Principles on Internal Displacement,[122] focusing his work on the preparation of such guidelines and their distribution and promotion.[123] The Guiding

[116] GA Res. 47/133, 18 December 1992.

[117] International Convention for the Protection of All Persons from Enforced Disappearance, adopted by GA Res. 61/177, 20 December 2006 (in force since 23 December 2010).

[118] *See* the recommendations of the Group enshrined in its reports UN Docs. E/CN.4/1985/15, at para. 302; and E/CN.4/1988/19, at para. 251(b).

[119] UN Doc. E/CN.4/1990/13, at paras. 28–38.

[120] *See* Revised Methods of Work of the Working Group on Enforced or Involuntary Disappearances, UN Doc. A/HRC/19/58/Rev.1, Annex II, adopted on 11 November 2011 and applicable from 1 January 2012, at para. 1.

[121] Until 2010, the mandate holder was a Representative of the Secretary General. On the decision to change the denomination, *see* HR Council Res. 14/6, 23 June 2010. For the original mandate, *see* UNCHR Res. 1991/25, 5 March 1991; UNCHR Res. 1992/73, 5 March 1992; and UNCHR Res. 1994/68, 9 March 1994.

[122] *See* UN Doc. E/CN.4/1998/53/Add.2 (1998). On the background and process of framing these principles, *see* Simon Bagshaw, "Internally Displaced Persons at the Fifty-Fourth Session of the United Nations Commission on Human Rights, 16 March–24 April 1998" 10(3) *International Journal of Refugee Law* (1998): 548; and Walter Kälin, *Guiding Principles on Internal Displacement: Annotations* (American Society of International Law, 2000).

[123] Latest mandate for this Special Procedure can be found in HR Council Res. 23/8, 13 June 2013.

Principles have been further complemented by a handbook[124] and legal annotations.[125]

In 2011 the Human Rights Council formally endorsed[126] the Guiding Principles on Business and Human Rights,[127] and a year later adopted[128] Guiding Principles on Extreme Poverty and Human Rights.[129] Also in 2012, the Human Rights Council endorsed Guiding Principles on Foreign Debt and Human Rights.[130] These sets of Guiding Principles were drafted by the Special Rapporteurs with mandates on the concerned topic. These three sets of Guiding Principles provide global policy guidelines on issues not codified in international law and are now widely used to evaluate state behavior in relation to displacement of people, poverty, and business and human rights.[131]

Some Guiding Principles have had a measurable impact on legislation and policies. The Guiding Principles on Business and Human Rights seeking the implementation of the "protect, respect and remedy" framework have been endorsed by governments, businesses, civil society, workers organizations, national human rights institutions, and investors.[132] The case of Colombia, where the Guiding Principles have been used as a basis for decisions of its Constitutional Court, is a particularly outstanding illustration of the impact of the Special Procedures on state practice.[133] Many other examples confirm the influence of Guiding Principles at national, regional, and international level.[134]

[124] UNHCR, *Handbook for the Protection of Internally Displaced Persons* (Global Protection Cluster Working Group, 2010).

[125] Kälin (n. 123).

[126] HR Council Res. 17/4, 16 June 2011, at operative para. 1.

[127] *See* n. 132. For a resource center devoted to the Guiding Principles, *see* http://business-humanrights.org/UNGuidingPrinciplesPortal/Home.

[128] HR Council Res. 21/11, 27 September 2012, at para. 2. In political terms it is important to notice that in this case the Council "adopts" rather than "endorses" the Guiding Principles.

[129] Sepúlveda Carmona, *Final draft of the guiding principles on extreme poverty and human rights*, UN Doc. A/HRC/21/38.

[130] *See* UN Doc. A/HRC/20/23/ 10 April 2011; and HR Council Res. 20/10, 5 July 2012.

[131] For instance, the Guiding Principles on extreme poverty were mentioned in the European Committee of Social Rights' decision on the merits in *Defence for Children International (DCI) v. Belgium* (69/2011) Merits, 23 October 2012, at para. 81.

[132] UN Doc A/HRC/17/31 (21 March 2011) para. 7.

[133] Cepeda Espinosa, "The Constitutional Protection of IDPs in Colombia" in Arango Rivadeneira (ed.), *Judicial Protection of Internally Displaced Persons: The Colombian Experience* (Brookings Institution/University of Bern, 2009): 1.

[134] Jessica Wyndham, "A Developing Trend: Laws and Policies on Internal Displacement" 14(1) *Human Rights Brief* (2006): 7; and Marion Couldrey and Maurice Herson (eds.), "Ten Years of the Guiding Principles on Internal Displacement" Special Issue *Forced Migration Review* (2008).

C. Handbooks and Guidelines

Mandate holders cooperate with the OHCHR in drafting manuals, guides, and other publications directly related to their mandates. These have not always been endorsed by a political body but nonetheless enjoy a particular weight in addressing and codifying the content of rights without clear legal boundaries. Besides the Handbook for the Protection of Internally Displaced Persons cited earlier, other examples include the participation of the Special Rapporteur on torture in the drafting of the Manual on the Effective Investigation and Documentation of Torture and Other Cruel, Inhuman or Degrading Treatment or Punishment (Istanbul Protocol)[135] and the Handbook for realizing the human right to safe drinking water and sanitation prepared by the Special Rapporteur on the human right to water.[136] The Special Rapporteur on hazardous waste has prepared guidelines for good practice in relation to the human rights obligations related to the environmentally sound management and disposal of hazardous substances and wastes.[137]

In the context of the preparation of international human rights conferences, the experts in charge of Special Procedures have, since 2015, also contributed to studies that clarify existing normative frameworks and draw attention to the need for new regulations where appropriate.[138]

[135] *See* HR/P/PT/8/Rev.1. The Manual was itself inspired by the *Manual on the Effective Prevention and Investigation of Extra-Legal, Arbitrary and Summary Executions*, UN Doc. A/54/426, (10 October 1999) paras. 53–5.

[136] *See Realising the Human Rights to Water and Sanitation: A Handbook by the UN Special Rapporteur Catarina de Albuquerque* (2004), available at: http://www.ohchr.org/Documents/Issues/Water/Handbook/Book1_intro_.pdf; OHCHR, *United Nations Special procedures: Facts and Figures 2013* (OHCHR, 2014): at 6 and 7. This document highlights other contributions to standard setting during 2013 by the mandates on the use of mercenaries, trafficking in persons, countering terrorism, torture, summary executions, and freedom of religion.

[137] UN Doc. A/HRC/36/41 (20 July 2017).

[138] *See*, for instance, the two thematic studies by the Special Rapporteur on religious freedom prepared, in 2000, for the International Conference on Racism, analyzing the issue of "aggravated discrimination": UN Doc. A/CONF.189/PC.1/7, Annex; and "legal and factual aspects of racial discrimination in education": UN Doc. A/CONF.189/PC.2/22, Annex 2. *See also*, in relation to the same conference, the contribution made by the Special Rapporteur on the rights of migrants, UN Doc. A/CONF.189/PC.2/23.

D. Risk of Fragmentation: The Case of "Hate Speech"

The controversy over the cartoons portraying the Prophet Muhammad, published on September 30, 2005, by the Danish newspaper *Jyllnadds-Posten*,[139] provides a striking example of contradictory approaches by Special Procedures mandates. In this instance, the Human Rights Council requested a joint report by its mandate holders on racism and on freedom of religion on the question of incitement to racial and religious hatred.[140] In their final reports, the two mandate holders took divergent positions, which had the effect of fueling rather than assuaging the controversy.[141]

The Special Rapporteur on contemporary forms of racism, racial discrimination, xenophobia, and related intolerance, Doudou Diène, unequivocally expressed his condemnation of the cartoons, labeling them "racist." As explained by Keane,[142] the position of Doudou Diène was already well established in the context of drawing the conceptual contours of his report "Defamation of religion and Global Efforts to Combat Racism: Anti-Semitism, Christianophobia and Islamophobia,"[143] in which he based his analysis on Article 18 (freedom of religion) and Article 19 (freedom of expression) of the ICCPR.[144] According to the Special Rapporteur, the cartoons reflected "an alarming resurgence of defamation of religions . . . [and] failed to show the commitment and vigilance that [the Danish government] normally displays in combating religious intolerance and incitement to religious hatred."[145] Diène used the joint report[146] to reaffirm his previous position on the defamation of religions and what he viewed as the relationship with racist trends promoting racial and religious hatred in the context of the post-9/11 "war on terror."

[139] *See* Marion Müller and Esra Özcan, "The Political Iconography of Muhammad Cartoons: Understanding Cultural Conflict and Political Action" 40(2) *Political Sciences and Politics* (2007): 287.

[140] *See* HR Council Decision 1/107, 30 June 2006, decided by a recorded vote of 33 votes to 12, with 1 abstention. The votes against came from Canada, the Czech Republic, Finland, France, Germany, Japan, the Netherlands, Poland, Romania, Switzerland, the Ukraine, and the United Kingdom; the Republic of Korea abstained.

[141] Joint Report, "Incitement to Racial and Religious Hatred and the Promotion of Tolerance," UN Doc. A/HRC/2/3 (20 September 2008).

[142] David Keane, "Cartoon Violence and Freedom of Expression" 30(4) *Human Rights Quarterly* (2008): 845.

[143] *See* report submitted by Diène, UN Doc. E/CN.4/2006/17, following the request in UNCHR Res. 2005/3, 12 April 2005, at para. 16.

[144] UN Doc. E/CN.4/2006/17 (2006) paras. 23–47.

[145] Ibid. para. 25.

[146] UN Doc. A/HRC/2/3 (n. 141).

Meanwhile the Special Rapporteur on freedom of religion or belief, Asma Jahangir, adopted a more cautious approach toward limiting freedom of expression. Rather, that Special Rapporteur emphasized the distinction between racism and religious defamation.[147]

At the heart of these seemingly contradictory positions are the different normative frameworks and interpretations used by each mandate holder in addressing the topic. The Human Rights Council had requested the mandate holders to examine the question under Article 20(2) of the ICCPR which prohibits "hate speech";[148] however, the joint report also engaged Article 4 of the International Convention on the Elimination of All Forms of Racial Discrimination (ICERD).[149] In Keane's words:

> Jahangir's comments are representative of the legal instruments that govern racial discrimination and religious intolerance. While racist speech is prohibited under Article 4 of the binding International Convention on the Elimination of Racial Discrimination 1965, no comparable international instrument exists in the area of religion. Her analysis was conducted solely under Article 20(2) ICCPR, and the Danish cartoons do not reach the required level to constitute incitement under this provision. Diène seems to associate the cartoons with racist propaganda, as prohibited by Article 4 ICERD. Jahangir appears not to agree with this assessment.[150]

In 2008, the Special Rapporteur on freedom of expression, Ambeyi Ligabo, provided his own understanding of the legal restrictions on freedom of expression.[151] Without referring to the report of his peers, he underlined his strong stance against defamation laws, a stance already published in 2002 along with the Organisation for Security and Co-operation in Europe (OSCE) Representative on freedom of the media, and the Organization of American

[147] *See* Javaid Rehman, "The Sharī'ah, International Human Rights Law and the Right to Hold Opinions and Free Expression: After Bilour's Fatwā" in Marie-Luisa Frick and Andreas Th. Müller (eds.), *Islam and International Law: Engaging Self-Centrism from a Plurality of Perspectives* (Martinus Nijhoff, 2013): 244, particularly at 252.

[148] Article 20(2) ICCPR provides: "Any advocacy of national, racial or religious hatred that constitutes incitement to discrimination, hostility or violence shall be prohibited by law."

[149] Article 4 ICERD provides: "States Parties condemn all propaganda and all organizations which are based on ideas or theories of superiority of one race or group of persons of one colour or ethnic origin, or which attempt to justify or promote racial hatred and discrimination in any form, and undertake to adopt immediate and positive measures designed to eradicate all incitement to, or acts of, such discrimination."

[150] Keane (2008) (n. 142): 872.

[151] UN Doc. A/HRC/7/14, at paras. 30–53.

States (OAS) Special Rapporteur on freedom of expression.[152] Complicating matters further, the Committee on the Elimination of Racial Discrimination, which monitors implementation of the ICERD, took a similar stance as the Special Rapporteur on racism.[153] For their part, the successors as Special Rapporteurs on religion and racism took a slightly different approach to their predecessors, underlining the importance of framing this issue within the existing human rights framework instead of viewing it as a matter of defamation of religion.[154]

These divergent approaches to the same topic within the United Nations were a catalyst for dialogue and cooperation among the Special Rapporteurs involved in the interpretation and implementation of international standards on freedom of expression, freedom of religion, and racial discrimination. This resulted in the emergence of consensus regarding some of the most controversial issues, such as blasphemy laws, and a departure from a focus on "defamation of religion."[155] On April 22, 2009, the Special Rapporteurs on racism, freedom of religion, and freedom of expression issued a joint statement enshrining a common view on "defamation of religion."[156] The Office of the High Commissioner for Human Rights hosted a multilateral discussion on the relationship between Articles 19 and 20 of the ICCPR, which took place in the context of expert workshops held in 2011, in Europe, Africa, and Asia. The aim of these workshops was to arrive at a "comprehensive assessment of the implementation of legislation, jurisprudence and policies regarding advocacy of national, racial or religious hatred that constitutes incitement to discrimination, hostility or violence at the national and regional levels, while

152 Ibid. at para. 43.

153 Keane (2008) (n. 142): 873–4.

154 A summary of the discussion and the positions held by the Chair of the Committee on the Elimination of Racial Discrimination at the time, Anwar Kemal, and the newly appointed Special Rapporteurs on racism, Githu Muigai, and on freedom of religion and belief, Heiner Bieledfedt, can be found in International Service for Human Rights (ISHR), "Support for 'defamation of religion' continues to decline; draft resolutions passes by only 12 votes," Press Release, November 25, 2010, available at: http://www.ishr.ch/news/support-defamation-religion-continues-decline-draft-resolution-passes-only-12-votes.

155 However, this does not mean that states within the Organisation of Islamic Cooperation have abandoned their positions on this topic; *see* Javaid Rehman and Stephanie Berry, "Is 'Defamation of Religions' Passé? The United Nations, Organisation of Islamic Cooperation, and Islamic State Practices: Lessons from Pakistan" 44(3) *The George Washington International Law Review* (2012): 431.

156 Joint Statement by Mr. Githu Muigai, Special Rapporteur on contemporary forms of racism, racial discrimination, xenophobia and related intolerance, Ms. Asma Jahangir, Special Rapporteur on freedom of religion and belief, and Mr. Frank La Rue, Special Rapporteur on the promotion and protection of the right to freedom of opinion and expression, "Freedom of expression and incitement to racial or religious hatred," April 22, 2009, available at: http://www2.ohchr.org/english/issues/racism/rapporteur/docs/Joint_Statement_SRs.pdf.

encouraging full respect for freedom of expression as protected by international human rights law."[157] Members of the Human Rights Committee, the Committee on the Elimination of Racial Discrimination, and the mandate holders of Special Procedures on racism, freedom of religion, and freedom of expression participated in several working groups.[158] The outcome report states a common UN position on the interpretation of Articles 19 and 20 of the ICCPR and Article 4 of the ICERD, with specific recommendations to states on how to incorporate human rights legislation at domestic level.

The conclusions regarding policies aimed at states, the United Nations, and other stakeholders do little beyond acknowledging the importance of cooperating and sharing information between the various regional and cross-regional mechanisms working on these issues worldwide. Still, it can only be welcome that the dialogue served as the immediate precedent for the adoption of General Comment No. 34 on freedoms of opinion and expression by the Human Rights Committee in July 2011.[159] The interpretation of the ICCPR by the three special rapporteurs was considered in the drafting process of the general comment.[160] The discussion also seems to have prompted the Committee on the Elimination of Racial Discrimination to revisit Article 4 of the ICERD and to issue its General Recommendation No. 35 on combating racist hate speech, in September 2013.[161] While the Committee reiterates its belief that laws are needed to combat racist speech, it also took a more balanced view to the issue, favoring the Jahangir rather than the Diène approach, and seeking a more synchronized approach with other UN treaties.

5. Conclusions

Mandate holders have drawn on the potential advantages of vague political mandates to implement practices that would have needed years of

[157] *See* "Rabat Plan of Action," OHCHR Press Release, 2013, available at: http://www.ohchr.org/EN/Issues/FreedomReligion/Pages/RabatPlanOfAction.aspx.

[158] The documentation resulting from these workshops, stakeholders' positions and background papers is available at: http://www.ohchr.org/EN/Issues/FreedomOpinion/Articles19-20/Pages/Index.aspx.

[159] General Comment No. 34, Article 19: Freedoms of opinion and expression, CCPR/C/GC/34.

[160] Michael O'Flaherty, "Freedom of Expression: Article 19 of the International Covenant on Civil and Political Rights and the Human Rights Committee's General Comment No 34" 12(4) *Human Rights Law Review* (2012): 627, at 648 and 650–1.

[161] General Recommendation No. 35: Combating racist hate speech, CERD/C/GC/35.

negotiations with uncertain outcomes if they had to be enshrined in a legal or quasi-legal document. However, for the system to gain further robustness, it remains important that several weaknesses presented here are eliminated and that the entire system gain a degree of transparency that would assist all stakeholders and, particularly, victims of human rights violations. Wearing a double hat as being independent from, but simultaneously representing the United Nations, is a legal impossibility that is nonetheless performed by Special Procedures on a regular basis. Their methods of work in handling communications, undertaking missions on the ground, and contributing to the normative development of international human rights law typify the influence of the unique combination of politicization and independence characterizing Special Procedures analyzed throughout the former chapters.

Independent experts apply legal standards in assessing the relevance of communications on human rights violations in terms of compliance of human rights standards by states and, increasingly, non-state actors. Many crucial issues have been resolved including the legitimacy of receiving and acting on communications and the prospect of their being handled by a number of different channels simultaneously. The implicit or explicit endorsement by states of the interference into their sovereignty through the methods of work adopted by Special Procedures, without requiring standardized admissibility criteria has widened access to Special Procedures to all individuals, groups, and communities worldwide. However, the absence of these constraints also yields discretionary approaches, leaving victims, states, and other sources of information in the dark regarding what to expect from different mandates and mandate holders. Increased cooperation among Special Procedures, reflected in the mainstreaming of joint actions, may mean significant costs in terms of effectiveness.

Different interpretation of mandates and roles, depending on the personality of the expert, financial resources or political sensitivity permeates the modus operandi of Special Procedures and makes them, at times, unpredictable. It is not always possible to identify the rationale underpinning decisions about individual communications or visits on the ground that may breach their own rules, depending on political opportunism. Their relationship with the Human Rights Council and the General Assembly provides a direct door to impact changes in international law norms.

The disconnected and negotiated political environment that decides the creation of mandates allows experts to continue to operate as individual mechanisms, immune to any form of "collective discipline." Nor is it desirable. Irrespective of the differentiated history of the Special Procedures, they are now configured and perceived as a unit. As a consequence, a misguided decision of one expert may well undermine the work of the others. In this context it is imperative that Special Procedures' mandate holders reflect further on potential bad practices regarding the use of public channels at their disposal to reinforce their actions. The appointment of new mandate holders, based on their expertise, does not ensure enough understanding of the institutions in which they must develop their work. A remedial measure could be introduced through more effective induction materials, available to all candidates aspiring to a position within the system of Special Procedures. The ambiguity between "official" and "unofficial" is close to a misunderstanding that is construed between the "personal" and the "professional." This short-term haziness may appear attractive and may prove beneficial in the short and medium terms, enabling capitalization on specific opportunities to further progress a given right or geographic mandate. However, it would cause longer-term damage unless consistent expectations are provided and communicated in a transparent manner that seek to safeguard, enhance, and strengthen the Special Procedures as a whole.

Six

Politics of "Independence"

Position of Special Procedures within the United Nations

1. Introduction

Special Procedures are conducted by independent expert who must live up to high standards of impartiality and objectivity to become eligible candidates and perform their functions without damaging the legitimacy of the mandates under their competence. However, political considerations permeate every aspect of the work of mandate holders even before they are appointed. The selection process of mandate holders of Special Procedures has been reformulated on several occasions and has become better regulated while remaining deeply anchored to political considerations and subject to a wide margin of discretion.

The mandate holders hold an unpaid and part-time position and are largely unregulated in terms of their legal standing within the UN machinery. They are normally appointed for three years (thematic mandates) or one year (country mandates) with a maximum tenure of six years. The content of their mandate may also suffer significant modifications derived from annual decisions of the Human Rights Council or the General Assembly, both intergovernmental bodies. The Security Council has no formal relationship with the Special Procedures, but mandate holders have interacted with its members using existing channels and pioneering others. The following paragraphs also outline the decisive role of the Office of the High Commissioner on Human Rights on Special Procedures.

Despite the categorization of Special Procedures as a "system" and their long trajectory within the UN machinery, the institutional status of mandate holders remains an unresolved issue potentially impacting their authority and legitimacy. The following pages will also explore the normative, conceptual, and practical issues associated with this anomaly, analyzing arguments that support divergent views. The ambiguity of the legal status of Special

In Defense of Politicization of Human Rights. Elvira Domínguez-Redondo, Oxford University Press (2020).
 DOI: 10.1093/oso/9780197516706.001.0001

Procedures has been used profusely by mandate holders to advance their agendas, achieving remarkable results. However, it makes them more vulnerable to attacks from states, and at times, specific mandate holders have adopted misguided understandings of their independence without considering their position within the UN system. While gray areas have benefited more than disadvantaged the work of Special Procedures, this is not the case in relation to their institutional position since it determines the relevance, nature, and status of their outputs and the validity of their activities. A more thoughtful approach to this issue, within the politicized environment surrounding their work, will also benefit the complex relationship between Special Procedures and the Office of the High Commissioner.

2. The Politics of Selecting and Naming Mandate Holders

Special Procedures are subsidiary bodies of the Human Rights Council, which is also the body appointing mandate holders. The first mandate holders' appointment did not follow a uniform procedure. The Economic and Social Council Resolution 9(II) of June 21, 1946, precursor of current practice, was used as normative basis for some cases (e.g., Working Group on South Africa and the Special Rapporteur on Equatorial Guinea). Other mandate holders (e.g., Working Groups on Chile and occupied territories) were appointed on the basis of the Economic and Social Council Resolution 100 (V) of August 12, 1947. The first mandate holders were appointed in their personal capacity but were selected from among the governmental representatives of the Commission of Human Rights, raising questions about their independence at the time.[1] Subsequent decisions determined that mandate holders could not be members of any intergovernmental organ. Following well-established practice, formalized by the Commission on Human Rights Resolution 1993/94 of March 11, 1993, and Decision 2000/109 of April 26, 2000, experts were appointed by the President of the Commission following consultations with the Bureau and the regional groups. The decision in 2000 requested the Office of the High Commissioner for Human Rights to maintain an updated list of

[1] *See, e.g.*, Theo van Boven, "Fact-finding in the field of human rights" 3 *Israel Yearbook of Human Rights* (1973): 93, 97; Robert Miller, "United Nations Fact-finding Missions in the Field of Human Rights" *Australian Year Book of International Law* (1970–73): 40, 44, and 54; and "Membership of the Working Group on Enforced and Involuntary Disappearances: Opinion of the Officer of Legal Affairs, Dated 15 September 1989" in Bertrand Ramcharan, *The principle of legality in International Human Rights Institutions. Selected Legal Opinions* (Martinus Nijhoff Publishers, 1997): 135.

candidates published on its website, containing their names and curriculum vitae. States, the Secretariat, and all other possible sources, including non-governmental organizations with consultative status before the Economic and Social Council, were encouraged to propose candidates. The President of the fifty-seventh session of the Commission (2001) expressly authorized all non-governmental organizations to suggest candidates. In practice, it was unclear how the Secretariat or non-governmental organizations could put forward candidates since no procedure existed for such endeavors. The Office of the High Commissioner took over five years to implement this mandate, revealing reticence in enabling greater transparency in the selection of mandate holders.

The institution-building resolution of the Council outlined a new procedure of selection and appointment of mandate holders in 2007, which is more complex but also more transparent than former arrangements.[2] Eligible candidates must demonstrate a high level of expertise, experience in the field of the mandate, independence, impartiality, personal integrity, and objectivity. Individuals have been added to the list of entities that can propose candidates, opening the door to self-nominate, which has become the prevalent practice since then. In 2011, Resolution 16/21 of April 25, 2011, improved the system of selection requiring that all candidates submit a written application, including biographical data and a motivation letter, which are made available on the website of the Office of the High Commissioner.[3] The President/Chairperson of the Bureau makes the decision on the appointment, but it is now supported by a Consultative Group, composed of one representative of each regional group but serving in a personal capacity. The decision of the President requires the approval of the Human Rights Council, which is normally considered a formality.

Resolution 16/21 requires that all short-listed candidates are interviewed by the Consultative Group, a provision that has forced the introduction of a formal process to short-list candidates.[4] The short list is elaborated by the

[2] On debated proposals to change the process of selection, including the possibility of direct election by the Council, *see* Meghna Abraham, "Building the New Human Rights Council. Outcome and analysis of the institution-building year" *Dialogue on Globalization* (Friedrich-Ebert-Stiftung Occasional Papers, August 2007): 25–7.

[3] *See* OHCHR website at: https://www.ohchr.org/EN/HRBodies/HRC/SP/Pages/Nominations.aspx. On the selection process, *see* Marc Limon and Ted Piccone, "Human Rights Special Procedures: Determinants of Influence" in *Brookings Institutions & Universal Rights Group Policy Report* (Universal Rights Group, 2014): 13.

[4] Surya P. Subedi, "Human rights experts in the United Nations: a review of the role of United Nations Special Procedures" in Monika Ambrus, Karin Arts, Ellen Hey, and Helena Raulus (eds.), *The Role of "Experts" in International and European Decision-Making Processes* (Cambridge University Press, 2014): 241, 245.

Consultative Group, submitting a final short list of three candidates, by order of preference to the President, who then decides the nominations after consulting with regional groups. The selection process has improved significantly but remains vulnerable to undue pressures by states, particularly in vetoing undesired candidates. Those political interferences happen in the background, and it is impossible to know the maneuvers or lobbying that may lead the President to choose candidates different from those ranked first, although those reasons must be provided. In practice, the President has normally followed the advice of the Consultative Group, though this has been changed in some remarkable cases. For instance, during the process of selection held during the thirty-fifth session of the Council, the President of the Council, Ambassador of El Salvador Maza Martelli, did not appoint any of the favorite candidates suggested by the Consultative Group for the mandates on solidarity, minority issues, human rights of migrants, and countering terrorism.[5]

Another welcome innovation is the publication of the statistics on mandate holders by regional distribution and gender.[6] On paper, the new procedure has been rather successful in addressing imbalances in geographical representation and gender. By December 2018, 45 percent of mandate holders were women; 23.75 percent of mandate holders came from member states belonging to the African Group, 13.75 percent from the Asia-Pacific Group, 10 percent from the Eastern European Group, 22.25 percent from the Latin American and Caribbean Group, and 31.25 percent from the Group of Western European and Other States.[7] A closer look at the short-listed candidates and those finally appointed reveals a majority based in institutions located in countries belonging to the Western Group, many of them academics. As explained in the following sections, the unpaid nature of the job and its demands partly explain this situation.[8]

[5] Relevant documents are available at the relevant page of the OHCHR: https://www.ohchr.org/EN/HRBodies/HRC/SP/Pages/HRC35.aspx.

[6] *See* OHCHR website at: https://www.ohchr.org/EN/HRBodies/HRC/SP/Pages/Nominations.aspx.

[7] *Report on the twenty-fifth annual meeting of special rapporteurs/representatives, independent experts and chairs of working groups of the special procedures of the Human Rights Council (Geneva, 4 to 8 June 2018), including updated information on special procedures*, UN Doc. A/HRC/40/38 (12 March 2019) chap. II.

[8] *See also* statistics provided in Limon and Piccone (2014) (n. 3): 12–3.

3. Independent from Whom? Mandate Holders' Standing within and outside the United Nations

Special Procedures are served by independent experts, a feature that cements their credibility. When performing their work as mandate holders of Special Procedures, experts cannot receive or follow instructions from civil society organizations, victims, or any of the wide range of interlocutors they interact with. They should perform their functions according to their mandates, free from external governmental or non-governmental influence, a principle supported by Article 3 of the Code of Conduct. They cannot seek or accept instructions, honors, gifts, or remuneration from any source or use their position for private gain. Since mandate holders have traditionally sought and obtained external resources to increase their limited resources, the rule has been implemented by declaring these additional resources and their provenance.

The requirement of independence is particularly relevant in relation to state actors, with mandate holders enjoying a legal status deemed equivalent to "experts on mission" for the purposes of the Convention of Privileges and Immunities of the United Nations, as asserted by the Office of the Legal Counsel of the United Nations in 1988 and the International Court of Justice in 1989 in the *Mazilu* case.[9] In its second advisory opinion on this matter, the Court clarified that the UN Secretary General is normally the competent organ in deciding whether particular acts of a Special Rapporteur fall within the scope of her or his mission and therefore whether to waive or maintain the privileges and immunities of experts on mission.[10] While it falls outside the realm of this book, it is worth noting the relevance of the

[9] *Legal Status of Members of the Sub-Commission: Opinion of the Legal Counsel Dated 23 August, 1988—Dated 30 August, 1988*, reproduced in Ramcharan (ed.), (1997) (n. 1): 153–7; *Applicability of Article VI, Section 22, of the Convention on the Privileges and Immunities of the United Nations*, Advisory Opinion, ICJ Reports 1989, 177. *See also* Francesc-Xavier Pons Rafols, "Aplicabilidad de la sección 22 del artículo VI de la Convención sobre los privilegios e inmunidades de las Naciones Unidas" XLIII(1) *Revista Española de Derecho Internacional* (1991): 39–56; and Eric David, "L'avis de la Cour Internationale de Justice du 15 décembre 1989 sur l'applicabilité de la section 22 de l'article VI de la Convention sur les privilèges et immunités des Nations Unies (Aff. Mazilu)" XXXV *Annuaire Français de Droit International* (1989): 298–324.

[10] *Difference relating to immunity from legal process of a Special Rapporteur of the Commission on Human Rights. Advisory Opinion of 29 April 1999*, ICJ reports 1999, 62. *See* Hazel Fox, "The Advisory Opinion on the Difference Relating to Immunity from Legal Process of a Special Rapporteur of the Commission of Human Rights: Who Has the Last Word on Judicial Independence?" 12 *Leiden Journal of International Law* (1999): 889-918; Chanaka Wickremasinghe, "Difference relating to immunity from legal process of a special rapporteur of the Commission on Human Rights" 49(3) *International and Comparative Law Quarterly* (2000): 724–30.

second advisory opinion in relation to other international law issues such as the competence of the Economic and Social Council to change the terms of an advisory consultation request; whether an intervention by the UN Secretary General requesting a change of decision by the judiciary from a government constitutes a problematic intervention in domestic affairs; and the binding nature of advisory opinions through external agreement.[11] In any case, the condition of experts on mission being protected by immunities is uncontested and has been codified in Article 4 of the Code of Conduct of Special Procedures in 2007. Special Procedures mandate holders are also subject to the relevant provisions of the *Regulations Governing the Status, Basic Rights and Duties of Officials other than Secretariat Officials and Experts on Mission*.[12]

In 2008, the Assistant Secretary General for Legal Affairs and the Office of the High Commissioner's Legal Adviser briefed Special Procedures during their annual meeting in relation to amicus curiae or other expert opinions that several mandate holders have submitted before domestic, regional, and international courts. According to the Secretariat, when submitting amicus curiae briefs, Special Procedures were considered "experts on mission" and accorded immunity from personal arrest, granted immunity in respect of their written or verbal communications as well as their actions, and granted immunity from legal processes of every kind. However, they were also reminded that:

> amicus briefs should be carefully worded and that a disclaimer should be issued explaining that mandate-holders were expressing their own views, which did not necessarily reflect those of the United Nations or those of the Secretary-General.[13]

The Office of the High Commissioner for Human Rights provides support to Special Procedures, but mandate holders are not linked by any contract to the administrative structure of the United Nations and they have also

[11] *See, e.g.*, Peter Bekker, "Difference Relating to Immunity from Legal Process of a Special Rapporteur of the Commission on Human Rights" 93(4) *American Journal of International Law* (1999) 913–23; and Carlos Espósito, *La jurisdicción consultiva de la Corte Internacional de Justicia* (McGraw Hill, 1996): 155–8.

[12] UN Doc. ST/SGB/2002/9 (2002).

[13] *Report of the fifteenth meeting of special rapporteurs/representatives, independent experts and chairpersons of working groups of the special procedures of the Council, held in Geneva from 23 to 27 June 2008*, UN Doc. A/HRC/10/24 (17 November 2008), para. 52.

disassociated themselves expressly from the High Commissioner and its Office on several occasions.[14] The Office has no obligation to follow Special Procedures' instructions either and responds to its own hierarchical structure. In practice it has important leverage over the mandate holders because every official aspect of their activities, including the publication of their reports, is handled through the Office of the High Commissioner.

Mandate holders do not belong to the intergovernmental structure of the United Nations either. However, they are subsidiary organs of the Human Rights Council and, through this organ, of the General Assembly, with the requirement of submitting reports to both bodies. Their creation, renewal, and scope of competence is governed by their parent organ. Their categorization as bodies belonging to the structure of the United Nations since 1967 is reflected in the terminology used to describe them as "Charter bodies"—a reference to their relationship with the organs created by the UN Charter. As detailed in chapter three, they have evolved toward what is commonly now referred to as the "system of Special Procedures," emphasizing the institutionalization of the different thematic and geographic mandates belonging to the category within the Organization.

The answer provided to whether mandate holders are independent from the Human Rights Council determines the relevance of their actions as potentially attributable to the United Nations, apart from the competence of the Council over mandate holders. If absolute independence is argued, the Human Rights Council has no power to interfere in the work of independent experts, even if they act beyond their mandate or fail to fulfill it in anyway incompatible with decisions of the Council. This position has been frequently advocated by mandate holders themselves. For instance, the Special Rapporteur on torture and the Working Group on Arbitrary Detention have resisted mandates to carry out country visits that do not meet the standards established in their methods of work. The mandate holder of the Special Procedure on Torture, Rodley, decided not to visit the occupied territories by Israel, as requested by the Commission, because he had not received enough allegations of the gravity required to justify a visit according to his published methods of work.[15] Similarly, the Working Group on Arbitrary Detention

[14] Jane Connors, "Special Procedures: Independence and Impartiality" in Aoife Nolan, Rosa Freedman, and Thérèse Murphy (eds.), *The United Nations Special Procedures System* (Brill, 2017): 52, 71.

[15] UN Doc. E/CN.4/2003/68 (17 December 2012), para. 14. *See also* section 3.C. and n. 99 in chapter three. The discussions are reproduced in *Summary of the 77th meeting of the 57th session of the Commission on Human Rights, held on 25 April 2001*, UN Doc. E/CN.4/2001/SR.77 (12 December

disobeyed the petition to visit Cuba because its methods of work dictated that the Group would not visit a territory for which a Special Procedure already existed, as was the case at the time.[16] All Special Procedures have defended their independence, expressing their discomfort with the decision of the Commission 1997/125 of April 18, 1997, which sought to modify the content of the report of the Special Rapporteur on contemporary forms of racial discrimination, xenophobia, and related intolerance.[17]

Several mandate holders have acted as if the outcomes of their work belong to them and not the United Nations. Increasingly, they have created their own websites to publish their findings, bring issues into focus, and disseminate their own reports. On October 4, 2000, the UN Secretary General felt compelled to deny that mandate holders' acts could be attributed to the United Nations in the light of the controversial declarations made by Jiri Dienstbier, then Special Rapporteur for human rights in the former Yugoslavia, stating his opposition to the indictments of Yugoslav President Slobodan Milosevic. Under the rubric "Secretary-General surprised by human rights Rapporteur's suggestion that war crimes indictment against Slobodan Milosevic be dropped," the Secretary General issued a statement clarifying that "Special Rapporteurs of the Commission on Human Rights act in their personal capacity as independent experts and do not represent the views of the Secretary-General or of any inter-governmental organ."[18] Some of the language encountered in the Code of Conduct and other documents addressing mandate holders' independence seem to support the position of absolute independence.[19]

Strong arguments support the hypothesis that Special Procedures are independent from the United Nations and, particularly, the Human Rights Council. However, the Human Rights Council constitutes the final authority

2001), paras. 28–44. *See also* Michael J. Dennis, "The Fifty-Seventh Session of the UN Commission on Human Rights" 96 (1) *American Journal of International Law* (2002): 181, 188, and *Summary record of the 75th meeting of the 57th session of the Commission on Human Rights, held on 24 April 2001*, UN Doc. E/CN.4/2001/SR.75 (30 April 2001).

[16] The request of the Commission can be found in its Resolution 1994/71 (9 March 1994), para. 8. The methods of work were then published in UN Doc. E/CN.4/1995/31 (1995), para. 22. For the explanation of the Group, *see* UN Doc. E/CN.4/1996/40 (1996).

[17] The relevant report is UN Doc. E/CN.4/1997/71, para. 27.

[18] *See* UN Doc. SG/SM/7574 (4 November 2000).

[19] Philip Alston "Hobbling the Monitors: Should U.N. Human Rights Monitors be Accountable?" 52(2) *Harvard International Law Journal* (2011): 561, 624–5; *see also* Miko Lempinen, "When loyalty towards the United Nations limits the independence of special procedure mandate holders" 21(4) *Nordic Journal of International Law* (2003): 456.

over the activity of the experts. In the words of Article 15 of the Code of Conduct, mandate holders are "accountable to the Council." If the Council estimates that they have behaved beyond their conferred powers or in any other manner incompatible with their mandate, it can determine corrective measures, including the modification of their methods of work, as the Commission did in 1997 in relation to the terminology used by the Working Group on Arbitrary Detention[20] or the modification of the report of the Special Rapporteur on racism mentioned earlier, despite the protest of mandate holders. The Council also has the authority to determine the review of mandates and, ultimately, the termination of a Special Procedure.

The experts are accountable to a political body and therefore subject to political decisions. Calling out "politicization" when those decisions that inform the full life cycle of Special Procedures are perceived as antagonistic with the work of one or all mandate holders can be useful in gathering enough support to hinder negative state agendas seeking to shield their human rights record from scrutiny. What is not useful is the denial of the institutional association between Special Procedures and the Organization from which they draw their authority.

The consideration of Special Procedures as independent from the intergovernmental organs to which they report, particularly the Human Rights Council, implies a conception of their status similar to that of external consultants entirely dissociated from the UN apparatus. In such role, the relevance of their work would be similar, at best, to the weight provided to scholars as subsidiary means for the determination of facts or the law. Such a conclusion is in open contradiction with the functions developed by Special Procedures and the quasi-diplomatic treatment they are granted in their relationship with international actors. Over decades of practice codified in several resolutions, states have endorsed competences to carry out missions on the ground, intervene in individual cases and assess the compliance of human rights.[21]

[20] About this incident, *see* chapter two.

[21] *See* chapters one and two.

4. The Politics of Funding: Office of the High Commissioner for Human Rights

Mandate holders come from multiple backgrounds; they are elected by a political body based on their expertise in a field and may not be familiar with the institutional framework of the UN Organization or the Special Procedures. The Office of the High Commissioner for Human Rights plays a fundamental role in providing coherence to the system of Special Procedures by articulating common methodologies, providing continuity to Special Procedures when new mandate holders take over, and coordinating the activities of a growing number of mechanisms. Most activities of mandate holders, including country visits, are assisted by a member of the Office. Its staff members deal with almost all information addressed to Special Procedures, undertake relevant research for thematic reports or visits on the ground, and draft communications and, sometimes, significant parts of the reports. The personnel assigned to Special Procedures are the main points of contact for those reaching out to the Special Procedures.

The Office has also developed and maintains databases and multiple sources of information that are fundamental for the functioning of Special Procedures and to stakeholders engaging with them.[22] The progressive centralization of the institutional structures supporting Special Procedures through a dedicated branch of the Office (the Special Procedures Branch) has a major influence in the mitigation of difference in methods of work.[23]

The nature of the relationship between Special Procedures and the Office of the High Commissioner is peculiar, which can easily lead to misunderstandings and erroneous expectations. Successive High Commissioners have also understood their mission differently, further complicating the establishment of fluid and stable coexistence with Special Procedures.[24] Mandate holders are independent from the High Commissioner and from the Office; they work pro bono and are not employed by the Secretariat. The personnel supporting them, on the other

[22] *See* chapter three.

[23] In addition to bibliography cited in chapter three, *see* Theo van Boven, "Five years after strengthening the United Nations. Recasting the Office of the High Commissioner for Human Rights," Ineke Boerefijn and Jenny Goldschmidt (eds.), *Changing Perceptions of Sovereignty and Human Rights. Essays in Honour of Cees Flinterman* (Intersentia, 2008): 145–60, 152.

[24] *See* Felice Gaer, "The High Commissioner and the Special Procedures: Colleagues and Competitors" in Felice Gaer and Christen Broecker (eds.), *The United Nations High Commissioner for Human Rights. Conscience for the World* (Martinus Nijhoff, 2014): 133, 137–51.

hand, are UN staff pursuing their own civil servant careers within a distinct hierarchical structure, who are assigned to specific Special Procedures mandate holders but are not their personal or research assistants nor their employees.[25] While the Office serves Special Procedures, there is no formal relationship between them and no clear model to follow to respect the independence of both mandate holders and the Secretariat. The relationship between mandate holders and the Office is governed by the "Guiding principles regarding the working relations between special procedures mandate holders and OHCHR staff," which outlines their division of work and responsibilities. These guidelines are included as Annex II of the Manual of Special Procedures. However, the annexes are not reproduced in the version of the Manual available online, and none of these documents are published as official papers. At the time of writing, the guiding principles could be found at a cached online address containing the 2006 version of the Manual.[26]

The reaction of mandate holders when these guiding principles were introduced by the Office of the High Commissioner, under the rubric "Guidelines," exemplifies the underlying suspicion that permeates their relationship with the Office. Mandate holders questioned the overall nature of the document and the potential misinterpretation of their independence, suggesting the change of title from "guidelines" to "guiding principles."[27]

The human rights pillar of the United Nations suffers from a chronic resource deficit despite improvements in the past fifteen years. The regular budget assigned to the Office of the High Commissioner for the years 2002 and 2003 amounted to 1.8 percent of the overall regular budget, compared to over double in 2019 (3.7 percent). The absence of resources involves a hefty reliance on voluntary funds with a profound impact on the already complex institutional liaison between Special Procedures and the Office. The political interest of donors, overwhelmingly consisting of states, politicizes the work of the Office of the High Commissioner and Special Procedures in ways different from direct interference with specific mandates. Contrary to commonly held perceptions, the main problems associated with voluntary funds are not the percentage of earmarked funds nor that donors prefer a particular

[25] Connors (2017) (n. 14): 52, 73.
[26] In files with the author.
[27] *Report on the ninth meeting of special rapporteurs/representatives, experts and chairpersons of working groups of the special procedures of the Commission on Human Rights and of the advisory services programme, which took place in Geneva from 24 to 28 June 2002*, UN Doc. E/CN.4/2003/6 (22 August 2002), para. 20. *See also* report of the tenth annual session, UN Doc. E/CN.4/2004/4 (5 August 2003), para. 64.

category of rights.[28] The crucial factor is the reliance on voluntary funds, some of them earmarked, which constitute almost 60 percent of the budget of the High Commissioner.[29] This situation necessarily implies some leverage of the biggest donors over the Office of the High Commissioner because a significant percentage of its work is funded by unpredictable funds that need to keep coming to sustain core activities. Budget shortfalls have meant the cancellation of country visits for which the consent of a state was secured, reliance on interpreters and other resources provided by governments under investigation, the threat to cancel human rights bodies' meetings, and non-renewal of contracts.[30]

Many of those serving Special Procedures directly or indirectly are on temporary contracts and interns (unpaid) are used to complete substantive work. In the past, opaque decisions regarding the administrative division of the Office had strong implications on who could benefit from unified institutional support and databases depending on the mostly political categorization of rights, but this has been largely resolved.[31]

The nature of the work of a Special Procedure mandate holder implies reliance on personal or external resources since the position is not paid and requires flexibility and a time commitment, estimated as approximately three months per year, including attendance at the Human Rights Council sessions. This explains that advances made in a wider geographical representation of mandate holders is largely nominal. While those appointed may hold passports from developing and developed countries, the majority are employed by institutions located in OECD countries, and many work in the academic sector. Earmarked funding as well as external support can compromise the independence of experts in charge of Special Procedures. There is no formal requirement to report about extra support; yet the majority of mandate holders do. By the end of 2018, sixty-seven mandate holders (out of eighty) informed the Coordination Committee about external support received. Of those, only twenty-eight had received support, mostly in kind, including research assistance, use of facilities, or funding of specific research

[28] Connors (2017) (n. 14): 52, 75–83.

[29] All data on funding and budget of the OHCHRs is available in its Annual Reports and other relevant documents, available at: https://www.ohchr.org/EN/AboutUs/Pages/FundingBudget.aspx.

[30] *See, e.g.*, the report of the former Special Rapporteurs on the situation of human rights in Rwanda (UN Doc. E/CN.4/1997/61, paras. 2–5) or Myanmar (UN Doc. E/CN.4/1996/65, para. 19); *see also* OHCHR Press Release, *UN budget shortfalls seriously undermine the work of the Human: Rights treaty bodies* (Geneva, 17 May 2019).

[31] *See* chapter four.

or events. A reading of the details provided by those receiving external assistance reveals significant variations in the level of support as well as the difference of information disclosed by mandate holders.[32]

5. Relationship with Other UN Organs: General Assembly and Security Council

The reform of the United Nations that resulted in the creation of the Human Rights Council involved an institutional "upgrade" of the main human rights body of the Organization. The Human Rights Council is a subsidiary of the General Assembly instead of the Economic and Social Council, as was its predecessor. This seems to have promoted a closer relationship between Special Procedures and the General Assembly to which most of them report.[33] This proximity brings obvious advantages since it forces attention and greater visibility to Special Procedures by all states of the United Nations, rather than the fifty-four represented in the Economic and Social Council.

Considering the normative weight associated to resolutions of the General Assembly and that many human rights treaties find their origin in them, the contribution of Special Procedures to the development of human rights standards is greatly reinforced by the direct link with the General Assembly. The General Assembly has endorsed many human rights instruments submitted by the Human Rights Council, many of which have been drafted by mandate holders of Special Procedures or with their input, including the Convention for the Protection of all Persons from Enforced Disappearances; the Optional Protocol to the International Covenant on Economic, Social and Cultural Rights on a communication procedure; and the Optional Protocol to the Convention on the Rights of the Child on a communication procedure, the Declaration on Human Rights Education and Training and the Guiding Principles on Business and Human Rights.[34]

[32] *Report on the twenty-fifth annual meeting of special rapporteurs/representatives, independent experts and chairs of working groups of the special procedures of the Human Rights Council (Geneva, 4 to 8 June 2018), including updated information on special procedures*, UN Doc. A/HRC/40/38 (12 March 2019), para. 56; *see also* Facts and figures for 2018, detailed in UN Doc. A/HRC/40/38/Add.1, ch. XI.

[33] See chapter four on submissions of annual reports.

[34] On the contribution of Special Procedures to normative developments, *see* chapter four. On the approval by the General Assembly of the listed instruments, *see* Emmanuel Bichet and Stephani Rutz, *The Human Rights Council as a subsidiary organ* (URG, October 2016), available at: https://www.universal-rights.org/urg-policy-reports/human-rights-council-subsidiary-organ-evaluating-relationships-un-general-assembly-un-security-council/.

However, the relationship between the Human Rights Council and the General Assembly has not been clearly defined and has the potential to undermine the work of Special Procedures.[35] There were positive aspects of the institutional distance between the former Commission on Human Rights and the General Assembly.[36] In the former structure, the Economic and Social Council acted as a rubber stamp of the Commission's decisions, with very few exceptions. They shared a similar composition and a tacit division of "labor" with the Economic and Social Council mostly detached from the human rights agenda. This is not the case for the General Assembly, especially when the agenda of its Third Committee and the Human Rights Council overlaps substantially. The new institutional position of the Council has introduced a higher level of uncertainty as to how the General Assembly may exercise its authority over the Human Rights Council and whether states unhappy with a Human Rights Council decision can gather enough majority to overturn it. This danger materialized immediately after the creation of the Human Rights Council when the General Assembly did not approve the draft declaration to protect indigenous peoples.[37]

Admittedly, this scenario arises when a resolution has already been approved with a very minor margin within the Human Rights Council, as was the case of those addressing sexual orientation and gender identity. In 2013, the General Assembly overturned a resolution of the Human Rights Council on the topic.[38] Three years later a thematic Special Procedure was created by 23 votes to 18 with 6 abstentions.[39] During its subsequent session, the General Assembly tried to halt the establishment of the Independent Expert but the proposal was narrowly defeated by 84 votes against 77 with 17 abstentions.[40] The mandate, renewed in July 2019, by 27 votes against 12 with 7 abstentions, remains on fragile ground, and similar manoeuvres can be expected in the future.[41] The history of Special Procedures suggests that mandates born with great controversy have been consolidated over time,

[35] *See* International Service for Human Rights, "The General Assembly and Human Rights" *Human Rights Monitor* 64/2006 (February 2007): *esp*. 82–3.

[36] Miko Lempinen, "The United Nations Human Rights Council: The Next Victim of Illusions and False Expectations" 26(2) *Nordic Journal of International Law* (2008): 182, 186.

[37] *See* Amnesty International, UN: Third Committee rejects strong draft Declaration to protect Indigenous Peoples, AI Doc. IOR 41/025/2006, 28 November 2006.

[38] Bichet and Rutz (n. 34).

[39] HRC Res. 32/2, 30 June 2016.

[40] International Service for Human rights *LGBT Rights | World's human rights organisations marshal support ahead of November 21's crucial vote on UN's first sexual orientation and gender identity expert* (ISHR, 21 November 2016).

[41] HRC Res. 40/8, 12 July 2019.

partly because of the difficulty in reversing decisions establishing them. This difficulty has decreased with the oversight of the General Assembly. In any case, Special Procedures that provoke a significant level of opposition will suffer from a legitimacy deficit, complicating their operations. Testing the absence of political support in the plenary organ of the United Nations may contribute to meaningful debate and progress over groundbreaking topics in the human rights agenda.

The creation of the Human Rights Council opened a window of opportunity to ensure that the main UN human rights body was equipped with better tools than its predecessor in dealing with security threats deriving from human rights violations. However, the Human Rights Council, established at the same time as the Peacebuilding Commission, has not been provided with adequate tools to address the fundamental deficit of the UN human rights machinery in dealing with armed conflict and other emergencies that threaten international peace and security.

The failure of the Organization to articulate an apparatus that can respond effectively to such situations can be mainly attributed to lack of political will. A range of geopolitical positions and interests explain how the proclaimed interlink between human rights and security has not found easy accommodation at institutional level within the United Nations. Some states have strongly opposed involving the Security Council with human rights issues because, inter alia, they see the introduction of thematic discussions in the realm of this restricted membership body, with five veto-wielding permanent members, as a further concession of competences to the Security Council to the detriment of the General Assembly.[42] Others have advocated for periodic communication between the Human Rights Council, the Human Rights Commissioner, the Security Council, and the Peacebuilding Commission.[43]

[42] *See*, for instance, statements made by the representative of the government of Algeria, Belarus or Mauritius included in the Official Records of the 74th and 75th meetings of the 61st session of the GA (UN Docs. A/61/PV.74–75, General Assembly Official Records, 61st Session, 74th and 75th Meetings, New York, 11 and 12 December 2006). *See also* the positions of the government of Pakistan and Cuba in the 55th session of the GA reflected in the UN Press Releases GA/9789, 18 October 2000, and GA/AB/3421, 14 December 2000. For the positions of states around this issue in the early 1990s, *see* Philip Alston, "The Security Council and Human Rights: Lessons to be learned from the Iraq-Kuwait crisis and its aftermath," 13 *Australian Yearbook of International Law* (1990–1991): 107, 129–34.

[43] *Report of the Facilitators to the President of the General Assembly on the Consultations Regarding "The Question of Equitable Representation on an Increase in the Membership of the Security Council and Other Matters Related to the Security Council"* (United Nations, 23 April 2007): 18; and *Note transmitting report of the High-Level Panel on Threats, Challenges and Change, entitled "A More Secure Word: Our Shared Responsibility*, UN Doc. A/59/565 (2 December 2004), para. 289.

The latest serious attempt to reform the Security Council included the "S-5 proposal" preventing the use of veto-wielding powers in cases of genocide, crimes against humanity, or serious violations of international humanitarian law.[44] During the institution-building process of the Human Rights Council, Pakistan, speaking on behalf of the Organisation of the Islamic Conference, along with Bangladesh, Cuba, Indonesia, the Russian Federation, and South Africa, expressed their opposition to a Canadian proposal that would have allowed Special Procedures to brief the Security Council.[45]

Ultimately, the Human Rights Council and its subsidiary bodies, including Special Procedures, were not endowed with the competence to raise recommendations to the Security Council, hindering possible benefits in synchronizing both Councils' agendas. Other progress in this direction have, once again, depended on individual and/or informal initiatives that remain unregulated and unpredictable but also more flexible and adaptable to changing scenarios. At the institutional level, direct communication between Special Rapporteurs and the Security Council has been increasingly frequent under the so-called "Aria Formula." The Security Council has progressively stretched the interpretation of its competences, covering human rights issues when responding to threats to international peace and security, including those adopted under Chapter VII of the UN Charter,[46] and it often refers to the activities of Special Procedures and of the Office of the High Commissioner, demonstrating increased political willingness to engage with the human rights machinery.[47]

The work of the Special Representative on the question of children in armed conflict, who reports to the Human Rights Council when the General

[44] "Improving the Working Methods of the Security Council," Draft Resolution UN Doc. A/60/L.49, March 2006 submitted by Costa Rica, Jordan, Liechtenstein, Singapore, and Switzerland. *See also* International Service for Human Rights.

[45] International Service for Human Rights, "A Stock-Taking of the Human Rights Council's Institution Building Process," *Human Rights Monitor* 64/2006 (February 2007): 18.

[46] David Petrasek, "The UN Security Council and Human Rights," in Gordon DiGiacomo and Susan Kang (eds.), *The Institutions of Human Rights* (University of Toronto Press, 2019): 44; *see also* David P. Forsythe and Baekkwan Park, "The Changing of the Guard: From the UN Human Rights Commission to the Council" 29(1–5) *Human Rights Law Journal* (2008) 3–14.

[47] *See, e.g.*, Françoise Hampson and Ibrahim Salama, "Working paper on the relationship between human rights law and international humanitarian law," UN Doc. E/CN.4/Sub.2/2005/14 (2005), paras. 25–6 and 56. *See also* Bertrand G. Ramcharan, *The Security Council and the Protection of Human Rights* (Brill, 2002); Sandrine Turgis, "Les moyens d'alerte du Conseil de sécurité des Nations Unies en cas de violation des droits de l'homme" 41(2) *Civitas Europa* (2018): 33; and Elvira Domínguez-Redondo, "Making the connection: security and human rights" in Cherif Bassiouni and William Schabas (eds.), *New Challenges of the Human Rights Machinery: what future for the UN treaty body system and the Human Rights Council procedures* (Intersentia, 2011): 255; Bichet and Rutz (n. 34).

Assembly requests it and was temporarily treated as a Special Procedure in the past, has been decisive for the inclusion of the question of children in armed conflict on the agenda of the Security Council leading to the approval of its first ever thematic resolution in 1999.[48] This precedent opened the door for other thematic human rights issues, including on questions such as terrorism; protection of civilian in armed conflict; women, peace, and security; and HIV/AIDS. Another visible effect of the work of this hybrid mechanism was the introduction of Special Advisors on Children and Women in several Peacekeeping Operations. A further manifestation, at the operational level, is the rising frequency of human rights components in the design of Peacekeeping Operations.

For the first time ever, in March 2018, the Chair of the Coordination Committee sent a letter, circulated as an official document through the Dutch delegation, to all the members of the Security Council, sharing findings of Special Procedures addressing peace and security issues.[49] This remarkable document outlines the relevance of Special Procedures in sounding the alarm on situations involving threats to peace and security, highlighting the well-known case of Rwanda and also more recent examples related to Burundi, the Central African Republic, and Myanmar.[50] It draws attention to the framework approach to prevention developed by the Special Rapporteur on the promotion of truth, reparations, and guarantees of non-recurrence as well as to other thematic reports addressing prevention, early warning, conflict and post-conflict situations, and humanitarian crisis, covering the topic of the impact of fundamentalism and extremism on cultural rights; the right to food in conflict situations; private military and security companies; the vulnerability of children to sale, trafficking, and other forms of exploitation in situations of conflict; and transitional justice in weakly institutionalized post-conflict settings. The letter also highlights the relevance of specific country visits undertaken by different mandate holders to Chad, Iraq, Afghanistan, Cyprus, Serbia, Kosovo, Israel, the occupied Palestinian Territory and the government of the state of Palestine, Nigeria, Libya, and the Democratic People's Republic of Korea.

[48] *See* Resolution 1261 (1999) 25 August 1999. The latest report of the Special Representative to the HRC can be found in UN Doc. A/HRC/40/49 (12 December 2018). On the consideration of this mechanism as a Special Procedure, *see* chapter three.

[49] *Note verbale dated 28 March 2018 from the Permanent Mission of the Netherlands to the United Nations addressed to the President of the Security Council*, UN Doc. S/2018/280 (2 April 2018).

[50] *See also* Turgis (2018) (n. 47): 33.

This communication with all members of the Security Council, through the Chair of the Coordination Committee, represents the first systematic approach to informing the Security Council about the wealth of findings and analyses produced by Special Procedures that are relevant to that organ. The compilation in a short document of relevant reports is a promising format, potentially more effective than random mandate holders attempting to access directly or indirectly the Security Council when they deemed it necessary.

6. Conclusions

Multidimensional factors influence the real or perceived independence of mandate holders. Some are explored in other parts of this book. For instance, the decisions on different nomenclature (Special Rapporteur or independent expert) denote certain political expectations on the nature of the mandate and are, at times, reflected in the functions assigned in the resolution creating and renewing Special Procedures. Most Special Procedures are entrusted to a single person, but some thematic mandates are held by a five-person working group, significantly increasing the independence of the body and its reinforced ability to withstand political pressure.

The process of selection of mandate holders involves governmental input and consequent politicization. It has been improved significantly since the creation of the Human Rights Council in terms of transparency and regulation, substituting a system totally dependent on the proximity of some individuals to the UN human rights machinery and the discretion of the President of the Bureau. Weaknesses inherent to relying on the decision of one governmental representative remains, and the process is still vulnerable to hidden manipulation. Outcomes such as those outlined earlier for the thirty-fifth period of sessions of the Human Rights Council undermine the credibility of the final selection by questioning the competence of the Consultative Group in charge of analyzing all applications, short-listing, and interviewing the candidates. It is not necessary to reform the process to reach this outcome. Other states should demand that decisions to overturn the views of the Group are well reasoned rather than providing generic statements that fail to provide any clarity. The Human Rights Council can also overturn decisions of the President, but this can only undermine further the selection process. The imbalance in the gender and geographical distribution of mandate holders, a long-standing plight of countries not belonging to the Western Group, has been greatly redressed, albeit it remains of a cosmetic rather than substantial nature for many Special Procedures.

The independence of mandate holders from non-governmental and the governmental stakeholders they interact with is well established. This is strengthened by the extraordinary support of two advisory opinions of the International Court of Justice, the Code of Conduct, and other regulations, making this feature the best regulated among those characterizing the system of Special Procedures. This clarity is lost on the issue of independence vis-à-vis other organs of the United Nations, especially, the Human Rights Council. Mandate holders have contributed to the haziness in this area, insisting at times on their absolute independence while keeping the authority that the blue stamp the United Nations provides to their activities. The not-so-diverse background of mandate holders probably partly explains the issue. The overwhelming presence of academics among mandate holders is a direct consequence of the demands of a selection based on expertise, extreme flexibility, and no funding. Academics are accustomed to derive their authority from their institutional affiliation while preserving academic freedom, because their words never represent those of the university they belong to, unless specifically instructed.

When they seek the input of a Special Procedure, victims of human rights violations and other members of civil society are effectively approaching the United Nations, not just any expert. A wide range of governmental and intergovernmental actors grant quasi-diplomatic status to their interactions with mandate holders, and states must ensure their immunity from prosecution. The intergovernmental leverage provided by their association with the United Nations has a political cost. Speaking on behalf of the United Nations involves the possibility of being monitored by a political body. This is an inescapable reality and defending total independence from the United Nations' organs is a shortsighted strategy.

Mandate holders should also accept their dependence on the work of the Office of the High Commissioner for Human Rights as inevitable, engaging in a cooperative manner with its structure and staff members. Attempts to escape its chains by drawing on personal resources to support mandates may seem solutions, but they confuse those who are outside the system, particularly victims. Mandate holders should make every effort to use the resources available to them in coordination with the Office, despite its flaws. In an ideal world, the Office of the High Commissioner's management and staff members should understand their only purpose is to serve the human rights machinery rather than a soulless pursuit of survival to enable bureaucratic coherence.

Unless the rules governing the relationship between organs of the United Nations are radically reformed, the Human Rights Council is vulnerable to the forces at work in the General Assembly. There is no independence of the Council in relation to its parent organ in the current system. Mandates of Special Procedures that prove controversial within the Human Rights Council may suffer a bleak fate within the General Assembly. Perhaps states should be credited more for having endorsed almost every decision of its subsidiary body, providing great autonomy to the Human Rights Council and, as a result, Special Procedures.

The overall improvement of the treatment of human rights issues by the Security Council and the creation of some institutional relationship between this body and the Human Rights Council can only be welcome. Some of the political constraints for this relationship to flourish are also well founded. The absence of a formal link between the institutions in charge of human rights and peace and security continues to hinder decision-making processes by the Security Council. However, any enlargement of the competences of the Security Council in addressing human rights issues directly involves a wider range of issues under the control of the most undemocratic organ of the United Nations.

Final Remarks

Public international law scholars are familiar with different doctrinal debates questioning the legal standing of the rules governing inter-state relationships[1] or probing its "internationality" from Marxist,[2] feminist,[3] third world,[4] or comparative perspectives,[5] among others.[6] Skepticism toward the "legality" of international law and its "internationality" conflate as they seek to understand, explain, and/or analyze the role of power in creating, designing, and implementing law and vice versa. In other words, the relationship between politics and law is at the core of the endless identity crisis international law seems to suffer from. This debate permeates every aspect regulated by international law. Legal academics and practicing lawyers tend to reflect on the "politicization" issue as a negative phenomenon, particularly among human rights lawyers because it implies that different standards are used to address similar situations, depending on power dynamics. Lacking central structures monopolizing power to create and enforce norms, the politicization of international law defies the logic that associates law with a system of rules and enforcement mechanisms able to deliver the same consequences for equivalent events. The legal and political construct of state sovereignty implies a central role for the consent of states in reacting to similar scenarios, a characteristic that mystifies lawyers and the public at large.

There is no mechanism to ensure respect for the elements associated with conventional conceptions of the rule of law, no matter how minimalist. In the

[1] Anthony D'Amato, "Is International Law Really Law?" 79 *Northwestern University Law Review* (1984–5): 1293–1314; James Crawford, "International Law as Discipline and Profession" 106 *American Society of International Law Proceedings* (2012): 471–86; Frédéric Mégret, "International law as law" in James Crawford and Martti Koskenniemi (eds.), *The Cambridge Companion of International Law* (Cambridge University Press, 2012): 64–91.

[2] Robert Knox, "Marxist Approaches to International Law" in Anne Orford and Florian Hoffmann, *The Oxford Handbook of the Theory of International Law* (Oxford University Press, 2016): 306–26.

[3] Hilary Charlesworth, Sam Chaiton, and Christine Chinkin, *The boundaries of international law: A feminist analysis* (Manchester University Press, 2000).

[4] Bhupinder S. Chimmi, "Third World Approaches to International Law: A Manifesto" 8 *International Community Law Review* (2006): 3–27; Luis Eslava and Sundhya Pahuja, "Between Resistance and Reform: TWAIL and the Universality of International Law" 3(1) *Trade, Law and Development* (2011): 103–30.

[5] Anthea Roberts, *Is International Law International?* (Oxford University Press, 2017).

[6] Bhupinder S. Chimmi, *International law and world order: A critique of contemporary approaches* (Cambridge University Press, 2017).

In Defense of Politicization of Human Rights. Elvira Domínguez-Redondo, Oxford University Press (2020).
 DOI: 10.1093/oso/9780197516706.001.0001

transnational space, states do not abide with the principle of supremacy of the law—with the exception perhaps of the disputed existence of peremptory norms of international law: equality before the law, fairness in its application, and independent adjudication. The concept of an international "rule of law" is evasive and largely vacuous[7] despite grand declarations proclaiming the importance of the rule of law at international level.[8]

Politicization, understood as the application of double standards that undermine the essence of the rule of law, is inevitable. However, Lebovic and Voeten have empirically demonstrated that, in the field of human rights, double standards are less prominent than is often supposed. After analyzing the work of the Commission on Human Rights, between 1979 and 2005, focusing on its actions in targeting states that the authors benchmarked using the Political Terror Scale scores, they concluded that targeting and condemnation of countries were directly related to the situation of human rights in the country. Double standards were still present: a considerable percentage of the states with the worst Political Terror Scale scores had not been the object of a decision of the Commission on Human Rights. However, their data revealed that human rights performance mattered and that over time, the Commission became progressively better at giving it more weight to decide specific actions compared to political strategic alignment.[9] While some states were more outspoken than ever about the "selectivity" of the actions of the Commission and its politicization, leading to its disappearance, the data compiled demonstrates that the Commission on Human Rights had become less prone to country resolutions during its last three years, opting for "softer" actions.[10]

[7] Simon Chesterman, "An international rule of law?" 56(2) *The American Journal of Comparative Law* (2008): 331–62. For a slightly different view, *see* Bhupinder S. Chimmi, "Legitimising the international rule of law" in James Crawford and Martti Koskenniemi (eds.), *The Cambridge Companion of International Law* (Cambridge University Press, 2012): 290–307. *See also* Knox (n. 2).

[8] *See esp. Declaration of the High-level Meeting of the General Assembly on the Rule of Law at the National and International Levels*, UNGA Res. 67/1 of 27 September 2012; *see also Declaration on Principles of International Law concerning Friendly Relations and Co-operation among States in accordance with the Charter of the United Nations*, UNGA Res. 2625(XXV) 24 October 1970, preamble; *United Nations Millennium Declaration*, UNGA Res. 55/2, 8 September 2000, paras. 23, 24, and 30.

[9] *See* James H. Lebovic and Erik Voeten, "The politics of shame: The condemnation of country human rights Practices in the UNHCR" 50(4) *International Studies Quarterly* (2006): 54, and James H. Lebovic and Erik Voeten, "The Cost of Shame: International Organizations and Foreign Aid in the Punishing of Human Rights Violations" 46(1) *Journal of Peace Research* (2009): 79. Their results are analyzed in David P. Forsythe and Baekkwan Park, "The Changing of the Guard: From the UN Human Rights Commission to the Council" 29(1–5) *Human Rights Law Journal* (2008): 3.

[10] Forsythe and Park (2008) (n. 9): 3–14, 7.

Lebovic and Voeten's findings, corroborated by others, dismantle the perception that actions adopted by intergovernmental bodies are mostly, if not entirely, based on the national interest of countries composing those organs.[11] Further statistical analysis reveals that the impact of the actions of the Human Rights Council relies, at least partially, on its political nature. Information about human rights violations does not seem to have a tangible effect on bilateral relations between states, in particular those related to the provision of international aid.[12] Instead, states seem to delegate "punishment" to multilateral institutions. When the Human Rights Council adopts a negative resolution chastising a country, it results in significant reduction in multilateral aid, particularly funds managed by the World Bank. In practice, it implies that the World Bank is acting as a "selective enforcer of international human rights norms."[13]

The impact of the Council's decisions on the ground is an entirely different matter. The studies available suggest such impact is negligible, at best.[14] They also reveal that actions of the Human Rights Council may negatively impact the situation of human rights of those under the jurisdiction of the states targeted because they may result in reductions of international aid.

Contemporary scholars investing time in making the case for the continued value and efficacy of human rights have become alarmingly scarce.[15] Baxi, Shivji, Mutua, Odinkalu, and Kapur are among those who have advanced published critiques of the individualist liberal ideals informing the human rights project and its perception as a neocolonialist tool, at best unable to confront the structural inequalities of the international order; and, at worst, as a facilitator of transforming the human rights movements into human rights markets that have replaced the Universal Declaration of

[11] Ibid., 3.

[12] A slightly different conclusion is reached in Justin Easery and Jacqueline H.R. DeMeritt, "Political context and the consequences of naming and shaming for human rights abuse" 43(4) *International interactions* (2017): 589; *see also* Eric Neumayer, "Do human rights matter in bilateral aid allocation? A quantitative analysis of 21 donor countries" 84(3) *Social Science Quarterly* (2003): 650.

[13] Lebovic and Voeten (2009) (n. 9): 79.

[14] In relation to the former Commission on Human Rights, *see* Forsythe and Park (2008) (n. 9): 3–14.

[15] For notable exceptions, *see* Kathryn Sikkink, *Evidence for Hope. Making Human Rights Work in the 21st Century* (Princeton University Press, 2017), and Beth A. Simmons, *Mobilizing for Human Rights: International Law in Domestic Politics* (Cambridge University Press, 2009). A summary of other works articulating achievements of the human rights agenda, can be found in Stephen Hopgood, Jack Snyder, and Leslie Vinjamuri, "Introduction: Human Rights Past, Present, and Future" in Hopgood, Snyder, & Vinjamuri (eds.), *Human Rights Futures* (Cambridge University Press, 2017): 1.

Human Rights paradigm with a trade-related, market-friendly human rights paradigm.[16] The arguments underpinning this line of reasoning have gained unprecedented attention in the last decade, after they have been further articulated and reframed by some Western academics platformed abundantly in mainstream media, and whose publications have been unceasingly analyzed by other scholars, governments, and civil society organizations in multiple fora. As a consequence, the human rights discourse and its mechanisms are increasingly portrayed as so fragile and/or inadequate that a complete new human rights narrative with a different approach to politics and law is required to make human rights a meaningful tool for diagnosis and remedy.[17] The most pessimistic have simply heralded the end of a machinery no longer fit for purpose.[18] Different hypotheses have been tested to identify the causes explaining the crisis of confidence in human rights. One factor often invoked is the triumph of the capitalist model, globalization, and market liberalization associated with the end of the Cold War. Human rights are a "powerless companion" of market fundamentalism, unable by design to deliver on its promises.[19] Posner has argued that the root cause of this defeat lies in the design of non-enforceable international human rights norms and their hidden cost since they interference with other governmental welfare-promoting activities.[20] Wuerth takes this idea further. According to her, the human rights–driven transformation of international law and sovereignty have weakened international law, making it less able to generate compliance, harming interstate relations and increasing the potential for interstate friction and conflict. She emphasizes the magnitude of costs involved in maintaining and enforcing international human rights requires a dramatic solution and advocates that international law and international institutions, including the work of the United Nations, should focus on a narrower range of core legal rules to

[16] Upendra Baxi, *The future of human rights* (Oxford University Press, 2002). *See also* Issa G. Shivji, *The concept of human rights in Africa* (African Books Collective, 1989); Makau Mutua, "Savages, victims, and saviors: The metaphor of human rights" 42(1) *Harvard International Law Journal* (2001): 201; Ratna Kapur, "Human Rights in the 21st Century: Take a Walk on the Dark Side," 28 *Sydney Law Review* (2006): 665; Chidi A. Odinkalu, "Why More Africans Don't Use Human Rights Language" 2(1) *Human Rights Dialogue* (2000): 3.

[17] Susan Marks, "Human rights in disastrous times" in James Crawford & Martti Koskenniemi (eds.), *The Cambridge Companion of International Law* (Cambridge University Press, 2012): 309–26; *see also* Knox (n. 2).

[18] Stephen Hopgood, *The Endtimes of Human Rights* (Cornell University Press, 2013).

[19] Samuel Moyn, "A powerless companion: Human rights in the age of neoliberalism" 77(4) *Law & Contemporary Problems* (2014): 147.

[20] Eric Posner *The Twilight of Human Rights Law* (Oxford University Press, 2014), and "Human Welfare, Not Human Being" 108(7) *Columbia Law Review* (2008): 1758.

protect and prevent threats to peace and security but not human rights. In her view, the latter is a role that ought to be confined to domestic and regional legal systems.[21]

At the core of these criticisms is the alleged inability of the international human rights agenda to deliver on its promises. One key obstacle in engaging with a critique of the international human rights framework from this perspective is determining what those unfulfilled promises are since the range of human rights standards, mechanisms, and actors involved in their implementation continue to evolve. This evolution is extremely visible in Special Procedures whether we look at their changing nature from isolated fact-finding missions to a "system," the development of methods of work, or the scope of topics they cover worldwide. The analysis of that evolution suggests that human rights have not succeeded in combating inequality and structural imbalances of the international order precisely because the standards and mechanisms developed under the human rights umbrella remain isolated in this task. International human rights normative and institutional frameworks are suffering from the failure of enabling other regulatory and monitoring institutions to address non-state actors' grievances. The unique features of human rights mechanisms and institutions in terms of accessibility have resulted in unrealistic hopes placed on bodies and rules designed for one set of purposes, but expected to deliver those assigned to other international mechanisms and normative frameworks.

International human rights have been configured as subjective rights articulated against abuses of state power. The rules and bodies created around that idea work insofar as the state is the supreme power, capable of enforcing—and violating—the law, a principle on which all international law is based. Arguably, the idea that human rights are a Western-led normative project is easier to contest than the Western idea of state and statehood that most scholars assume when addressing human rights issues.[22] The innovation introduced by the human rights regime in international law was not that states became accountable for their legal commitment toward other states regarding the treatment of citizens under their jurisdiction. The revolutionary element lies rather in the consolidated possibility of individuals and

[21] Ingrid Wuerth, "International Law in the Post-Human Rights Era" 96(2) *Texas Law Review* (2017): 279.

[22] Thomas Risse, "Human Rights in Areas of Limited Statehood: From the Spiral Model to Localization and Translation" in Stephen Hopgood, Jack Snyder, and Leslie Vinjamuri (eds.), *Human Rights Futures* (Cambridge University Press, 2017): 135, 139.

other non-state actors bringing human rights claims before international mechanisms.

The incursion of human rights into a wide range of international actions, permeating nearly all policies at international level, has been portrayed as a consequence of their success and/or absence of clear conceptual boundaries. In the words of Koskenniemi:

> From advancing development to expanding free trade, from intervening in "failed states" to regulating (or not regulating) the internet, the benefits offered by such projects have been described in terms of the "rights" of the beneficiaries. Because there is no clear limit to such re-labelling, it often happens that both sides in a conflict invoke their "human right" say, a right to "freedom" or a right to "security."

This phenomenon is reflected in the ever-growing number of Special Procedures. While several proposals for reform analyzed in chapter two were aimed at "rationalizing" Special Procedures, states continued to approve resolutions creating new mandates. The reasons for this "success" and its damaging effects have been highlighted by commentators from different perspectives.[23] Here we emphasize that this phenomenon is the direct consequence of the failure of other mechanisms to deliver remedies in the context of the struggles of communities. When underrepresented people, such as the Tibetans, seek to raise awareness of their situation and self-determination aspirations at international level, human rights violations become the only focus of their plea because human rights bodies are the lone avenue open to formal interaction with an intergovernmental body. When developing countries failed in their push for the creation of a New International Economic Order, the topic has found, under various guises, accommodation in the human rights agenda, as manifested in the creation of several Special Procedures' mandates focusing on foreign debt, international solidarity, or development. Many organizations focusing on women's equality do not use human rights approaches as the main tool or idea informing their work, but

[23] *See, e.g.*, Jean d'Aspremont, "Expansion and the Sources of International Human Rights Law" 46 *Israel Yearbook on Human Rights* (2016): 223; Rosa Freedman and Jacob Mchangama, "Expanding or diluting human rights: the proliferation of United Nations Special Procedures mandates" 38(1) *Human Rights Quarterly* (2016): 164.

those seeking allies beyond their national boundaries may strategically adopt the language of human rights.[24]

In brief, other international institutions have remained closed avenues to addressing the aspirations of non-state actors. International human rights law has not introduced significant changes to traditional conceptions of sovereignty, despite some doctrinal claims. As a result, international rules and institutions remain largely state-centric and inaccessible to individuals and communities.[25] Thus when civil society organizations, peoples, women, environmental activists, or other stakeholders want to access international fora to raise global challenges and highlight structural inequalities, it becomes rapidly evident that they may only succeed in doing so through access to the UN Human Rights Council or other regional human rights mechanisms. Other international organizations and bodies within and outside the United Nations are hermetically sealed against meaningful non-state actors' participation. The few exceptions available are extremely limited in terms of access and the scope of concerns and demands that can be brought before them. The European Court of Justice within the European Union or the Ombudsperson figures created to allow non-state actors and individuals to have a voice before the Security Council or the International Settlement of Investment Disputes before the World Bank, are good examples of this.

The accessibility of human rights mechanisms in general, and Special Procedures in particular, to individuals and other non-state actors, remains a rara avis in international law. Klabbers has recently highlighted an interconnected issue: many branches of international law addressing the position of the individual are seldom considered international law. He illustrates his point by referring to treaties on taxation, refugee status, or labor. Incidentally, labor rights are among the few not covered by a Special Procedure. This raises issues beyond the inflated claims concerning the legal status of the individual as a subject of international law.[26] In other words, the role of individuals and

[24] Sally Engle Merry and Peggy Levitt, "The Vernacularization of Women's Human Rights" in Hopgood, Snyder, & Vinjamuri (eds.), *Human Rights Futures* (Cambridge University Press, 2017): 213, 233–6.

[25] On the resilience of international law vis-à-vis human rights agendas, *see* Frédéric Mégret, "Having It Both Ways: International Human Rights Law Cannot Both Be in Decline and Be (That) Problematic for International Law" 96 *Texas Law* Review (2017): 114, 131. On exaggerated claims about the impact of human rights on sovereignty, *see* Elvira Domínguez-Redondo and Edward R. McMahon, "More honey than vinegar: peer review as a middle ground between universalism and national sovereignty" 51 *Canadian Yearbook of International Law/Annuaire canadien de droit international* 51 (2014): 61, 80–90.

[26] Jan Klabbers, "On Epistemic Universalism and the Melancholy of International Law," 29(4) *European Journal of International Law* (2018): 1057.

other non-state actors to bring their voices to the international arena are nearly non-existent if they are not framed as human rights.

The openness of the human rights system is obviously one of its best features. There is little merit in creating standards and structures aimed at protecting human beings from abuses of power if the main beneficiaries cannot access them directly. However, the fact that it remains exceptional has pernicious consequences. This can be illustrated with two points. First, the human rights regime is also more open than others to constant criticism from within. The involvement of organized civil society, law practitioners, academics, and victims of breaches of international law with human rights mechanisms facilitates a contestation of double standards by non-state actors from within the mechanisms themselves that is difficult to imagine in other domains regulated by international rules. A revealing example is the abundance of scholarship produced as critique to the human rights system. However, openness to criticism is not the major weakness associated to the accessibility of human rights mechanisms. This study of Special Procedures shows how the absence of strict admissibility criteria for approaching mandate holders and the direct participation of non-state actors in the proceedings of the Human Rights Council makes them particularly accessible. The exponential growth of Special Procedures and agenda items under the Human Rights Council is one of the visible consequences. Yet this progress is not a concern by itself—beyond the availability of adequate human and financial resources to support them.[27] The real problem lies in the contradictions created within a system from which different objectives that are not always compatible are expected. Illustrating a wider issue affecting other international human rights mechanisms, mandate holders of Special Procedures often address human rights concerns that are more closely related to the development and security agenda of the United Nations. While the complementarity of human rights, development, and security are well established, the strategies, rules, and mechanisms to achieve those objectives are not always easy to combine.

Large-scale human rights violations occur in the shadow of violent conflict. The United Nations was founded against the backdrop of the Holocaust for the purpose of saving future generations from wars related to disrespecting

[27] Although it has been claimed that it affects their impact by Marc Limon and Ted Piccone, *Human Rights Special Procedures: Determinants of Influence* (Universal Rights Group, 2014): 16. *See also* Jane Connors, "Special Procedures: Independence and Impartiality" in Aoife Nolan, Rosa Freedman, and Thérèse Murphy (eds.), *The United Nations Special Procedures System* (Brill, 2017): 52, 57–60.

human rights. Human rights violations and impunity are widely acknowledged as drivers of conflicts.[28] Security is often framed as a feeling of being protected. In the same way that some have postulated that sovereignty is conditioned to the respect of human rights, others have grounded national and international security on individual security.[29] The well-intentioned attempt to reconcile security and human rights agendas has been translated into different initiatives to enhance the relationship between Special Procedures and the Security Council, outlined in chapter six. However, the recognition of peace and security as a condition for the enjoyment of human rights and vice versa does not resolve challenges in designing policies that are compatible with human rights enjoyment and/or security to fit specific scenarios.

As mentioned earlier, Wuerth has argued that human rights–driven innovations affecting international norms on immunity, jurisdiction, and territorial integrity of the state threaten peace and security.[30] This disputed line of argumentation serves nonetheless to prove that the harmonious complementarity and coexistence of human rights protection and security remain a contested aspiration. More broadly, it denotes that the decline of human rights might be better explained by the widespread acknowledgment that pursuing one objective always involves a cost.[31]

The introduction of targeted sanctions by the Security Council in 1992 illustrates the point. The design and implementation of "intelligent sanctions" to avoid the devastating humanitarian consequences of comprehensive sanctions has become progressively sophisticated, especially in combating financial support for terrorism. The ethical, theoretical, and practical benefits of this move are obvious.[32] However, the imposition of sanctions against individuals and non-state actors, rather than states, had a negative impact on well-established human rights that have been challenged before national and international mechanisms.[33] Responding to the criticisms, the Security Council undertook several reforms, including the establishment of

[28] *See*, for instance, the Statement by UNHCHR Michelle Bachelet, *Arria formula meeting of the UN Security Council "Human rights, accountability and justice: contributions to international peace and security,"* OHCHR, 11 March 2019, available at: https://www.ohchr.org/EN/NewsEvents/Pages/DisplayNews.aspx?NewsID=24293&LangID=E.

[29] Bertrand G. Ramcharan, *Human Rights and Human Security* (M. Nijhoff Publishers, 2002).

[30] Wuerth (2017) (n. 21): 279.

[31] Mégret (2017) (n. 25): 114, 122.

[32] Thomas J. Biersteker, "Targeted sanctions and individual human rights" 65(1) *International Journal* (2010): 99.

[33] Ibid., 103–6.

a Focal Point for De-Listing[34] and the Office of the Ombudsperson to the ISIL (Da'esh) and Al-Qaida Sanctions Committee.[35] While these measures constitute an improvement, they continue to fall short of complying with international human rights standards, an issue repeatedly raised by the Special Rapporteur on human rights and fundamental freedoms while countering terrorism.[36] The mere existence of this mandate, confirmed by the contents of all its reports, corroborates the conflicting nature of the security and human rights agendas.

Similar problems are raised by the growing use of unmanned aerial vehicles, or drones, in lethal operations. As technology revolutionizes contemporary forms of engagement in warfare, new risks to human rights have arisen. Like targeted sanctions, the drones seem, at first sight, a welcome development with the potential of minimizing casualties in the battleground and in other extraterritorial lethal operations. However, they have attracted important criticism from a human rights perspective, as reflected in several reports of the Special Procedures on extrajudicial, summary, or arbitrary executions and on fundamental rights while countering terrorism.[37]

Solid arguments also sustain the complementarity of development and human rights, their interdependence, and the potential of human rights approaches to sharpen strategies for achieving development goals and vice versa.[38] The mandates of Special Procedures focused on economic, social, and cultural rights frequently refer to the 2030 Agenda for Sustainable Development, diluting the boundaries between human rights and development only for a category of mandates. Several mandate holders have addressed the development agenda since the adoption of the Millennium Development Goals.[39] The human rights and development agendas are

[34] SC Res. 1730/2006, 19 December 2006. Other relevant resolutions and information about the Focal-Point can be found at: https://www.un.org/securitycouncil/sanctions/delisting/resolutions.

[35] SC Res. 1904/2009, 17 December 2009. Other resolution and information about the Ombudsperson can be found at: https://www.un.org/securitycouncil/ombudsperson.

[36] *See*, for instance, a report to the General Assembly focusing on the Compliance with human rights by the United Nations when countering terrorism, UN Doc. A/65/258 (2010), paras. 17–80; *see also* reports contained in UN Docs. A/HRC34/61 (2017); A/73/453 (2017); and A/HRC/40/32 (2019).

[37] *See* reports of the Special Rapporteur on executions, UN Docs. A/68/382 (13 September 2013) and A/HRC/26/36 (1 April 2014); and the Special Rapporteur on counter-terrorism, UN Doc. A/HRC/25/59 (10 March 2014).

[38] *See, e.g.*, Salil Shetty, "Millennium Declaration and Development Goals: Opportunities for Human Rights" 2(2) *SUR-International Journal on Human Rights* (2005): 6; Inga T. Winkler and Margaret L. Satterthwaite, "Leaving no one behind? Persistent inequalities in the SDGs" 21(8) *The International Journal of Human Rights* (2017): 1073.

[39] *See, e.g., Report of the Independent Expert on the enjoyment of human rights by persons with albinism*, UN Doc. A/73/181 (2018); *Report of the Independent Expert on international solidarity*, UN

extremely congruent in the objective of ameliorating the well-being of individuals, but their harmonization presents conceptual, methodological, and practical challenges that have been translated into development and human rights practitioners performing their day-to-day activities in "splendid isolation."[40]

The legal valence attached to human rights hinders the incorporation of a human rights based approach by development practitioners or aid agencies. This value often renders rights as ill-suited to trade-offs that are considered necessary when implementing development agendas.[41] Well-founded political stances promote a separation of the development and human rights agendas. For instance, some states fear that human rights approaches to development would be the entry point for the imposition of conditionalities to development assistance at UN level.[42] There are many unknowns about the specific relationship between development policies and human rights. For instance, strong evidence supports the argument that structural adjustment programs have led to less respect for human rights but an improvement in democratic institutions.[43] These difficulties cannot be overcome by merely incorporating development goals in the scope of mandates of human rights mechanisms or mainstreaming human rights within the development machinery.[44]

The issues of security, development, and human rights are deeply intertwined. States should consider human rights when they design security, economic, and financial policies and normative frameworks at international

Doc. A/72/171 (19 July 2017), paras. 33–66; or *Reports of the Special Rapporteur on water and sanitation*, UN Docs. A/67/270 (8 August 2012); and A//71/302 (5 August 2016); *Report of the Independent Expert on minority issues: Achieving the Millennium Development Goals for minorities*, UN Doc. A/HRC/4/9/Add.1 (2 March 2007); *see also* summary of relevant reports on Sustainable Development Goals by several mandate-holders in *Report on the twenty-fifth annual meeting of special rapporteurs/representatives, independent experts and chairs of working groups of the special procedures of the Human Rights Council (Geneva, 4 to 8 June 2018), including updated information on special procedures*, UN Doc. A/HRC/40/38 (12 March 2019), paras. 21 and 36.

[40] Peter Uvin, *Human Rights and Development* (Kumarian Press, 2005): 1.

[41] Ibid. (Uvin) 30–1.

[42] Non-Aligned Movement and G77, *Joint Statement by G-77 and NAM on Informal Consultations of the General Assembly on United Nations System-wide Coherence* (24 July 2007), available at: https://www.g77.org/statement/2007.html.

[43] Rodwan Abourharb and David Cigranelli, *Human Rights and Structural Adjustment* (Cambridge University Press, 2007); the latest report of the independent expert on foreign debt and structural adjustment programmes focuses precisely on the responsibility for complicity of international financial institutions in human rights violations, UN Doc. A/74/178 (16 July 2019).

[44] On the limitations of this approach, *see* Elvira Domínguez-Redondo, "The Millennium Development Goals and the human rights-based approach: reflecting on structural chasms with the United Nations system" 13(1) *The International Journal of Human Rights* (2009): 29.

level. Likewise, human rights bodies cannot retreat from security and development implications enshrined within the human rights agenda. Yet, human rights bodies are not equipped to address many of the development and security implications of normative, institutional, and political frameworks through their current configuration. However, until other international fora open their space and mechanisms to non-state actors seeking to remedy rising inequality linked to specific economic policies, repression of the right to self-determination or violent conflict, human rights mechanisms remain the only available option. The operational flexibility, visibility, status, and methods of work of Special Procedures make them the most directly accessible mechanisms of the international human rights machinery to governmental officials, civil society, the media, other international organizations, and the victims of human rights violations. At the mercy of the resources and expertise of individuals working part-time, Special Procedures' capacity to fill the gaps of other international institutions are self-evident. However, their plasticity also permits navigation of different international law normative frameworks and direct contact with other transnational actors that are out of reach for other human rights mechanisms with stronger legal foundations and stricter rules of procedure.

One strongly held belief informing human rights narratives is the idea of human rights as a Western-led project, despite critical revisions accounting for the foundational and long-lasting impact of non-Western actors.[45] Within the United Nations, the voting weight gained by African and Asian states from the mid-1960s determined a change of direction in the General Assembly toward greater consideration of human rights that was soon reflected in the amplified scope of competence assumed by the Commission on Human Rights.[46] The first attempt to create a World Court of Human Rights can be traced back to an unsuccessful Australian proposal in 1947. With the support of Switzerland, this idea was revived by proposals put forward by Scheinin and Nowak in the 2000s,[47] which culminated with a draft statute for

[45] Steven L.B. Jensen, *The Making of International Human Rights: The 1060s, Decolonization, and the Reconstruction of Global Values* (Cambridge University Press: 2016).

[46] *See* Warren Weinstein, "Africa's Approach to Human Rights at the United Nations," 6(4) *African Issues* (1976): 14.

[47] *See* Manfred Nowak, "The Need for a World Court of Human Rights" 7(1) *Human Rights Law Review* (2007): 251; *see also* Manfred Nowak, "The right of victims of human rights violations to a remedy: The need for a world court of human rights" 32(1) *Nordic Journal of Human Rights* (2014): 3; Martin Sheinin, "Towards a world court of human rights" *Agenda on Human Rights, Swiss Initiative* (2009), available at: https://www.eui.eu/Documents/DepartmentsCentres/AcademyofEuropeanLaw/CourseMaterialsHR/HR2009/Scheinin/ScheininClassReading1.pdf.

the suggested World Court in 2010.[48] However, the scholarship on this issue mostly fails to acknowledge that, already in 1968, the Attorney General of Nigeria prepared a study for the International Conference on Human Rights advocating the establishment of a UN committee with the aim of assessing proposals leading to the creation of an International Court of Human Rights.[49]

The enlargement of the members of the UN Commission on Human Rights and the different geographic distribution of state representative in the UN Human Rights Council with a greater representation of states from the Asian and African Group has not resulted in the negative consequences envisaged by many.[50] These assumptions are related to their "negative reform agenda" and their attempts to remove country resolutions or curtail the power of mandate holders of Special Procedures. These initiatives, as explained in detail in chapter two, have been largely unsuccessful. Countries from the African Group, the Asian Group, and the Group of Latin America Caribbean Countries have been fundamental in introducing positive outcomes. They have promoted and facilitated the focus on economic, social, and cultural rights, collective rights, and solidarity rights. They have also helped correct the geographical imbalance in the representation of mandate holders, and have sponsored positive reforms such as limits to the terms of mandate holders. They have also promoted the approval of a Code of Conduct that provides better legal foundations than ever before to some of the methods of work applied by mandate holders.

Existing data suggests that countries in the African and Asian States Groups are more likely to be the object of a negative human rights resolution, and countries belonging to the Western Group are more likely to promote such decisions.[51] However, an analysis of voting patterns and sponsorship of resolutions covering thematic and country-specific issues defy preconceived conventions about the "North" and the "South." Developing countries are not unified under a "sovereignty-trumps-all" approach to human rights nor under any other distinguishable position aligning with initiatives normally associated with members of the Western Group.[52] Even when a regional

[48] Julia Kozma, Manfred Nowak, and Martin Scheinin, *A world court of human rights: consolidated statute and commentary* (Neuer Wissenschaftlicher Verlag, 2010).
[49] Weinstein (1976) (n. 46): 14, 15.
[50] See chapter one.
[51] *The Human Rights Council in 2018. Leadership, resolve and cooperation at the UN's main human rights body* (yourHRC.org, 2019): 25–6.
[52] Debunking traditional misconceptions, *see* Jonathan Fisher and Danielle Beswick, "The African State and Special Procedures: Agency, Leverage and Legitimacy" in Aoife Nolan, Rosa Freedman,

group has established a concerted position on specific issues, individual votes vary. An analysis of the Human Rights Council's actions published in 2014 revealed that the Western Group was responsible for the creation of a significant number of mandates on economic, social, and cultural rights, while the African Group was behind the creation of most country mandates.[53] Different reports covering the Human Rights Council's sessions between 2015 and 2018 confirm that the North-South divide is often alleged for political purposes but is not actually reflected in practice.[54] Most African members have voted against country resolutions but joined consensus when no vote was called. However, there are a significant number of exceptions to this general pattern.[55] A similar picture emerges from the initiatives and voting behaviors exhibited by the Asian and Pacific Group, with an overall favorable position toward voting in favor of thematic human rights issues.[56] The trend among the Eastern European Group's membership has been to position themselves against mandates focusing on economic, social, and cultural rights in roll-called voting situations, with the exceptions being the mandates on the right to food and to water and sanitation.[57] Different members of the Latin American and Caribbean Countries Group have sponsored resolutions pertaining to country and thematic mandates, but they have not presented a united front in their political endorsement of country mandates. Conversely, they have supported thematic mandates pertaining to all categories of rights, with few exceptions.[58] The Western European and Other States Group has displayed the most uniform performance. Its countries have endorsed geographic mandates with divisions only manifesting in relation to the mandate on the Occupied Palestinian Territories. They have tended to support thematic mandates, with some minor exceptions such as the use of mercenaries as a means of violating human rights and impeding the exercise of the right of peoples to self-determination and cross-cutting

and Thérèse Murphy (eds.), *The United Nations Special Procedures System* (Brill/Martinus Nijhoff, 2016): 385; *see also* Sibylle Scheipers, "Civilization vs Toleration: The New UN Human Rights Council and the Normative Foundations of the International Order" 10(3) *Journal of International Relations & Development* (2007): 219, 234–6.

53 Limon and Piccone (2014) (n. 27): 15.

54 *See* the annual reports on the Human Rights Council written by "yourHRC.org" for 2015–2018 at: http://yourhrc.org/. All relevant data is compiled in the reports "Facts and Figures with regard to the Special Procedures," (*see* chapter three *esp.* n. 38).

55 *The Human Rights Council in 2018* (2019) (n. 51).

56 Ibid.

57 Ibid.

58 Ibid.

matters, voting against resolutions on foreign debt, international solidarity, or democratic and equitable international order.[59]

The absence of a firm legal framework and the political decisions underpinning the creation and renewal of Special Procedures contrasts with the "jurisdictional development" of their methods of work. This combination provides a perfect scenario to test the role of politicization on human rights mechanisms. Special Procedures' history, reform, methods of work, and legal status demonstrate that states' involvement in the functioning of expert-led mechanisms, through intergovernmental bodies, may be more beneficial than detrimental to the advancement of human rights. Compared with the difficulties judges from the same background often face in agreeing on the interpretation of a shared normative framework, little credit is given to the skills and diplomatic mindset driving states to reach negotiated compromises despite strong differences of national agendas. Conversely, too much recognition has been awarded to the leadership of some countries in promoting the human rights agenda, fueling criticisms against human rights bodies as Western tools that promote their own interests. The increased availability of data facilitates empirically based conclusions regarding the functioning of human rights mechanisms. Acknowledging the positive aspects of the politicization of the human rights agenda does not mean compromising and bargaining with powerful human rights violators with the hope of raising rates of compliance with human rights standards. As this book has sought to demonstrate, vague political mandates, autonomy, and independence are limited by the standards that human rights mechanisms led by experts must follow at all times, even if they may hinder their efficacy in the short term.

[59] Ibid.

ANNEX

Number of Communications Sent. Data from OHCHR between December 1, 2009, and July 15, 2010.

Thematic Mandates	Established	Sent to States	Sent to Nonstate Actors
African Descent	2002	79	1
Albinism	2015	12	0
Arbitrary Detention	1991	1,126	14
Business	2011	343	103
Cultural Rights	2009	128	1
Development	2016	92	0
Disabilities	2014	118	4
Disappearances	1980	418	11
Education	1998	53	5
Environment	2012	257	37
Executions	1982	1,061	25
Food	2000	133	29
Foreign Debt	2000	90	10
Freedom of Assembly & Association	2010	1,338	27
Freedom of Opinion & Expression	1993	2,096	48
Hazardous Substances & Waste	1995	185	52
Health	2002	653	53
Housing	2000	207	18
Human Rights Defenders	2000	2,040	47
Judges & Lawyers	1994	701	8
Indigenous Peoples	2001	385	37
Internally Displaced People	2004	69	0
International Order	2011	137	4
International Solidarity	2005	54	1
Leprosy	2017	2	0
Mercenaries	2005	52	5
Migrants	1999	251	18
Minority Issues	2005	302	9
Older Persons	2013	39	0
Poverty	1998	108	10
Privacy	2015	60	5
Racism	1993	190	5

(Continued)

Thematic Mandates	Established	Sent to States	Sent to Nonstate Actors
Religion	1986	349	9
Sale of Children	1990	35	0
Sexual Orientation	2016	44	1
Slavery	2007	99	24
Terrorism	2005	289	3
Torture	1985	1,379	18
Trafficking	2004	68	7
Truth, Justice, & Reparations	2011	74	1
Unilateral Coercive Measures	2014	1	0
Violence Against Women	1994	402	6
Water & Sanitation	2008	232	31
Discrimination Against Women	2010	350	7

In 2019, communications sent by Special Procedures included four communications to states with the participation of the Inter-American Commission on Human Rights.

Country Mandates	Established	Sent to States	Sent to Nonstate Actors
Belarus	2012	13	0
Cambodia	1993	47	6
Central African Republic	2013	2	0
Democratic Republic of Korea	2004	13	0
Eritrea	2012	1	0
Iran	2011	180	0
Mali	2013	0	0
Myanmar	1992	76	0
Occupied Palestinian Territories	1993	55	0
Somalia	1993	16	2
Sudan	1993	40	0

Bibliography

Abourharb, Rodwan and David Cigranelli, *Human Rights and Structural Adjustment* (Cambridge University Press, 2007).

Abraham, Meghna, *A New Chapter for Human Rights: A Handbook on Issues of Transition from the Commission on Human Rights to the Human Rights Council* (Friedrich-Ebert-Stiftung and International Service for Human Rights, June 2006).

Abraham, Meghna, *Building the New Human Rights Council. Outcome and Analysis of the Institution-Building Year* (Friedrich-Ebert-Stiftung Occasional Papers, August 2007).

Alfredsson, Gudmundur, "Concluding Remarks: More Law and Less Politics," Gudmundur Alfredsson et al. (eds.), *International Human Rights Monitoring Mechanisms: Essays in Honour of Jakob Th. Möller* (Martinus Nijhoff Publishers, 2001).

Alfredsson, Gudmundur et al. (eds.), *International Human Rights Monitoring Mechanisms: Essays in Honour of Jakob Th. Möller* (Martinus Nijhoff Publishers, 2001).

Almeida, José A., *Reform of the United Nations Commission on Human Rights: Proposals to Restore the Commission's Credibility, Coherence and Consistency* (International Centre for Human Rights and Democratic Development, March 2004).

Almqvist, Jessica and Felipe Gómez Isa (eds.), *The Human Rights Council: Challenges and Opportunities* (FRIDE, 2006).

Alston, Philip, "Extreme Inequality as the Antithesis of Human Rights," *Open Global Rights* (August 27, 2015).

Alston, Philip, "Hobbling the Monitors: Should U.N. Human Rights Monitors Be Accountable?," 52(2) *Harvard International Law Journal* (2011): 561.

Alston, Philip, "Individual Complaints: Historical Perspectives and the International Covenant on Economic, Social and Cultural Rights," in Sarah Pritchard (ed.), *Indigenous Peoples, the United Nations and Human Rights* (Zed Books Ltd., The Federation Press, 1998): 81.

Alston, Philip, "Neither Fish nor Fowl: The Quest to Define the Role of the UN High Commissioner for Human Rights," 8 *European Journal of International Law* (1997): 321.

Alston, Philip, "Reconceiving the UN Human Rights Regime: Challenges Confronting the New UN Human Rights Council," 7(1) *Melbourne Journal of International Law* (2006): 185.

Alston, Philip, "Richard Lillich Memorial Lecture: Promoting the Accountability of Members of the New UN Human Rights Council," 15(1) *Journal of Transnational Law and Policy* (2005–2006): 49.

Alston, Philip, "The Security Council and Human Rights: Lessons to Be Learned from the Iraq-Kuwait Crisis and Its Aftermath," 13 *Australian Yearbook of International Law* (1990–1991): 107.

Alston, Philip (ed.), *The United Nations and Human Rights. A Critical Appraisal* (Clarendon Press, 1992).

Alston, Philip, "The U.S. and the Right to Housing: A Funny Thing Happened on the Way to the Forum," 1 *European Human Rights Law Review* (1996): 120.

Alston, Philip and Sarah Knuckey, "The Transformation of Human Rights Fact-Finding. Challenges and Opportunities," in Philip Alston and Sarah Knuckey (eds.), *The Transformation of Human Rights Fact-Finding* (Kindle ed., Oxford University Press, 2015).

Alston, Philip and Sarah Knuckey, *The Transformation of Human Rights Fact-Finding* (Kindle ed., Oxford University Press, 2015).

Alston, Philip, Jason Morgan, and William Abresch, "The Competence of the UN Human Rights Council and Its Special Procedures in Relation to Armed Conflicts," 18(1) *European Journal of International Law* (2008): 183.

Ambrus, Monika, Karin Arts, Ellen Hey, and Helena Raulus (eds.), *The Role of "Experts" in International and European Decision-Making Processes* (Cambridge University Press, 2014).

Amnesty International, *2003 UN Commission on Human Rights: A Time for Deep Reflection*, AI doc. IOR 41/025/2002, December 1, 2002.

Amnesty International, *UN Commission on Human Rights Ends on a Disappointing Note. New Council Deserves a Better Start*, AI doc. IOR 41/003/2006, March 28, 2006.

Amnesty International, *UN: Third Committee Rejects Strong Draft Declaration to Protect Indigenous Peoples*, AI doc. IOR 41/025/2006, November 28, 2006.

Aracil, Rafael, Joan Oliver, and Antoni Segura, *El mundo actual. De la Segunda Guerra Mundial a nuestros días* (2nd ed. Universitat de Barcelona, 1998).

Asian Indigenous and Tribal Peoples Network (AITPN), *LMG: Killing the Commission on Human Rights Softly*, UN Doc. E/CN.4/2005/NGO/8, February 5, 2005.

Bagshaw, Simon, "Internally Displaced Persons at the Fifty-Fourth Session of the United Nations Commission on Human Rights, 16 March–24 April 1998" 10(3) *International Journal of Refugee Law* (1998): 548.

Ballinger, R.B., "UN Action on Human Rights in South Africa," in Evan Luard (ed.), *The International Protection of Human Rights* (Thames and Hudson, 1967): 248.

Bassiouni, Cherif, "Appraising UN Justice-related Fact-finding Missions," 5 *Washington University Journal of Law and Policy* (2001): 35.

Bassiouni, Cherif and Christina Abraham (eds.), *Siracusa Guidelines for International, Regional and National Fact-Finding Bodies* (Intersentia, 2013).

Bassiouni, Cherif and William Schabas (eds.), *New Challenges for the UN Human Rights Machinery: What Future for the UN Treaty Body System and the Human Rights Council Procedures* (Intersentia, 2011).

Baxi, Upendra, *The Future of Human Rights* (Oxford University Press, 2002).

Bekker, Peter, "Difference Relating to Immunity from Legal Process of a Special Rapporteur of the Commission on Human Rights, 93(4) *American Journal of International Law* (1999): 913.

Berman, Eric G., *Bringing a New Life to UN Human Operations* (United Nations Associations of the United States of America, 1998).

Bernard, Jean-Marie, "La situation des droits de l'homme au Chili: enquête de la Commission des droits de l'homme des Nations Unies," 22 *Annuaire Français de Droit International* (1976): 305.

Bernhardt, Rudolf et al. (eds.), *Zeitschrift für Ausländisches Öffentliches Recht Und Völkerrecht. Begründet von Viktor Bruns* (Kohlhammer, 1985).

Bichet, Emmanuel and Stephani Rutz, *The Human Rights Council as a Subsidiary Organ* (URG, October 2016), available at https://www.universal-rights.org/

urg-policy-reports/human-rights-council-subsidiary-organ-evaluating-relationships-un-general-assembly-un-security-council/.

Biersteker, Thomas J., "Targeted Sanctions and Individual Human Rights," 65(1) *International Journal* (2010): 99.

Blatt, Deborah, "Recognizing Rape as a Method of Torture," 19(4) *New York University Review of Law and Social Change* (1992): 821.

Boerefijn, Ineke and Jenny Goldschmidt (eds.), *Changing Perceptions of Sovereignty and Human Rights. Essays in Honour of Cees Flinterman* (Intersentia, 2008).

Booth, Robert, "Amber Rudd's to Lodge Complaint over UN's Austerity Report," *The Guardian*, May 22, 2019.

Bossuyt, Marc, *The Human Rights Council: A Doubtful Reform?* (KU Leuven Faculty of Law paper, 2006), available at https://www.law.kuleuven.be/iir/nl/activiteiten/archief/documentatie/OldActivities/HRCBossuyt.pdf.

Bossuyt, Marc, *International Human Rights Protection. Balanced, Critical, Realistic* (Intersentia, 2016).

Bossuyt, Marc, "La distinction juridique entre les droits civil et politiques et les droits économiques, sociaux et culturels," VIII(4) *Revues des droits de l'Homme/Human Rights Journal* (1975): 783.

Bossuyt, Marc, "The United Nations and Civil and Political Rights in Chile," 27(2) *International and Comparative Law Quarterly* (1978): 462.

Boven, Theo van, "Chartering New Grounds in Human Rights," in Coomans et al. (eds.), *Human Rights from Exclusion to Inclusion; Principles and Practice. An Anthology from the Work of Theo van Boven* (Kluwer Law International, 2000): 3.

Boven, Theo van, "Creative and Dynamic Strategies for Using United Nations Institutions and Procedures: The Frank Newman Files," in Fons Coomans et al. (eds.), *Human Rights from Exclusion to Inclusion; Principles and Practice. An Anthology from the Work of Theo van Boven* (Kluwer Law International, 2000): 89.

Boven, Theo van, "Fact-finding in the Field of Human Rights" 3 *Israel Yearbook of Human Rights* (1973): 93.

Boven, Theo van, "Five Years after Strengthening the United Nations. Recasting the Office of the High Commissioner for Human Rights," in Ineke Boerefijn and Jenny Goldschmidt (eds.), *Changing Perceptions of Sovereignty and Human Rights. Essays in Honour of Cees Flinterman* (Intersentia, 2008): 145.

Boven, Theo van, "'Political' and 'Legal' Control Mechanisms: Their Competition and Coexistence," in Eide and Hagtvet (eds.), *Human Rights in Perspective. A Global Assessment* (Basil Blackwell Ltd., 1992): 36.

Boven, Theo van, "The United Nations Commission on Human Rights and Violations of Human Rights and Fundamental Freedoms," 18 *Netherlands International Law Review* (1968): 374.

Boven, Theo van, "United Nations and Human Rights. A Critical Appraisal," in Cassese (ed.), *UN Law/Fundamental Rights. Two Topics in International Law* (Sijthoff Noordhoff, 1979): 119.

Boyle, Kevin (ed.), *New Institutions for Human Rights Protection* (Oxford University Press, 2009).

Boyle, Kevin, "The United Nations Human Rights Council: Origins, Antecedents, and Prospects," in Kevin Boyle (ed.), *New Institutions for Human Rights Protection* (Oxford University Press, 2009): 29.

Brett, Rachel, *To Be or Not to Be. Report of the 61st Session of the UN Commission on Human Rights* (Quaker United Nations Office, Geneva, August 2005).

Bruegel, Johan W., "The Right to Petition an International Authority," 2 *International and Comparative Law Quarterly* (1953): 542.

Buckley, Carla, Alice Donald, and Philip Leach (eds.), *Towards Coherence in International Human Rights Law: Approaches of Regional and International Systems* (Brill, 2017).

Callamard, Agnes, Tamara Cofman Wiittes, and Ted Piccone, "Investigating the Khashoggi Murder: Insights from UN Special Rapporteur Agnes Callamard" (Podcast, The Brookings Institute, July 2, 2019), available at https://www.brookings.edu/events/investigating-the-khashoggi-murder-insights-from-un-special-rapporteur-agnes-callamard/.

Cançado Trindade, Antônio, "Co-existence and Co-ordination of Mechanisms of International Protection of Human Rights (at Global and Regional Levels," 202 *Collected Courses of the Hague Academy of International Law* (1987).

Carey, John, "The United Nations' Double Standards on Human Rights Complaints," 60 *American Journal of International Law* (1996): 792.

Carey, John, "United Nations Scrutiny of South African Prisons," I(4) *Revue de Droits de l'Homme/Human Rights Journal* (1968): 531.

Cassese, Antonio, "The Admissibility of Communications to the United Nations on Human Rights Violations," 5 *Human Rights Journal* (1972): 375.

Cassese, Antonio, "The Nicaragua and Tadić Tests Revisited in Light of the ICJ Judgment on Genocide in Bosnia," 18(4) *European Journal of International Law* (2007): 649.

Cassese, Antonio (ed.), *UN Law/Fundamental Rights. Two Topics in International Law* (Sijthoff Noordhoff, 1979).

Cassin, René, "La déclaration universelle et la mise en œuvre des droits de l'homme," 79(II) *Collected Courses of the Hague Academy of International Law* (1951): 237.

Castellino, Joshua and Sarah Bradshaw, "Sustainable Development and Social Inclusion: Why a Changed Approach Is Central to Combating Vulnerability," 24 *Washington International Law Journal* (2015): 459.

Cepeda Espinosa, Manuel J. "The Constitutional Protection of IDPs in Colombia," in Rodolfo A. Rivadeneira (ed.), *Judicial Protection of Internally Displaced Persons: The Colombian Experience* (Brookings Institution/University of Bern, 2009): 1.

Charlesworth, Hilary, Sam Chaiton, and Christine Chinkin, *The Boundaries of International Law: A Feminist Analysis* (Manchester University Press, 2000).

Charpentier, Jean, "Contrôle par les Organisations Internationales de l'exécution des obligations des Etats," 182(IV) *Collected Courses of the Hague Academy of International Law* (1983): 147.

Chesterman, Simon, "An International Rule of Law?," 56(2) *The American Journal of Comparative Law* (2008): 331.

Chesterman, Simon, Thomas M. Franck, and David M. Malone, *Law and Practice of the United Nations* (Oxford University Press, 2008).

Chimmi, Bhupinder S., *International Law and World Order: A Critique of Contemporary Approaches* (Cambridge University Press, 2017).

Chimmi, Bhupinder S., "Legitimising the International Rule of Law," in James Crawford and Martti Koskenniemi (eds.), *The Cambridge Companion of International Law* (Cambridge University Press, 2012): 290.

Chimmi, Bhupinder S., "Third World Approaches to International Law: A Manifesto," 8 *International Community Law Review* (2006): 3.

Clapham, Andrew, "Human Rights Obligations of Non-state Actors in Conflict Situations," 88 *International Review of the Red Cross* (2006): 491.
Connors, Jane, "Special Procedures: Independence and Impartiality," in Aoife Nolan, Rosa Freedman, and Thérèse Murphy (eds.), *The United Nations Special Procedures System* (Brill, 2017): 52.
Cook, Helena M., "International Human Rights Mechanisms. The Role of the Special Procedures in the Protection of Human Rights. The Way Forward After Vienna," 50 *Brooklyn Law Review* (1993): 31.
Coomans, Fons et al. (eds.), *Human Rights from Exclusion to Inclusion; Principles and Practice. An Anthology from the Work of Theo van Boven* (Kluwer Law International, 2000).
Couldrey, Marion and Maurice Herson (eds.), "Ten Years of the Guiding Principles on Internal Displacement," *Special Issue Forced Migration Review* (2008), available at http://www.refworld.org/pdfid/4c6cf2372.pdf.
Crawford, James, "International Law as Discipline and Profession," 106 *American Society of International Law Proceedings* (2012): 471.
Crawford, James, *State Responsibility* (Cambridge University Press, 2013).
Crawford, James and Martti Koskenniemi (eds.), *The Cambridge Companion of International Law* (Cambridge University Press, 2012).
Crook, John R., "The Fiftieth Session of the UN Commission on Human Rights," 88(4) *American Journal of International Law* (1994): 806.
Crook, John R., "The Fifty-first Session of the UN Commission on Human Rights," 90(1) *American Journal of International Law* (1996): 126.
D'Amato, Anthony, "Is International Law Really Law?," 79 *Northwestern University Law Review* (1984–1985): 1293.
d'Aspremont, Jean, "Expansion and the Sources of International Human Rights Law," 46 *Israel Yearbook on Human Rights* (2016): 223.
David, Eric, "L'avis de la Cour Internationale de Justice du 15 décembre 1989 sur l'applicabilité de la section 22 de l'article VI de la Convention sur les privilèges et immunités des Nations Unies (Aff. Mazilu)," XXXV *Annuaire Français de Droit International* (1989): 298.
Davoise, Marie, "Open Letter in Response to UN Special Rapporteur's Op-Ed on Julian Assange," *Medium*, July 1, 2019, available at https://medium.com/@mariedavoise/response-to-un-special-rapporteurs-op-ed-on-julian-assange-e911e0684182.
Daws, Sam, "The Origin and Development of UN Electoral Groups," in Ramesh Thakur (ed.), *What Is Equitable Geographic Representation in the 211 Century?* (UN University, 1999): 11.
Dennis, Michael J., "The Fifty-Second Session of the UN Commission on Human Rights," 91(1) *American Journal of International Law* (1997): 167.
Dennis, Michael J., "The Fifty-Seventh Session of the UN Commission on Human Rights," 96(1) *American Journal of International Law* (2002): 181.
Dennis, Michael J., "The Fifty-Sixth Session of the UN Commission on Human Rights," 95(1) *American Journal of International Law* (2001): 213.
Dennis, Michael J., "The Fifty-Third Session of the UN Commission on Human Rights," 92(1) *American Journal of International Law* (1998): 112.
DiGiacomo, Gordon and Susan Kang (eds.), *The Institutions of Human Rights* (University of Toronto Press, 2019).

Dodo Dulay, Atty, "UN Rapporteur Garcia-Sayán Violated UN Code of Conduct," *Manila Times*, June 8, 2018.

Domínguez-Redondo, Elvira, "Human Rights Through the Backdoor: The Contribution of Special Procedures to the Normative Development of International Human Rights Law," in Carla Buckley, Alice Donald, and Philip Leach (eds.), *Towards Coherence in International Human Rights Law: Approaches of Regional and International Systems* (Brill, 2017): 543.

Domínguez-Redondo, Elvira, "La Comisión de Derechos Humanos a Debate: El Procedimiento 1503," 2 *Revista Iberoamericana de Derechos Humanos* (2006): 34.

Domínguez-Redondo, Elvira, *Los procedimientos Públicos Especiales de la Comisión de Derechos Humanos* (Tirant lo Blanc, 2005).

Domínguez-Redondo, Elvira, "Making the Connection: Security and Human Rights," in Cherif Bassiouni and William Schabas (eds.), *New Challenges for the UN Human Rights Machinery: What Future for the UN Treaty Body System and the Human Rights Council Procedures* (Intersentia, 2011): 255.

Domínguez-Redondo, Elvira, "The Millennium Development Goals and the Human Rights–based Approach: Reflecting on Structural Chasms with the United Nations System," 13(1) *The International Journal of Human Rights* (2009): 29.

Domínguez-Redondo, Elvira, "Rethinking the Legal Foundations of Control in International Human Rights Law—The Case of Special Procedures," 29(3) *Netherlands Quarterly of Human Rights* (2011): 261.

Domínguez-Redondo, Elvira, "The Universal Periodic Review of the UN Human Rights Council: An Assessment of the First Session," 7(3) *Chinese Journal of International Law* (2008): 721.

Domínguez-Redondo, Elvira, "UN Public Special Procedures under Damocles' Sword—Two Particular Innovations: Mechanisms for the Appointment of Mandate-holders and the Adoption of a Code of Conduct for Special Procedures Mandate-holders of the Human Rights Council," 29 *Human Rights Law Journal* (2009): 32.

Domínguez-Redondo, Elvira and Magdalena Sepúlveda Carmona, "Contextualizando el Informe Cassese: La dictadura que cambió el sistema de derechos humanos de Naciones Unidas y su legado en el monitoreo de derechos económicos, sociales y culturales," in Juan P. Bohoslavsky, Karinna Fernández, and Sebastian Smart (eds.), *Un país desigual a la fuerza: Complicidad económica con la dictadura chilena* (LOM, 2019): 97.

Domínguez-Redondo, Elvira and Edward R. McMahon, "More Honey than Vinegar: Peer Review as a Middle Ground between Universalism and National Sovereignty," 51 *Canadian Yearbook of International Law/Annuaire canadien de droit international* (2014): 61.

Droege, Cordula, "Elective Affinities? Human Rights and Humanitarian Law," 90 *International Review of the Red Cross* (2008): 501.

Easery, Justin and Jacqueline H.R. DeMeritt, "Political Context and the Consequences of Naming and Shaming for Human Rights Abuse," 43(4) *International Interactions* (2017): 589.

Egret, Pauline, "Outcomes of the 1503 and 1235 Procedures," in Meghna Abraham, *A New Chapter of Human Rights* (International Service for Human Rights and Friedrich Elbert Stifung, 2006).

Eide, Asbjørn, "The Sub-Commission on Prevention on the Elimination of Racial Discrimination," in Philip Alston (ed.), *The United Nations and Human Rights. A Critical Appraisal* (Clarendon Press, 1992): 211.

Eide, Asbjørn and Bern Hagtvet (eds.), *Human Rights in Perspective. A Global Assessment* (Basil Blackwell Ltd., 1992).

Ermacora, Felix, "Human Rights and Domestic Jurisdiction (Article 2 Paragraph 7 of the Charter," 124 *Collected Courses of the Hague Academy of International Law* (1968): 375.

Ermacora, Felix, "International Enquiry Commission in the Field of Human Rights," I(2) *Revue de Droits de l'Homme/Human Rights Journal* (1968): 180.

Ermacora, Felix, "Procedure to Deal with Human Rights Violations. A Hopeful Start in the United Nations?," 7 *Human Rights Journal* (1974): 670.

Ermacora, Felix, "UN and Human Rights in Chile," 1(2) *The Human Rights Review* (1976): 145.

Escobar-Hernández, Concepción, *La Comisión de Derechos Humanos de Naciones Unidas y la violación de los derechos humanos y libertades fundamentales: un estudio de los procedimientos especiales.* Doctoral Thesis (3 volumes) (Madrid, Universidad Complutense de Madrid, 1988).

Eslava, Luis and Sundhya Pahuja, "Between Resistance and Reform: TWAIL and the Universality of International Law," 3(1) *Trade, Law and Development* (2011): 103.

Espósito, Carlos, *La jurisdicción consultiva de la Corte Internacional de Justicia* (Madrid: McGraw Hill, 1996).

Fagan, Andrew, "Poverty and Inequality in the UK: Proud to be British?," *Human Rights Centre Blog* (University of Essex, June 27, 2019), available at https://hrcessex.wordpress.com/2019/06/27/poverty-inequality-in-the-uk-proud-to-be-british/.

Faleh Pérez, Carmelo, "El Grupo de Trabajo sobre la Detención Arbitraria de la Comisión de Derechos Humanos de las Naciones Unidas," 0 *Revista de la Facultad de Ciencias Jurídicas de la Universidad de Las Palmas* (1995): 103.

Fareed, Nabiel J., *The United Nations Commission on Human Rights and Its Work for Human Rights and Fundamental Freedoms* (Diss. Washington State University, 1979).

Farer, Tom J., "The UN and Human Rights: More than a Whimper, Less than a Roar," in Adam Roberts and Benedict Kingsbury (eds.), *United Nations, Divided World. The UN's Roles in International Relations* (Clarendon Press, 1988): 95.

Farer, Tom J. and Felice Gaer, "The UN and Human Rights: At the End of the Beginning," in Roberts and Kingsbury (eds.), *United Nations, Divided World. The UN's Role in International Relations* (2nd ed., Clarendon Press, 1993): 240.

Fisher, Jonathan and Danielle Beswick, "The African State and Special Procedures: Agency, Leverage and Legitimacy," in Aoife Nolan, Rosa Freedman, and Thérèse Murphy (eds.), *The United Nations Special Procedures System* (Brill/Martinus Nijhoff, 2016): 385.

Flood, Patrick J., *The Effectiveness of UN Human Rights Institutions* (Praeger Publishers, 1998).

Forsythe, David D. and Baekkwan Park, "The Changing of the Guard: From the UN Human Rights Commission to the Council," 29(1) *Human Rights Law Journal* (2008): 3.

Fox, Hazel, "The Advisory Opinion on the Difference Relating to Immunity from Legal Process of a Special Rapporteur of the Commission of Human Rights: Who Has the Last Word on Judicial Independence?," 12 *Leiden Journal of International Law* (1999): 889.

Franck, Thomas and Scott H. Fairley, "Procedural Due Process in Human Rights Fact-finding by International Agencies," 74 *American Journal of International Law* (1980): 308.

Freedman, Rosa and Jacob Mchangama, "Expanding or Diluting Human Rights: The Proliferation of United Nations Special Procedures Mandates" 38(1) *Human Rights Quarterly* (2016): 164.

Frick, Marie-Luisa and Andreas Th. Müller (eds.), *Islam and International Law: Engaging Self-Centrism from a Plurality of Perspectives* (Brill, 2013).

Frouville, Olivier de, *Les procédures thématiques: une contribution efficace des Nations Unies à la protection des droits de l'homme* (A. Pedone, 1996).

Frouville, Olivier de, "Working Out a Working Group: A View from a Former Working Group Member," in Aoife Nolan, Rosa Freedman, and Thérèse Murphy (eds.), *The United Nations Special Procedures System* (Brill, 2017): 223.

Gaer, Felice, "The High Commissioner and the Special Procedures: Colleagues and Competitors," in Felice Gaer and Christen Broecker (eds.), *The United Nations High Commissioner for Human Rights. Conscience for the World* (Martinus Nijhoff, 2014): 133.

Gaer, Felice, "Picking and Choosing? Country Visits by Thematic Special Procedures," in Aoife Nolan, Rosa Freedman, and Thérèse Murphy (eds.), *The United Nations Special Procedures System* (Brill, 2017): 87.

Gaer, Felice and Christen Broecker (eds.), *The United Nations High Commissioner for Human Rights. Conscience for the World* (Martinus Nijhoff, 2014).

Galbraith, Jean, "United States Withdraws from the UN Human Rights Council, Shortly after Receiving Criticism about Its Border Policy," 112(4) *American Journal of International Law* (2018): 745.

Gallagher, Anne, "The Human Rights Protection System of the United Nations and of Its Specialized Agencies," *Recueil des Cours* (Strasbourg: Institut International des Droits de l'Homme, 1998): 197.

Glendon, Mary A., "The Forgotten Crucible: The Latin American Influence on the Universal Human Rights Idea," 16 *Harvard Human Rights Journal* (2003): 27.

Gomez, Jim, "Duerte Tells UN Expert 'to Go to Hell' over Criticism," *AP News*, June 3, 2018.

Gonzáles, Theresa, "The Political Sources of Procedural Debates in the United Nations: Structural Impediments to Implementation of Human Rights," 13 *New York University Journal of International Law* (1981): 427.

Groom, A.J.R., "The Trusteeship Council: A Successful Demise," in Paul Taylor and A.J.R. Groom, *The United Nations at the Millennium. The Principal Organs* (Continuum, 2000): 142.

Guest, Ian, *Behind the Disappearances. Argentina's Dirty War against Human Rights and the United Nations* (University of Pennsylvania Press, 1990).

Gütter, Jeroen, "Special Procedures and the Human Rights Council: Achievements and Challenges Ahead," 7(1) *Human Rights Law Review* (2007): 93.

Gütter, Jeroen, *Thematic Procedures of the United Commission on Human Rights and International Law: In Search of a Sense of Community* (Intersentia, 2006).

Hampson, Françoise J., "An Overview of the Reform of the Human Rights Machinery," 7(1) *Human Rights Law Review* (2007): 7.

Hampson, Françoise J., "The Relationship between International Humanitarian Law and Human Rights Law from the Perspective of a Human Rights Treaty Body," 90 *International Review of the Red Cross* (2008): 549.

Hampson, Françoise J. and Ibrahim Salama, *Working Paper on the Relationship between Human Rights Law and International Humanitarian Law*, UN Doc. E/CN.4/Sub.2/2005/14 (June 21, 2005).

Hannum, Hurst, "Human Rights and the United Nations: Progress at the 1980 U.N. Sub-Commission on Prevention of Discrimination and Protection of Minorities," 3 *Human Rights Quarterly* (1981): 1.

Haver, Peter, "The United Nations Sub-Commission on Prevention of Discrimination and Protection of Minorities," 21 *Columbia Journal of Transnational Law* (1982): 103.

Herndl, Kurt, "Recent Developments Concerning United Nations Fact-finding in the Field of Human Rights," in Manfred Nowak, Dorothea Sterurer, and Hannes Tretter (eds.), *Progress in the Spirit of Human Rights. Festchrift für Felix Ermacora* (Engel, 1988): 1.

Hopgood, Stephen, *The Endtimes of Human Rights* (Cornell University Press, 2013).

Hopgood, Stephen, Jack Snyder, and Leslie Vinjamuri (eds.), *Human Rights Futures* (Cambridge University Press, 2017).

Howard, Tolley, *The UN Commission on Human Rights* (Westview Press, 1987).

Humphrey, John P., *Human Rights and the United Nations: A Great Adventure* (Transnational Publishers, Inc. 1984).

International Commission of Jurist, "UN Commission on Human Rights (Commentaries, 36th Session)," 24 *International Commission of Jurists. The Review* (1980): 29.

International Service for Human Rights, "The General Assembly and Human Rights," *Human Rights Monitor* 64/2006, February 2007.

International Service for Human Rights, "A Stock-Taking of the Human Rights Council's Institution Building Process," *Human Rights Monitor* 64/2006 (February 2007).

International Service for Human Rights, "Support for 'Defamation of Religion' Continues to Decline; Draft Resolution Passes by Only 12 Votes," *Press Release*, November 25, 2010.

Ize-Charrin, M. Francisca, "1503: A Serious Procedure," in Alfredsson Gudmundur, et al. (eds.), *International Human Rights Monitoring Mechanisms: Essays in Honour of Jakob Th. Möller* (Martinus Nijhoff Publishers, 2001): 293.

Jekewitz, Jürgen et al. (eds.), *Des Menschen Recht zwischen Freiheit und Verantwortung. Festchrift für Josef Partsh zum 75. Geburstag* (Duncker & Humblot, 1989).

Jensen, Steven L.B., *The Making of International Human Rights: The 1060s, Decolonization, and the Reconstruction of Global Values* (Cambridge University Press, 2016).

Jensen, Steven L.B., "Putting to Rest the Three Generations Theory of Human Rights," *Open Global Rights*, November 15, 2017, available at https://www.openglobalrights.org/putting-to-rest-the-three-generations-theory-of-human-rights/.

Jernow, Allison, "Ad-hoc and Extraconventional Means for Human Rights Monitoring," 28(4) *New York University Journal of International Law & Policy* (1996): 785.

Joosten, Veronique, *The UN Human Rights Council at Work: From High Hopes Back to Reality* (United Nations Association Flanders Belgium, 2006).

Joseph, Sarah and Eleanor Jenkin, "The United Nations Human Rights Council: Is the United States Right to Leave This Club?," *American University International Law Review* (2019) (forthcoming).

Kälin, Walter, *Guiding Principles on Internal Displacement: Annotations* (American Society of International Law, 2000).

Kamminga, Menno T., *Inter-State Accountability for Violations of Human Rights* (University of Pennsylvania Press, 1992).

Kapur, Ratna, "Human Rights in the 21st Century: Take a Walk on the Dark Side," 28 *Sydney Law Review* (2006): 665.

Kaufman, Stephen B, "The Necessity for Rules of Procedure in Ad Hoc United Nations Investigations," 18(4) *The American University Law Review* (1969): 739.

Keane, David, "Cartoon Violence and Freedom of Expression," 30(4) *Human Rights Quarterly* (2008): 845.

Klabbers, Jan, "On Epistemic Universalism and the Melancholy of International Law," 29(4) *European Journal of International Law* (2018): 1057.

Klabbers, Jan, "The Virtues of Expertise," in Monika Ambrus et al. (eds.), *The Role of Experts in International and European Decision-Making Processes* (Cambridge University Press, 2014): 82.

Knox, Robert, "Against Law-sterity," 6 *Salvage*, November 2018, available at http://salvage.zone/in-print/against-law-sterity/?fbclid=IwAR17KyPW03hOM_MjJJk4mFwszuZO8_oC-tlSJsSplD_0_6SL9paIQPBMnuM.

Knox, Robert, "Marxist Approaches to International Law," in Anne Orford and Florian Hoffmann (eds.), *The Oxford Handbook of the Theory of International Law* (Oxford University Press, 2016): 306.

Kommers, Donald and Gilburt Loescher (eds.), *Human Rights and American Foreign Policy* (University of Notre Dame Press, 1979).

Kooijmans, Peter, "Introduction to the International Systems of Protection of Human Rights," *Recueil des Cours* (Strasbourg Institut International des Droits d l'Homme, 1986): 6.

Kozma, Julia, Manfred Nowak, and Martin Scheinin, *A World Court of Human Rights: Consolidated Statute and Commentary* (Neuer Wissenschaftlicher Verlag, 2010).

Kramer, David and David Weissdbrodt, "The 1980 U.N. Commission on Human Rights and the Disappeared," 3 *Human Rights Quarterly* (1981): 18.

Lane, Eric, "Mass Killing by Governments: Lawful in the World Legal Order?," 12 *New York University Journal of International Law & Politics* (1979): 239.

Lauren, Paul G., "To Preserve and Build on Its Achievements and to Redress Its Shortcomings: The Journey form the Commission on Human Rights to the Human Rights Council," 29 *Human Rights Quarterly* (2007): 307.

Lauterpacht, Hersch, *International Law and Human Rights* (Praeger, 1950).

Lazarus, Liora, "The United Nations Working Group on Arbitrary Detention Decision on Assange: 'Ridiculous' or 'Justifiable'?," *Ejil: Talk*, February 9, 2016, available at http://www.ejiltalk.org/the-united-nations-working-group-on-arbitrary-detention-decision-on-assange-ridiculous-or-justifiable/.

Lebovic, James H. and Erik Voeten, "The Cost of Shame: International Organizations and Foreign Aid in the Punishing of Human Rights Violations," 46(1) *Journal of Peace Research* (2009): 79.

Lebovic, James H. and Erik Voeten, "The Politics of Shame: The Condemnation of Country Human Rights Practices in the UNHCR," 50(4) *International Studies Quarterly* (2006): 54.

Lempinen, Miko, *Challenges Facing the System of Special Procedures of the United Nations Commission on Human Rights* (Åbo Academi University, 2001).

Lempinen, Miko, *The United Nations Commission on Human Rights and the Different Treatment of Governments* (Åbo Akademi University Press, 2005).

Lempinen, Miko, "The United Nations Human Rights Council: The Next Victim of Illusions and False Expectations," 26(2) *Nordic Journal of International Law* (2008): 182.

Lempinen, Miko, "When Loyalty towards the United Nations Limits the Independence of Special Procedure Mandate Holders," 21(4) *Nordic Journal of International Law* (2003): 456.

Lillich, R.B. and Hurst Hannum, *International Human Rights. Problems of Law, Policy and Practice* (3rd ed. Aspen Publishers, 1995).

Limon, Marc, *Reform of the UN Human Rights Petitions System* (Universal Rights Group, January 2018).

Limon, Marc, "US Departure from the Human Rights Council: What Really Happened and What Will Happen Next?" *Universal Rights Group Blog* (June 27, 2018), available at https://www.universal-rights.org/blog/us-departure-from-the-human-rights-council-what-really-happened-and-what-will-happen-next/.

Limon, Marc and Toby Lamarque, *The 2015 Human Rights Council* (Universal Rights Group, November 17, 2014), available at https://www.universal-rights.org/blog/the-2015-human-rights-council/.

Limon, Marc and Ted Piccone, *Human Rights Special Procedures: Determinants of Influence* (Brookings Institutions and Universal Rights Group, 2014).

Limon, Marc and Hilary Power, *History of the United Nations Special Procedures Mechanism: Origins, Evolution and Reform* (Universal Rights Group, 2014).

Liskofsly, Sidney, "Coping with the 'Question of the Violation of Human Rights and Fundamental Freedoms,'" VIII(4) *Human Rights Journal* (1975): 883.

Louys, Diane, "*I'll Kill You along with Drug Addicts"—President Duterte's War on Human Rights Defenders in the Philippines* (The Observatory for the Protection of Human rights Defenders, 2019).

Luard, Evan (ed.), *The International Protection of Human Rights* (Thames and Hudson, 1967).

Luard, Evan, *The United Nations. How It Works and What It Does* (2nd ed. Macmillan, 1994).

Lubell, Noam, "Challenges in Applying Human Rights Law to Armed Conflict," 87(860) *International Review of the Red Cross* (2005): 737.

Lubell, Noam and Nathan Derejko, "A Global Battlefield? Drones and the Geographical Scope of Armed Conflict," 11(1) *Journal of International Criminal Justice* (2013): 65.

Luck, Edward C., *Reforming the United Nations: Lessons from a History in Process* (Academic Council on the United Nations System, 2003).

M'jid, Najat M., "The UN Special Procedures System: The Role of the Coordination Committee of Special Procedures," in Aoife Nolan, Rosa Freedman, and Thérèse Murphy (eds.), *The United Nations Special Procedures System* (Brill, 2017): 131.

Mallory, Conall, "Membership and the UN Human Rights Council," 2(1) *Canadian Journal of Human Rights* (2013): 1.

Marks, Susan, "Human Rights in Disastrous Times," in James Crawford and Martti Koskenniemi (eds.), *The Cambridge Companion of International Law* (Cambridge University Press, 2012): 309.

McGonagle, Tarlach, *New General Recommendation Combating Racist Hate Speech* (IRIS, 2013).

McGonagle, Tarlach and Yvonne Donders (eds.), *The United Nations and Freedom of Expression and Information: Critical Perspectives* (Cambridge University Press, 2015).

Mégret, Frédéric, "Having It Both Ways: International Human Rights Law Cannot Both Be in Decline and Be (That) Problematic for International Law," 96 *Texas Law Review* (2017): 114.

Mégret, Frédéric, "International Law as Law," in James Crawford and Martti Koskenniemi (eds.), *The Cambridge Companion of International Law* (Cambridge University Press, 2012): 64.

Melzer, Nils, "Demasking the Torture of Julian Assange," *Medium*, June 26, 2019, available at https://medium.com/@njmelzer/demasking-the-torture-of-julian-assange-b252ffdcb768.

Mendel, Toby, "The UN Special Rapporteur on Freedom of Opinion and Expression: Progressive Development of International Standards Relating to Freedom of Expression," in Tarlach McGonagle and Yvonne Donders (eds.), *The United Nations and Freedom of Expression and Information: Critical Perspectives* (Cambridge University Press, 2015): 235.

Meron, Theodore, "The Humanization of Humanitarian Law," 94(2) *American Journal of International Law* (2000): 239.

Merry, Sally E. and Peggy Levitt, "The Vernacularization of Women's Human Rights," in Stephen Hopgood, Jack Snyder, and Leslie Vinjamuri (eds.), *Human Rights Futures* (Cambridge University Press, 2017): 213.

Miller, Robert, "United-Nations Fact-Finding Missions in the Field of Human Rights," *Australian Year Book of International Law* (1970–1973): 40.

Morgan-Foster, Jason, "Third Generation Rights: What Islamic Law Can Teach the International Human Rights Movement," 8 *Yale Human Rights & Development Law Journal* (2005): 67.

Morphet, Sally, "States Groups at the United Nations and Growth of Member States at the United Nations," in Paul Taylor and A.J.R. Groom (eds.), *The United Nations at the Millennium. The Principal Organs* (Continuum, 2000): 224.

Moyn, Samuel, "A Powerless Companion: Human Rights in the Age of Neoliberalism," 77(4) *Law & Contemporary Problems* (2014): 147.

Müller, Marion and Esra Özcan, "The Political Iconography of Muhammad Cartoons: Understanding Cultural Conflict and Political Action," 40(2) *Political Sciences and Politics* (2007): 287.

Mutua, Makau, "Savages, Victims, and Saviors: The Metaphor of Human Rights," 42(1) *Harvard International Law Journal* (2001): 20.

Neumayer, Eric, "Do Human Rights Matter in Bilateral Aid Allocation? A Quantitative Analysis of 21 Donor Countries," 84(3) *Social Science Quarterly* (2003): 650.

Nifosi, Ingrid, *The UN Special Procedures in the Field of Human Rights* (Intersentia, 2005).

Nolan, Aoife and Alice Donald, "Human Rights Case against Welfare Reforms Keeps Growing," *The Conversation*, July 10, 2014, available at https://theconversation.com/human-rights-case-against-welfare-reforms-keeps-growing-28990.

Nowak, Manfred, "The Need for a World Court of Human Rights," 7(1) *Human Rights Law Review* (2007): 251.

Nowak, Manfred, "The Need for a World Court of Human Rights," in Jessica Almqvist and Felipe Gómez Isa (eds.), *The Human Rights Council: Challenges and Opportunities* (FRIDE, 2006).

Nowak, Manfred, "Proposals for Improving the UN Human Rights Programme," 11 *Netherlands Quarterly of Human Rights* (1993): 153.

Nowak, Manfred, "The Right of Victims of Human Rights Violations to a Remedy: The Need for a World Court of Human Rights," 32(1) *Nordic Journal of Human Rights* (2014): 3.

Nowak, Manfred, Dorothea Sterurer, and Hannes Tretter (eds.), *Progress in the Spirit of Human Rights. Festchrift für Felix Ermacora* (Engel, 1988).

O'Donnell, Daniel, "Trends in the Application of International Humanitarian Law by United Nations Human Rights Mechanisms," 38 *International Review of the Red Cross* (1998): 481.

O'Flaherty, Michael, "Freedom of Expression: Article 19 of the International Covenant on Civil and Political Rights and the Human Rights Committee's General Comment No 34," 12(4) *Human Rights Law Review* (2012): 627.

Odinkalu, Chidi A., "Why More Africans Don't Use Human Rights Language," 2(1) *Human Rights Dialogue* (2000): 3.

Oeter, Stefan, "Inspection in International Law. Monitoring Compliance and the Problem of Implementation in International Law," XXVIII *New York Journal of International Law* (1997): 129.

Ohlin, Jeans D., "Is *Jus in Bello* in Crisis?," 13(1) *Journal of International Criminal Justice* (2013): 27.

Orford, Anne and Florian Hoffmann (eds.), *The Oxford Handbook of the Theory of International Law* (Oxford University Press, 2016).

Parson, Donald P., "The Individual Right of Petition: A Study of Methods Used by International Organizations to Utilize the Individual as a Source of Information on the Violations of Human Rights," 13 *Wayne Law Review* (1966–1967): 678.

Pastor Ridruejo, José A., "Les procédures publique spéciales de la Commission de Droits de l'Homme des Nations Unies," 228(III) *Collected Courses of the Hague Academy of International Law* (1991): 183.

Peterson, M.J., "General Assembly," in Thomas Weiss and Sam Daws (eds.), *The Oxford Handbook on the United Nations* (Oxford University Press, 2007): 97.

Petrasek, David, "The UN Security Council and Human Rights," in Gordon DiGiacomo and Susan Kang (eds.), *The Institutions of Human Rights* (University of Toronto Press, 2019): 44.

Piccone, Ted, *Catalysts for Change: How the UN's Independent Experts Promote Human Rights* (Brookings Institute Press, 2012).

Pons Rafols, Francesc-Xavier, "Aplicabilidad de la sección 22 del artículo VI de la Convención sobre los privilegios e inmunidades de las Naciones Unidas," XLIII(1) *Revista Española de Derecho Internacional* (1991): 39.

Posner, Eric, "Human Welfare, Not Human Being," 108(7) *Columbia Law Review* (2008): 1758.

Posner, Eric, *The Twilight of Human Rights Law* (Oxford University Press, 2014).

Prasad, Maya, "The Role of Non-Governmental Organizations in the New United Nations Procedures for Human Rights Complaints," 5(1) *Denver Journal of International Law and Policy* (1975): 441.

Pritchard, Sarah (ed.), *Indigenous Peoples, the United Nations and Human Rights* (Zed Books Ltd., The Federation Press, 1998).

Ramcharan, Bertrand G. *The Concept and Present Status of the International Protection of Human Rights. Forty Years after the Declaration* (Martinus Nijhoff Publishers, 1989).

Ramcharan, Bertrand G. (ed.), *Human Rights and Human Security* (Martinus Nijhoff Publishers, 2002).

Ramcharan, Bertrand G. *International Human Rights Institutions. Selected Legal Opinions* (Martinus Nijhoff Publishers, 1997).

Ramcharam, Bertrand G., *The Principle of Legality in International Human Rights Institutions. Selected Legal Opinions* (Martinus Nijhoff Publishers, 1997).

Ramcharan, Bertrand G. *The Protection Roles of UN Human Rights Special Procedures* (Martinus Nijhoff Publishers, 2009).

Ramcharan, Bertrand G. (ed.), *The Right to Life in International Law* (Martinus Nijhoff Publishers, 1985).

Ramcharan, Bertrand G. *The Security Council and the Protection of Human Rights* (Brill, 2002).

Rehman, Javaid, "The Sharī'ah, International Human Rights Law and the Right to Hold Opinions and Free Expression: After Bilour's Fatwā," in Marie-Luisa Frick and Andreas Th. Müller (eds.), *Islam and International Law: Engaging Self-Centrism from a Plurality of Perspectives* (Brill, 2013): 244.

Rehman, Javaid and Stephanie Berry, "Is 'Defamation of Religions' Passé? The United Nations, Organisation of Islamic Cooperation, and Islamic State Practices: Lessons from Pakistan," 44(3) *The George Washington International Law Review* (2012): 431.

Riedel, Eibe, "Commission on Human Rights," in Wolfrum Rudicer and Christiane Philipp (eds.), *United Nations: Law, Policies and Practice* (vol. 1, Martinus Nijhoff, 1995): 116.

Riedel, Eibe H. and Jan-Micahel Arend, "Article 55(c)," in Bruno Simma (ed.), *The Charter of the United Nations: A Commentary* (2nd ed. Oxford University Press, 2002).

Risse, Thomas, "Human Rights in Areas of Limited Statehood: From the Spiral Model to Localization and Translation," in Stephen Hopgood, Jack Snyder, and Leslie Vinjamuri (eds.), *Human Rights Futures* (Cambridge University Press, 2017): 135.

Ritchie, Meabh, "Bedroom Tax Row: Grant Shapps v "Woman from Brazil," *Channel4 News*, September 11, 2013, available at https://www.channel4.com/news/bedroom-tax-un-grant-shapps-brazil-row.

Rivadeneira, Rodolfo (ed.), *Judicial Protection of Internally Displaced Persons: The Colombian Experience* (Brookings Institution/University of Bern, 2009).

Roberts, Adam and Benedict Kingsbury (eds.), *United Nations, Divided World. The UN's Roles in International Relations* (Clarendon Press, 1988 and 1993).

Roberts, Anthea, *Is International Law International?* (Oxford University Press, 2017).

Rodley, Nigel, "Monitoring Human Rights by the U.N. System and Nongovernmental Organizations," in Donald Kommers and Gilburt Loescher (eds.), *Human Rights and American Foreign Policy* (University of Notre Dame Press, 1979): 157.

Rodley, Nigel, *Towards a More Effective and Integrated System of Human Rights Protection by the United Nations*, UN Doc. A/CONF.157/PC/60/Add.6 (April 1, 1993).

Rodley, Nigel, *The Treatment of Prisoners Under International Law* (2nd ed., Clarendon Press, 1999).

Rodley, Nigel, "United Nations Action Procedures against Disappearances, Summary or Arbitrary Executions, and Torture," (4) *Human Rights Quarterly* (1986): 700.

Rodley, Nigel, "The United Nations and Human Rights in the Middle East," 38(2) *Social Research* (1971): 217.

Rodley, Nigel S., "The Evolution of the United Nations Charter-based Machinery of the Protection of Human Rights," 1 *European Human Rights Law Review* (1997): 4.

Roth, Ken, "Defending Economic, Social and Cultural Rights: Practical Issues Faced by an International Human Rights Organization," 26 *Human Rights Quarterly* (2004): 63.

Rozenberg, Joshua, "How Did the UN Get It So Wrong on Julian Assange," The Guardian, February 5, 2016).

Rubenstein, Leonard S., "How International Human Rights Organizations Can Advance Economic, Social, and Cultural Rights: A Response to Kenneth Roth," 26 *Human Rights Quarterly* (2004): 845.

Rudicer, Wolfrum and Christiane Philipp (eds.), *United Nations: Law, Policies and Practice* (Vol.1, Martinus Nijhoff, 1995).

Rudolf, Beate, "The Thematic Rapporteurs and Working Groups of the United Nations Commission on Human Rights," (4) *Max Planck Yearbook on UN Law* (2000): 289.

Sannagel, Janika, *Chasing Shadows, A Quantitative Analysis of the Scope and Impact of UN Communications on Human Rights Defenders (2000–2016)* (Global Public Policy Institute, January 2018).

Schabas, William, "*Lex Specialis*? Belt and Suspenders? The Parallel Operation of Human Rights Law and the Law of Armed Conflict and the Conundrum of *Jus Ad Bellum*," 40(2) *Israel Law Review* (2007): 592.

Scheipers, Sibylle, "Civilization vs Toleration: The New UN Human Rights Council and the Normative Foundations of the International Order," 10(3) *Journal of International Relations & Development* (2007): 219.

Schwelb, Egon and Philip Alston, "The Principal Institutions and Other Bodies Founded Under the Charter," in Karel Vasak (ed.), *The International Dimensions of Human Rights* (UNESCO, 1982, vol. 1): 232.

Sepúlveda Carmona, Magdalena and Elvira Domínguez-Redondo, "An Overview of Human Rights Instruments to Raise Concerns About Trade and Investment Policies," in Murphy and Paasch (eds.), *The Global Food Challenge: Towards a Human Rights Approach to Trade and Investment Policies* (Brot für Alle, 2009): 92.

Shaheed, Ahmed and Rose Parris Richter, "Coping Mechanisms for State Non-cooperation," in Aoife Nolan, Rosa Freedman, and Thérèse Murphy (eds.), *The United Nations Special Procedures System* (Brill, 2017): 155.

Sheinin, Martin, "Towards a World Court of Human Rights," *Agenda on Human Rights, Swiss Initiative* (2009), available at https://www.eui.eu/Documents/DepartmentsCentres/AcademyofEuropeanLaw/CourseMaterialsHR/HR2009/Scheinin/ScheininClassReading1.pdf.

Shelton, Dinah, "Standard-Setting by the United Nations Commission on Human Rights—An Overview from Its Inception I 1947 until the Creation of the Human Rights Council in 2006," 29(1–5) *Human Rights Law Journal* (2008): 15.

Shetty, Salil, "Millennium Declaration and Development Goals: Opportunities for Human Rights," 2(2) *SUR-International Journal on Human Rights* (2005): 6.

Shivji, Issa G., *The Concept of Human Rights in Africa* (African Books Collective, 1989).

Sikkink, Kathryn, *Evidence for Hope. Making Human Rights Work in the 21st Century* (Princeton University Press, 2017).

Simma, Bruno (ed.), *The Charter of the United Nations: A Commentary* (2nd ed. Oxford University Press, 2002).

Simma, Bruno, "Human Rights," in Christian Tomuschat (ed.), *The United Nations at Age Fifty. A Legal Perspective* (Kluwer Law International, 1995): 263.

Simma, Bruno and Philip Alston, "The Sources of Human Rights Law: Custom, Jus Cogens, General Principles," 12 *The Australian Yearbook of International Law* (1992): 82.

Simmons, Beth A., *Mobilizing for Human Rights: International Law in Domestic Politics* (Cambridge University Press, 2009).

Sohn, Louis B., "The Human Rights Law of the Charter," 12 *Texas International Law Journal* (1977): 129.

Steiner, Henry and Philip Alston, *International Human Rights in Context. Law, Politics, Morals. Text and Materials* (2nd ed. Oxford University Press, 2000).

Subedi, Surya P., "Human Rights Experts in the United Nations: A Review of the Role of United Nations Special Procedures," in Monika Ambrus, Karin Arts, Ellen Hey, and Helena Raulu (eds.), *The Role of Experts in International and European Decision-Making Processes* (Cambridge University Press, 2014): 241.

Sunga, Lyal, "The Special Procedures of the UN Commission on Human Rights," in Gudmundur Alfredsson et al. (eds.), *International Human Rights Monitoring Mechanisms* (Martinus Nijhoff, 2001): 233.

Sunga, Lyal, "What Effect If Any Will the UN Human Rights Council Have on Special Procedures?," in Gudmundur Alfredsson et al. (eds.), *International Human Rights Monitoring Mechanisms* (2nd ed. Brill Nijhoff, 2009): 169.

Tardu, Maxime E., "Human Rights Complaint Procedures of the United Nations: Assessment and Prospects," in Jürgen Jekewitz et al. (eds.), *Des Menschen Recht zwischen Freiheit und Verantwortung. Festschrift für Josef Partsh zum 75. Geburstag* (Duncker & Humblot, 1989): 287.

Tardu, Maxime E., *Human Rights: The International Petition System* Vol. I, Part I, Section IA (Oceana Publications, 1979).

Tauli-Corpus, Victoria, "A Silent War Is Being Waged on Philippine Indigenous Communities," *Financial Times*, March 29, 2018.

Taylor, Paul and A.J.R. Groom, *The United Nations at the Millennium. The Principal Organs* (Continuum, 2000).

Thakur, Ramesh (ed.), *What Is Equitable Geographic Representation in the 211 Century?* (UN University, 1999).

Tolley, Howard, "The Concealed Crack in the Citadel: The United Nations Commission on Human Rights' Response to Confidential Communications," 6 *Human Rights Quarterly* (1984): 420.

Tolley, Howard, "Decision-Making at the United Nations Commission on Human Rights, 1979–1982," 5(1) *Human Rights Quarterly* (1983): 25.

Tolley, Howard, *The U.N. Commission on Human Rights* (Westview Press, 1987).

Tomuschat, Christian, "Human Rights in a World-Wide Framework. Some Current Issues," in Rudolf Bernhardt et al. (eds.), *Zeitschrift für Ausländisches Öffentliches Recht Und Völkerrecht. Begründet von Viktor Bruns* (Kohlhammer, 1985): 547.

Tomuschat, Christian (ed.), *The United Nations at Age Fifty. A Legal Perspective* (Kluwer Law International, 1995).

Turgis, Sandrine, "Les moyen d'alerte du Conseil de Sécurité des Nations Unies en cas de violation des droits de l'homme," 2 *Civitas Europa* (2018): 33.

Universal Rights Group, *Vision 2021—What Is the General Assembly's 2021–2026 Review, and How Might the Human Rights Council Usefully Contribute* (Universal Rights Group, January 2019).

Uvin, Peter, *Human Rights and Development* (Kumarian Press, 2005).

Vasak, Karel (ed.), *The International Dimensions of Human Rights* (UNESCO, 1982, vol. 1): 232.

Vasak, Karel, "Pour une troisième generation des droits de l'homme," *Studies and Essays on International Humanitarian Law and Red Cross Principles* (Martinus Nijhoff Publishers, 1984): 837.

Vasak, Karel, "A 30-Year Struggle. The Sustained Efforts to Give Force of Law to the Universal Declaration of Human Rights," 30 *The UNESCO COURIER* (November 1977): 29.

Villán Durán, Carlos, *Curso de Derecho Internacional de Los Derechos Humanos* (Trotta, 2002).

Weinstein, Warren, "Africa's Approach to Human Rights at the United Nations," 6(4) *African Issues* (1976): 14.

Weiss, Thomas G. and Daws, Sam (eds.), *The Oxford Handbook on the United Nations* (Oxford University Press, 2007).

Weissbrodt, David, "Protecting the Right to Life: International Measures against Arbitrary or Summary Killings by Governments," in Ramcharan (ed.), *The Right to Life in International Law* (Martinus Nijhoff, 1985): 297.

Weissbrodt, David, "The Three 'Theme' Special Rapporteurs of the UN Commission on Human Rights," 80 *American Journal of International Law* (1986): 685.

Weissbrodt, David S. and Brittany Mitchell, "The United Nations Working Group on Arbitrary Detention: Procedures and Summary of Jurisprudence," 38(3) *Human Rights Quarterly* (2016): 655.

Wickremasinghe, Chanaka, "Difference Relating to Immunity from Legal Process of a Special Rapporteur of the Commission on Human Rights," 49(3) *International and Comparative Law Quarterly* (2000): 724.

Winkler, Inga T. and Catarina de Albuquerque, "Doing It All and Doing It Well? A Mandate's Challenges in Terms of Cooperation, Fundraising and Maintaining Independence," in Aoife Nolan, Rosa Freedman, and Thérèse Murphy (eds.), *The United Nations Special Procedures System* (Brill, 2017): 188.

Winkler, Inga T. and Margaret L. Satterthwaite, "Leaving No One Behind? Persistent Inequalities in the SDGs," 21(8) *The International Journal of Human Rights* (2017): 1073.

Wolfrum, Rüdiger, "The Progressive Development of Human Rights: A Critical Appraisal of UN Recent Efforts," in Jürgen Jekewitz et al. (eds.), *Des Menschen Recht zwischen Freiheit und Verantwortung. Festschrift für Karl Josef Partsch zum 75. Geburtstag* (Duncker & Humblot, 1989): 67.

Wright-Carozza, Paolo, "From Conquest to Constitutions: Retrieving a Latin American Tradition of the Idea of Human Rights," 25(2) *Human Rights Quarterly* (2003): 281.

Wuerth, Ingrid, "International Law in the Post-Human Rights Era," 96(2) *Texas Law Review* (2017): 279.

Wyndham, Jessica "A Developing Trend: Laws and Policies on Internal Displacement," 14(1) *Human Rights Brief* (2006): 7.

Index

For the benefit of digital users, indexed terms that span two pages (e.g., 52–53) may, on occasion, appear on only one of those pages.

Ad Hoc Working Group of Experts on the situation of human rights in southern Africa, 20–21, 84
Ad Hoc Working Group on the Situation of Human Rights in Chile, 25
admissibility criteria, 58–60
African descent
  Special Procedures, 118–19, 197
  Working Group, 109–10, 118–19
African Group
  admissibility criteria, 51
  Code of Conduct, 54, 55–56
  country mandates, 33–34
  geographic Special Procedures, 52
  Human Rights Council, 67, 193–95
  mandate holders, 164
  positive outcomes, 193
Agenda for Sustainable Development, (2030), 113–14, 190–91
albinism
  Special Procedures, 3, 82–83, 109–10, 197
  Special Rapporteur, 86–87, 109–10
Albuquerque, Catarina de, 142, 148
Al-Khaim prison, Lebanon, 147
allegation letters, 76–77, 127–28, 131
Alston, Philip, 61–62, 67, 86–87
Anaya, James, 86–87
Annan, Kofi, 11–12, 49n70, 49, 52–53, 107
annual meetings, 87–92, 96
annual report, publicity, 118–19
Aoláin, Fionnuala Ní, 106–7
arbitrary and summary executions. *See* executions, arbitrary and summary
arbitrary detention
  Assange, 120–21, 121n103
  Special Procedures, 3, 42n36, 112–13, 118–19, 120–21, 197
  Special Rapporteur, 134–35
  Working Group, 37–38, 42, 43–44, 58–59, 60, 61–62, 76, 78, 81, 109–10, 117–18, 128–30, 131–33, 135, 142–43, 147–49, 167–69
Argentina, human rights violations investigation, 27–28
armed conflicts, 102–4
Armenia, human rights violations investigation, 29–30
Article 2(7), 9–11
  overcoming, 9–10, 32, 33–34, 40–41
Asian Group
  admissibility criteria, 51
  Code of Conduct, 62–63
  country mandates, 33–34
  geographic Special Procedures, 52
  Human Rights Council, 67
  name change, 13n16
  positive outcomes, 193
  Recommendation 10, 50n80, 50
  Special Procedure weakening attempts, 45n51, 45–46, 48, 49–50n77, 49–50
Assange, Julian, 61–62, 120–22, 121n103, 136
assembly and association, Special Procedures, 140–42, 197
autonomy and fragmentation, methods of work, 101–8
  armed conflicts and international humanitarian law, 102–4
  nonstate actors, 104–8
Azerbaijan, human rights violations investigation, 29–30

Bassiouni, Cherif, 79–80
Baxi, Upendra, 183–85
Belgrade Minimum Rules of Procedure for International Human Rights Fact-Finding Missions, 79–80, 80n55
Bolton, John, 64–66
Bossuty, Marc, 111–12
business, 107–8
  Forum on Business and Human Rights, 107
  "Guiding Principles on Business and Human Rights," 113–14, 152, 173
  Special Procedures, 109–10, 197
  Special Representative, 113–14
  Working Group, 136

Callamard, Agnès, 63–64, 134–35
Cassin, René, 40–41
Centre for Human Rights, 93n134, 93–94
Chad, human rights violations investigation, 29–30
Charpentier, Jean, 40–41
Charter, UN
  Article 2(7), 9–11, 11n8, 32, 33–34, 40–41
  Article 68, ECOSOC creation and mission, 14–15
children
  disappearances, 145–46, 148
  Representative for children and armed conflicts, 88–90, 176–77
  rights of the child, 71
  sale of children and child prostitution, 112–13
  sale of children and the use of children in pornography, 39–40, 40n22, 82–83, 112–13
  sale of children and the use of children in pornography, Special Rapporteur, 130–31, 140n56
  separating from parents, 65–66
  thematic mandate, 73–74
children, sale of
  Convention on the Rights of the Child, 39–40, 40n22
  Special Procedures, 82–83, 112–13, 197
  Special Rapporteur, 130–31, 140n56
Chile
  human rights violations investigation, 24–26
  Working Group, challenging competence, 41–42
  Working Group on Chile, 84
  Working Group on the Situation of Human Rights in Chile, 126–27
China, contesting Working Group on Arbitrary Detention quasi-jurisdictional approach, 37–38
climate change mandate, 72
Code of Conduct for Special Procedures, Human Rights Council (2006-2019), 42–43, 55–64
  admissibility criteria, 58–60
  African Group on, 54, 55–56
  Article 3, 165
  Article 4, 165–66
  Asian Group on, 62–63
  ill-intentioned use, 61–64
  "Internal Advisory Procedure to Review Practice and Working Methods," 61, 92
  methods of work, 125–26
  as political mechanism, 67–68
  publicity, 57–58, 120
  purposes, 56–57
  support, 54
  tightening, 54–55
  visits, 142
codification and clarification, human rights standards, 143–57
  codification, new instruments, 150–52
  competence delimitation and issue conceptualization, 145–50
  competence delimitation and issue conceptualization, general comments and deliberations, 148–50
  competence delimitation and issue conceptualization, scope of mandates, 145–48
  handbooks and guides, 153
  hate speech and fragmentation risk, 154–57
codifying model rules, fact-finding, 79–80
coercive measures, unilateral
  Special Procedures, 144–45, 197
  Special Rapporteur, 115–16
collective mandates, 70–74, 95
  climate change, 72
  cross-cutting issues, 72–73

intimidation and reprisals against those cooperating with the United Nations mechanisms in the field of human rights, 70
justice, administration, 70
opinion and expression, right to freedom of, 70–71, 82–83, 112–13, 135n32, 156n156, 197
rights of the child, 71
terrorism, 71–72
women and girls, violence and discrimination against, 71
comments, general, 117–18, 148–50
Commission on Human Rights, UN, 143. *See also specific topics*
ad hoc monitoring bodies, 8
Asian and African Groups on, 193–95
competence, 38–39
creation, 14
Decision 2000/109, 162–63
"Further Promotion and Encouragement of Human Rights," 47–48
members, 14–15, 15n21
membership enlargement on, 193
North-South Divide, 193–95
politicization and demise, 3–4
reforms, 47–51
Resolution 16/21, 163
Resolution 1993/ 94, 162–63
Resolution 1997/ 125, 167–68
"Selebi Report," 47–48
Special Procedures, 7 (*see also* Special Procedures)
Special Procedures, reforms (1974-2006), 47–51
termination decision, 11–12
thematic and geographic mandates resolution, 73–74 (*see also* thematic mandates)
"Working Group on Enhancing the Effectiveness of the Mechanisms of the Commission on Human Rights," 47–48
Committee Against Torture, UN, 75–76n35, 75–76, 82, 142–43
Committee to Investigate Israel Practices Affecting the Human Rights of the Palestinian People and Other Arabs of the Occupied Territories, 22–23
communications, human rights monitoring, 125–37
1503 procedure, 18
ECOSOC Resolution 75, 17–18
handling, 131–34
individual, pioneering UN bodies' intervention on behalf of, 126–28
individual, treaties for handling, 43
mainstreaming, as standard practice, 128–31
system, 134–37
thematic mandates, 197
thematic mandates, to nonstate actors, 105
communications sent
country mandates, 198
thematic mandates, 197
competence
delimitation and issue conceptualization, 145–50
delimitation and issue conceptualization, general comments and deliberations, 148–50
delimitation and issue conceptualization, scope of mandates, 145–48
self-denied, 14–20, 32–33
Confidential Special Procedures, 7–8, 29–32, 33. *See also* Special Procedures
Convention against Torture and Other Cruel, Inhuman or Degrading Treatment or Punishment, 39–40
Convention for the Protection of all Persons from Enforced Disappearances, 173
Convention on the Elimination of All Forms of Discrimination against Women, 39–40
Convention on the Rights of Persons with Disabilities, 39–40
Convention on the Rights of the Child, 39–40, 173
coordination, between mandate holders, 75–78, 95–96
Coordination Committee, 91–92, 96
core human rights instruments, 39–40
country. *See also specific countries and topics*
mandates, communications sent, 198
thematic mandates, disparity and political influence, 108–11

Covenant on Civil and Political Rights, 39–42
Covenant on Economic, Social and Cultural Rights, 39–40, 90, 113–14, 115–16, 145–46
Cuba
  contesting treaties as normative bases for human rights violations, 42–43
  Working Group on Arbitrary Detention, 37–38, 38n8, 76
cultural rights, 111–16, 145–46
  Bolivia, 101–2
  Covenant on Economic, Social and Cultural Rights, International, 39–40, 90, 113–14, 115–16, 145–46
  fundamentalism and extremism on, 177
  geographic groups on, 193–95
  Human Rights Council, 33–34, 193
  Optional Protocol to the International Covenant on Economic, Social and Cultural Rights, 173
  Special Procedures, 39, 72–73, 83–84, 93–94, 97–98, 109–10, 112–17, 122, 190–91, 197
  Special Rapporteur, 110, 136

Decision 2000/109, Commission on Human Rights, 162–63
Declaration of Independence to Colonial Countries and Parties, Special Committee monitoring, 19–20
Declaration on Human Rights Education and Training and the Guiding Principles on Business and Human Rights, 173
Declaration on the Elimination of All Forms of Intolerance and of Discrimination Based on Religion or Belief (UNGA), 98–99n3, 150
Declaration on the Protection of All Persons from Enforced Disappearance, 151
Decolonization Committee, human rights monitoring, 16–17
"Defamation of religion and Global Efforts to Combat Racism: Anti-Semitism, Christianophobia and Islamophobia," 154
deliberations, 148–50
development
  Agenda for Sustainable Development, 113–14, 190–91
  human rights and, 9–10, 186–87, 188, 190–92
  Millennium Development Goals, 113–14, 190–91
  right to, 109–10
  Special Procedures, 72–73, 82–84, 197
  sustainable development goals, 73n25, 115–16
  Thematic Engagement, Special Procedures and Right to Development Division, 93–94
Diène, Doudou, 154
Dienstbier, Jiri, 167–68
disabilities
  Convention on the Rights of Persons with Disabilities, 39–40
  Inter-American Convention on Forced Disappearances of Persons, 150
  rights of children with, 71
  Special Procedures, 72–73, 82–83, 197
  Special Rapporteur, 106–7
disappearances
  Argentina, 27–29
  Convention for the Protection of all Persons from Enforced Disappearances, 173
  Declaration on the Protection of All Persons from Enforced Disappearance, 151
  International Convention for the Protection of All Persons against Enforced Disappearances, 39–40, 173
  Khashoggi, 135n32, 135
  Republic Democratic of Congo, 140n56
  Special Procedures, 27–29, 77–78, 109–10, 118–19, 197
discrimination against women, 197
dominant violation criteria, 77–78
droit de regard, 38–39
drones
  human rights issues, 190
  targeted killings, 102–3
Duterte, Rodrigo, 63–64

Economic and Social Council (ECOSOC), 10–11
creation, mission, and early work, 14–16
Resolution 75 (V), 17–18
Special Procedures creation and practice, 15–16
Sub-Commission for the Prevention of Discrimination and the Protection of Minorities, 15, 16
Sub-Commission on the Promotion and Protection of Human Rights, 15n23, 15
education
Declaration on Human Rights Education and Training and the Guiding Principles on Business and Human Rights, 173
racial discrimination, 153n138
Special Procedures, 72–73, 113–14, 115–16, 197
El Salvador, 103–4
enforced or involuntary disappearances, 118–19. *See also* disappearances; Working Group on Enforced or Involuntary Disappearances
Declaration on the Protection of All Persons from Enforced Disappearance, 151
International Convention for the Protection of All Persons against Enforced Disappearances, 39–40, 173
role, primary, 128–29
environment
Special Procedures, 197
Special Rapporteur, 83–84, 110
Equatorial Guinea, human rights violations investigation, 31–32
Ermacora, Felix, 41, 103–4
ethical stand, 4
executions, arbitrary and summary, 71n5
Republic Democratic of Congo, 140n56
Saudi Arabia, Khashoggi, 134n31
Siracusa Guidelines, 80n57
Special Procedures, 42n36, 190, 197
Special Rapporteurs, 62–64, 75–76, 82, 86–87, 95–96, 98–99, 101n16, 103–5, 128–30, 129n17, 134–35, 142n65, 146
expression, right to freedom of, 70–71
fact-finding mechanisms, codifying model rules for, 79–80
"Facts and Figures of Special Procedures," 76n38, 76–77, 91–92, 94–95, 105, 194n56
Farha, Leilani, 142
financial resources, 132–33
Focal Point for De-Listing, 189–90
food
Eastern European Group on, 193–95
Food and Agriculture Organization, 137–38
right to, 83–84, 115, 134–35, 144–45, 177, 193–95
Special Procedures, 83–84, 115, 134–35, 144–45, 197
Special Rapporteur, 86n104, 177
foreign debt, 145, 193–95
Guiding Principles on Foreign Debt ad Human Rights, 152
Special Procedures, 83–84, 109–10, 186–87, 191n45, 197
Special Rapporteur, 48, 109–10
fragmentation risk, hate speech and, 154–57
freedom of assembly and association, Special Procedures, 140–42, 197
freedom of opinion & expression, Special Procedure, 70–71, 82–83, 112–13, 135n32, 156n156, 197
freedom of religion or belief, Special Rapporteur, 98–99n3, 132–33, 138–39, 150, 155, 156n156
Frouville, Olivier de, 116
funding, Office of the High Commissioner for Human Rights, 170–73
"Further Promotion and Encouragement of Human Rights," 47–48

General Assembly, Human Rights Council and, 173–78
General Comments, 117–18, 148–50
geographic mandates, 3, 130. *See also specific countries and mandates*
African, 109–10
Agenda of the Human Rights Council, Item 3, 109–10
Commission on Human Rights resolution, 73–74

geographic mandates (*Cont.*)
country, 84–85, 108–9
field visits and action on behalf of individuals, 128
institutionalization, 167
mandate holders, 110–11
scope and number, 109–10
Western European and Other States Group, 193–95
geographic mandates, first, 22–26
geographic Special Procedures, 52, 98–99
Group of Asia and the Pacific Small Island Developing States, 13n16, *See also* Asian Group
Group of Experts on the Situation of Human Rights in Southern Africa, 126–27
growth, Special Procedures, 3, 69–96. *See also* Special Procedures, system and growth
number, 186–87, 188
risks, 4
guidelines, codifying model rules for fact-finding mechanisms, 79–80
guides, 153
Guiding Principles, 151–52, 170–71
Guiding Principles on Business and Human Rights, 113–14, 152, 173
Guiding Principles on Foreign Debt ad Human Rights, 152
Guiding principles regarding the working relations between special procedures mandate holders and OHCHR staff, 170–71

Haiti, human rights violations investigation, 29–30
Handbook for realizing the human right to safe drinking water and sanitation, 153
Handbook for the Protection of Internally Displaced Persons, 151–52
handbooks, 153
hate speech, 70–71, 154–57
hazardous substances and waste, 82–83, 128–29, 153, 197
health
Special Procedures, 134–35, 197
Special Rapporteur, 106–7, 113–14, 115, 130–31, 138–39
housing
right to, 115
Special Procedures, 82–83, 134–35, 197
Special Rapporteur, 61–62, 113–14, 115n90, 115
visits, 140–42
human resources, 132–33
human rights, international. *See also specific topics*
accessibility, 187–88
categories, methods of work, 111–17
conceptual, normative, and institutional challenges, 2
crisis of confidence, 183–85
fact-finding mission, South Vietnamese Buddhists, 19–20n51, 19–20
failures, 185
flaws, 2
implementation, states' political will and influence, 1–2
incursion, wide range, 186
openness, system, 188
politicization and professionalization, 4–5
as rights with normative force, 4–5
sovereignty, 1–2, 187
standards, codification and clarification, 143–57 (*see also* codification and clarification, human rights standards)
subjective rights, state abuses of power, 185–86
thematic procedures, 73–74
Western-led project, 185–86, 192–93
Human Rights Council, 1–2, 178–79, 180
creation, 3–4, 51–52
functions and powers, 13
General Assembly and Security Council relations, 173–78
membership, current, 12–13
origin and Kofi Annan, 11–12, 12n11
Human Rights Council (2006-2019), Special Procedures reforms, 51–66
Code of Conduct, 55–64 (*see also* Code of Conduct for Special Procedures, Human Rights Council (2006-2019))
reform waves, 52–55

withdrawing for reform: US and Council, 64–66
human rights defenders, 4–5, 63n148, 82–83
Special Procedures, 82–83, 120–21, 197
Special Rapporteur, 77–78, 129, 132–33, 135n32, 140–42
Special Representative, 77–78, 129
"human rights pillar," 9–22
"missing" UN main body, 10–13
Resolutions 1235 (XLII) and 1503 (XLVIII), 9–10, 10n3, 20–22, 25–26, 32–33, 126–27
self-denied competence, addressing human rights violations (1947-1967), 14–20, 32–33
human rights violations and investigations
addressing, self-denied competence, 14–20, 32–33
Argentina, 27–28
Armenia, 29–30
Azerbaijan, 29–30
Chad, 29–30
Chile, 24–26
communications, 1503 procedure for recirculating, 18
communications transmission, Resolution 75, 17–18
Equatorial Guinea, 31–32
Haiti, 29–30
Israel's occupied territories, post-Six-Day War, 22–24
Special Rapporteur, 25
Uganda, 29–30
Uzbekistan, 29–30
Human Rights Watch, 111–12
Humphrey, John, 17–18

ill-intentioned use, Human Rights Council Code of Conduct, 61–64
"independence," politics of, 161–80
funding, Office of the High Commissioner for Human Rights, 170–73
mandate holders, selecting and naming, 161, 162–64
mandate holders, standing within/outside UN, 165–69
relationships, General Assembly and Security Council, 173–78
indigenous peoples, 43–44, 134–35
draft declaration protecting, 174
Sami, 140–42
Special Procedures, 134–35, 197
Special Rapporteur, 62–64, 86–87, 137–38, 140–42
institutional coherence, 93–95
intelligent sanctions, 189–90
Inter-American Convention on Forced Disappearances of Persons, 150
"Internal Advisory Procedure to Review Practices and Working Methods," 61, 92
internally displaced
Handbook for the Protection of Internally Displaced Persons, 153
Special Procedures, 72–73, 82–83, 112–13, 129n17, 197
Special Rapporteur, 63–64, 83–84, 151–52
International Convention for the Protection of All Persons against Enforced Disappearances, 39–40, 173
International Convention on the Elimination of All Forms of Racial Discrimination (ICERD), 39–40, 155n149, 155
International Convention on the Protection of the Rights of All Migrant Workers and Members of Their Families, 39–40
International Covenant on Civil and Political Rights (ICCPR), 70–71, 145–46, 149, 154, 155n148, 155, 156–57
international order
Special Procedures, 82–83, 197
Special Rapporteur, 83–84, 109–10
structural inequalities, 183–85
Western European and Other Stats Group support, 193–95
international solidarity
Special Procedures, 82–84, 109–10, 186–87, 197
Special Rapporteur, 83–84, 109–10
Western European and Other States Group support, 186–87, 193–95

international treaties, benchmark
contesting, 37, 43–44
contesting, individual communications handling, 43
contesting, legal basis, 39–43
intimidation and reprisals against those cooperating with the United Nations mechanisms in the field of human rights mandate, 70
Israel, 102–3, 103n21
Istanbul Protocol, 153

Jahangir, Asma, 155
Jimenez-Damary, Cecilia, 63–64
joint activities, mandate holders, 75–78, 95–96
Jones, Constance, 1
judges and lawyers, independence
Special Procedures, 82–83, 112–13
Special Rapporteur, 63–64, 128–29
justice administration, 70

Kanyabashi, Joseph, 149
Kapur, Ratna, 183–85
Keane, David, 154, 155
Khashoggi, Jamal, 134n31, 134–35, 135n32
Klabbers, Jan, 187–88
Kooijmans, Peter, 146–47
Koskenniemi, Martti, 186
Kuwait, Iran's invasion (1990), 102

Lebovic, James, 182–83
leprosy, Special Procedure, 83, 118–19, 197
letter of allegations, 76–77, 127–28, 131
Ligabo, Ambeyi, 155–56
Like-Minded Group
geographic Special Procedures, 52
members, 46n53
Special Procedure weakening attempts, 45n51, 45–46, 46n53, 48, 49–50

mandate coordination, system building, 69–70
mandate holder initiatives, 74–95
annual meetings and Coordination Committee, 87–92, 96
codifying rules, fact-finding, 79–80
fundamentals, 74
joint activities and coordination, 75–78, 95–96
methods of work, publication and standardization, 81–87, 95–96
Office of the High Commissioner for Human Rights, 93–95
mandate holders
appointments and terms, 161
coordination, 35–36, 69–70, 95–96
geographic mandates, 110–11
"Guiding principles regarding the working relations between special procedures mandate holders and OHCHR staff," 170–71
institutional status, 161–62
methods of work, 97–123
monitoring, states' critiques, 35
nomenclature, 109–10
Office of the High Commissioner for Human Rights, 166–67, 179–80
selecting and naming, politics, 161, 162–64
standing within/outside UN, 165–69
statistics, publication, 164
thematic mandates, 110
mandates. *See also specific topics*
collective (*see* collective mandates)
multidimensional approaches, 99–100
scope, determining, 145–48
from Western Group, 193–95
Manual of Operations, Special Procedures, 79n54, 79–80, 96
Manual on the Effective Investigation and Documentation of Torture and Other Cruel, Inhuman or Degrading Treatment or Punishment (Istanbul Protocol), 153
Marie, Jean-Bernard, 41–42
Martelli, Maza, 163
Mavrommatis, Andreas, 132–33
meetings, annual, 87–92
Melzer, Nils, 121–22
mercenaries
Special Procedures, 82–83, 98–99, 109–10, 127–28, 145, 197
Special Rapporteur, 130–31

Western European and Other States Group, 193–95
methods of work. *See also specific working groups*
normative frameworks, lack, 125–26
publication and standardization, 81–87, 95–96
methods of work, development, 97–123
activist role, Special Procedures, 97, 99–100
autonomy and fragmentation, 101–8
autonomy and fragmentation, armed conflicts, 102–4
autonomy and fragmentation, nonstate actors, 104–8
awareness raising, 97
disparity and political influence, 108–17
disparity and political influence, country and thematic mandates, 108–11
disparity and political influence, human rights categories, 111–17
geographic Special Procedures, 98–99
history, early, 98–99
improvising, 98–117
multidimensional approaches, to mandates, 99–100
publicity, Special Procedures activities, 117–22
publicity, Special Procedures activities, annual report, 118–19
publicity, Special Procedures activities, challenges, 119–22
methods of work, implementation, 125–59
codification and clarification, human rights standards, 143–57
communications, 125, 136–37 (*see also* communications)
visits, 137–43
migrants
El Salvador, 163
Special Procedures, 82–83, 197
Special Rapporteur, 153n138
Yugoslavia, 149n104
Millennium Development Goals, 113–14, 190–91
Milosevic, Slobodan, 167–68
minority issues, 91n127
El Salvador, 163
Special Procedures, 197
Special Rapporteur, 110, 136
minority petitions system, 15–16
Mohr, Alberto Fuentes, 126–27
monitoring, human rights. *See also specific bodies and topics*
Declaration of Independence to Colonial Countries and Parties, 19–20
Decolonization Committee, 16–17
methods, 125
states, mandate holders, 35
multidimensional approaches, to mandates, 99–100
Mutua, Makau, 183–85

naming and shaming, 67, 108–9, 183n13
non-papers, 49n75, 49–50
nonstate actors, 104–8. *See also specific topics*
North-South Divide, 193–95
Nowak, Manfred, 61–62, 192–93

Office of the High Commissioner for Human Rights (OHCHR)
funding, 170–73
location, 11–12
mandate holders, 166–67, 179–80
role and institutional coherence, 93–95
Special Procedures Branch, 93–94
Special Procedures relationship, 166–67
Office of the Ombudsperson to the ISIL (Da'esh), 189–90
older persons
Special Procedures, 109–10, 118–19, 197
Special Rapporteur, 83–84
opinion, right to freedom of, 70–71, 82–83, 112–13, 135n32, 156n156, 197
Optional Protocol to the International Covenant on Economic, Social and Cultural Rights, 173

Pastor-Ridruejo, José Antonio, 104–5n33
Petit, Jean Manuel, 130–31
Picard, Michèle, 29–30
Poland, 101–2

Political Terror Scale scores, 182
politicization, 181
Commission on Human Rights, 3–4
as double standards, 182
Special Procedures, 4 (*see also* Special Procedures)
politicization on human rights, impact, 1–5
as pernicious, 2
positive progress, 2–3
politics of "independence," 161–80. *See also* "independence," politics of
Posner, Eric, 183–85
poverty, extreme
Guiding Principles on Extreme Poverty and Human Rights, 152n131, 152
Special Procedures, 43–44, 82–84, 86–87, 113–14, 134–35, 197
Special Rapporteur, 61–62, 110, 138–39
privacy, Special Procedures, 120–21, 197
public and confidential special procedures, 7–34. *See also* Special Procedures
publication
methods of work, 81–87, 95–96
statistics, mandate holders, 164
publicity, Special Procedures activities, 117–22
annual report, 118–19
challenges, 119–22
restrictions, Human Rights Council Code of Conduct, 57–58

racism
"Defamation of Religion and Global Efforts to Combat Racism: Anti-Semitism, Christianophobia and Islamophobia,," 154
International Convention on the Elimination of Racial Discrimination 1965, 155
Special Procedures, 82–83, 112–13, 154, 156–57, 197
Special Rapporteur, 154–55, 156n154, 156n156, 168–69
rationalizing Special Procedures, 45–66
strengthening, 35, 45–66
strengthening, Commission on Human Rights, reforms (1974-2006), 47–51
strengthening, Human Rights Council (2006-2019), 51–66 (*see also* Human Rights Council (2006-2019))
weakening tactic, 45n50, 45–46
Recommendation 8, 49–50, 50n78
Recommendation 10, 50n80, 50
reforming Special Procedures, 35–68. *See also* Special Procedures, reforming
regional groups, UN member states, 12–13, 13n16
Regulations Governing the Status, Basic Rights and Duties of Officials other than Secretariat Officials and Experts on Mission, 165–66
religion
Declaration on the Elimination of All Forms of Intolerance and of Discrimination Based on Religion or Belief, 98–99n3, 150
"Defamation of Religion and Global Efforts to Combat Racism: Anti-Semitism, Christianophobia and Islamophobia," 154
Special Procedures, 141n59, 154, 197
Special Rapporteur, 82, 98–99n3, 132–33, 138–39, 150, 154–57, 156n154, 156n156
Special Rapporteur on freedom of religion or belief, 98–99n3, 132–33, 138–39, 150, 155, 156n156
UN Charter, 14
reprisals against those cooperating with the United Nations mechanisms in the field of human rights mandate, 70
Resolution 16/21, 163
Resolution 20 (XXXVI), 27–28
Resolution 60/ 251, 45, 54
Resolution 728 F (XXVIII), 17–18, 18n40, 20–21, 25–26
Resolution 1235 (XLII), 9–10, 10n3, 20–22, 25–26, 32–33, 79–80, 126
Resolution 1503 (XLVIII), 18, 21–22, 25–26, 32–33, 40–41
Resolution 1993/ 94, Commission on Human Rights, 162–63
Resolution 2004/ 76, Commission on Human Rights, 49n71, 49
rights, human. *See* human rights, international

rights of the child mandate, 71. *See also* children
right to food, 83–84, 115, 134–35, 144–45, 177, 193–95. *See also* food
right to freedom of opinion and expression mandate, 70–71, 82–83, 112–13, 135n32, 156n156, 197
right to housing, 61–62, 82–83, 115n90, 115, 134–35, 140–42
Rodley, Nigel, 85
Roth, Ken, 111–12
rule of law, international, 181–82

Sakharov, Andrei, 126–27
sale of children. *See* children, sale of
Scheinin, Martin, 106–7, 192–93
security
  development, human rights and, 191–92
  violent conflict, 188–89
Security Council, Human Rights Council relations, 173–78
"Selebi Report," 47–48
sexual orientation
  Human Rights Council, 174–75
  Special Procedures, 82–84, 144–45, 197
Shivji, G., 183–85
Siracusa Guidelines, 79–80, 80n57
Six-Day War, human rights violations in occupied territories, 22–24
slavery, special procedure, 197
South Africa
  Ad Hoc Working Group of Experts on South Africa, 143–44
  Ad Hoc Working Group of Experts on Violations of Human Rights in Southern Africa, 126–27
  apartheid human rights investigation, 20–21
  Group of Experts on the Situation of Human Rights in Southern Africa, 126–27
Special Advisors on Children and Women, 176–77
Special Committee on Apartheid, 16–17
Special Committee on the Policies of Apartheid of the Government of South Africa, 20
Special Procedure Branch's Quick Response Desk, 94–95
Special Procedures, 1–2, 7–34. *See also* geographic mandates; thematic mandates
  ad hoc monitoring bodies, 8
  agreed framework, absence, 8
  Article 2(7), overcoming, 9–10, 32, 33–34, 40–41
  complaints, handling, 7–8
  comprehensive study, as system, 3
  Confidential, 7–8, 29–32, 33
  contributions, 4
  creation and practice, ECOSOC on, 15–16
  first, 7–8, 9–10
  geographic mandates, first, 22–26
  growth, 3, 4
  institutional standing, 4
  legal basis and powers, 36
  Manual of Operations, 79n54, 79–80, 96
  "missing" UN main body, 10–13
  number, growth, 186–87, 188
  origins, 7–8
  politicization, 4
  reform waves, 11–12
  regional groups, antagonism, 12–13
  Resolutions 1235 (XLII) and 1503 (XLVIII), 9–10, 10n3, 20–22, 25–26, 32–33, 126–27
  scope, broadened, 9–10
  self-denied competence, human rights violations, 14–20, 32–33
  special in, 2–3
  thematic mandates, first, 26–29
  on UN Commission on Human Rights, 7
  unintended creation, "human rights pillar," 9–22
  working methods, subverting state consent, 36
Special Procedures, reforming, 35–68
  international treaties benchmark, contesting, 37, 43–44
  international treaties benchmark, individual communications, 43
  international treaties benchmark, legal basis, 39–43
  states' criticism, 35, 37, 43

Special Procedures, reforming and rationalizing
strengthening, 35, 45–66
strengthening, Commission on Human Rights, reforms (1974-2006), 47–51
strengthening, Human Rights Council (2006-2019), 51–66 (*see also* Human Rights Council (2006-2019))
weakening tactic, 45n50, 45–46
Special Procedures, system and growth, 45, 69–96
mandate holder initiatives, 74–95
mandate holder initiatives, annual meetings and Coordination Committee, 87–92, 96
mandate holder initiatives, codifyingfor fact-finding rules, 79–80
mandate holder initiatives, joint activities and coordination, 75–78, 95–96
mandate holder initiatives, methods of work, publication and standardization, 81–87, 95–96
mandate holder initiatives, Office of the High Commissioner for Human Rights role, 93–95
political decisions, collective mandates, 70–74, 95 (*see also* collective mandates)
system building, mandate coordination, 69–70
Special Procedures Branch, thematic mandates, 93–95
Special Rapporteurs, 109–10. *See also specific topics and mandates*
mandate, 129
promotion of truth, reparations, and guarantees of nonrecurrence, 177
sale of children and the use of children in pornography, 130–31, 140n56
Special Representative. *See* Special Rapporteur
Special Representative on the question of children in armed conflict, 176–77
standardization, methods of work, 81–87, 95–96
standards, human rights, codification and clarification, 143–57. *see also* codification and clarification, human rights standards
Stavenhagen, Rodolfo, 62–63
Sub-Commission for the Prevention of Discrimination and the Protection of Minorities, 15, 16
Sub-Commission on the Promotion and Protection of Human Rights, 15n23, 15
Sub-Committee for the Prevention of Discrimination and the Protection of Minorities, 22
summary executions. *See* executions, arbitrary and summary
system, Special Procedures, 45, 69–96. *See also* Special Procedures, system and growth

Tadić, Duško, 149
Tauli-Corpuz, Victoria, 63–64, 86–87
Templeton, Hugh, 29–30
terrorism
hostage-taking, 72n11
Human Rights Council, 64–65
intelligent sanctions, 189–90
mandates, 163
Special Procedures, 71–72, 176–77, 190, 197
Special Rapporteur, 106–7, 149–50, 189–90
terrorism mandate, 71–72
Thematic Engagement, Special Procedures and Right to Development Division, 93–94
thematic mandates, 1–2, 3–4. *See also specific countries and mandates*
allegation transmission, 77–78
annual reports, 118
as authentic Special Procedures, 116
branches and transfer among, 93–94
vs. categories or rights, 130
Commission on Human Rights resolution on, 73–74
communications sent, 197
communications to nonstate actors, 105
country, disparity and political influence, 108–11
evolution (1980-1987), 98–99

first, 26–29
growth, 33–34
Human rights and thematic procedures, 73–74
Latin American and Caribbean sponsor, 193–95
letter of allegations and urgent appeals, 127–28
mandate holders, 110
mandate holders, appointment, 161
methods of work, country disparity and political influence, 108–11
post-Cold War (1990-1994), 107
scope and number, 1–2, 109–10
Special Procedures Branch, 93–95
standing invitations to, states, 142–43
tenure, security, 67
working group, 178
"three pillars," 10–11
Tolley, Howard, 21–22, 22n60
torture
Assange case, 136
Chile, 126–27
Committee Against Torture, UN, 75–76n35, 75–76, 82, 142–43
Convention against Torture and Other Cruel, Inhuman or Degrading Treatment or Punishment, 39–40
dominant violation criteria, 77–78
Manual on the Effective Investigation and Documentation of Torture and Other Cruel, Inhuman or Degrading Treatment or Punishment (Istanbul Protocol), 153
South Africa, 20
Special Procedures, 42n36, 167–68, 197
Special Rapporteur, 61–62, 75–76, 77–78, 82, 85, 120–22, 138–39, 142–43, 146–47, 147n87, 153, 167–68
Special Rapporteur, Assange case, 120–22, 136
Special Rapporteur on Torture, 77–78
trade in torture technologies, 146–47
UN Committee Against Torture, 75–76n35, 75–76, 82, 142–43
UN Declaration on the Protection of All Persons from Being Subjected to Torture and Other Cruel, Inhuman and Degrading Treatment, 146
toxic waste, Special Rapporteur, 107–8n55, 107–8
trafficking, human
Special Procedures, 177, 197
Special Rapporteur, 106n45, 153n136
treaty bodies
first, 19–20
replication, 148–50
Trusteeship System, 16–17
truth, justice, & reparations, Special Procedures, 197

Uganda, human rights violations investigation, 29–30
UN Charter
Article 2(7), 9–11, 11n8, 32, 33–34, 40–41
Article 68, ECOSOC creation and mission, 14–15
UN Commission on Human Rights. *See* Commission on Human Rights, UN
UN Committee Against Torture, 75–76n35, 75–76, 82, 142–43
unilateral coercive measures
Special Procedures, 144–45, 197
Special Rapporteur, 115–16
United Nations (UN). *See also specific bodies and topics*
regional groups, 12–13, 13n16
"three pillars," origins and purpose, 10–11
United States
Human Rights Council withdrawal, for reform, 64–66
human rights leader, 66
Universal Declaration of Human Rights, 70–71, 113–14, 183–85
Universal Periodic Review, 1–2, 12–13, 54, 55–56
urgent appeals, 50, 73–74, 126–28, 130–31n22
admissibility criteria, 58–60
joint actions, 76–77
Special Procedure Branch's Quick Response Desk, 94–95
Uzbekistan, human rights violations investigation, 29–30

Valko, Amos, 146
van Boven, Theo, 27–28, 85, 146–47
van der Stoel, Max, 132–33
Vasek, Karel, 111
violence against women, Special Procedures, 3, 42n36, 71n6, 71, 82–83, 197
violence and discrimination against women and girls, elimination mandate, 71
violent conflict, 188–89
visits, 137–43
Voeten, Erik, 182–83

Waldheim, Kurt, 27
water and sanitation
 Detroit, 140–42
 Eastern European Group on, 193–95
 Handbook for realizing the human right to safe drinking water and sanitation, 153n136, 153
 Special Procedures, 3, 83–84, 113–14, 144–45, 148, 197
 Special Rapporteur, 86–87, 110
Western European and Other States Group, 4, 164, 193–95
Wolfram, Rüdiger, 42
women
 Convention on the Elimination of All Forms of Discrimination against Women, 39–40
 Special Advisors on Children and Women, 176–77
 Special Procedures, 71, 109–10, 118–19, 197
 violence against, Special Procedures, 3, 42n36, 71n6, 71, 82–83, 197
 violence and discrimination against women and girls, collective mandate, 71
women and girls, violence and discrimination elimination, 71
Working Group on Arbitrary Detention, 43–44, 109–10, 112–13, 128–29, 135, 168–69
 annual report, 118–19
 armed conflicts, 103–4
 Assange case, 61–62, 120–22
 categories, violations, 132–33
 Code of Conduct, 43–44, 58–59
 communications database, 135
 Covenant on Civil and Political Rights, 42–43
 creation and mandate, 128–29
 criteria, detailed, 78
 Cuba condemnation of, 37–38, 38n8, 76
 deliberations, 148–49
 general comments/observations, 148
 individual case treatment, consistent, 132–33
 international treaties benchmark, contesting, 37n6, 37–44
 Khashoggi killing, 127n8, 134–35, 135n32
 Lebanon, Al-Khaim prison, 147
 methods of work, 81, 129–30, 131–33, 142–43, 167–68
 publicity, 117–18
 quasi-judicial process, 37–38, 131–32
Working Group on Chile, 84
Working Group on Enforced or Involuntary Disappearances, 27–28, 75–76, 77–78, 101n16, 127–29, 145–46
 allegation transmission to concerned mandates, 77–78
 Code of Conduct, 58–59
 coordination, 75–76
 general comments/observations, 148
 individual cases focus, 101–2
 methods of work, 129–30, 131–32
 nonstate actors, 104–5n33, 104–8
 violations of human rights, views, 60
"Working Group on Enhancing the Effectiveness of the Mechanisms of the Commission on Human Rights," 47–48
Working Group on the Situation of Human Rights in Chile, 126–27
Working Group on Transnational Corporations and Business Enterprises., 107–8
World Court of Human Rights, 192–93
Wuerth, Ingrid, 183–85, 189